Event Processing for Business

Event Processing for Business

Organizing the Real-Time Enterprise

DAVID LUCKHAM

WILEY

John Wiley & Sons, Inc.

Published by John Wiley & Sons, Inc., Hoboken, New Jersey.
Published simultaneously in Canada.

For general information on our other products and services or for technical support, please contact our Customer Care Department within the United States at (800) 762-2974, outside the United States at (317) 572-3993, or fax (317) 572-4002.

Wiley also publishes its books in a variety of electronic formats. Some content that appears in print may not be available in electronic books. For more information about Wiley products, visit our Web site at www.wiley.com.

Library of Congress Cataloging-in-Publication Data:

ISBN 978-0-470-53485-4; ISBN 978-1-118-17183-7 (ebk);
ISBN 978-1-118-17184-4 (ebk); ISBN 978-1-118-17185-1 (ebk)

Printed in the United States of America

10 9 8 7 6 5 4 3 2 1

Contents

Preface

This is a book about modern event processing and its current and future applications in business, government, and the Information Society. Modern event processing at the higher levels of business operations and management is a lot different from the kinds of event processing that are the foundations of computer networks and the Internet. The events are different, their significance and importance to various levels of management are different, and there are far fewer standards and a lot more chaos, confusion, and lack of defined terminology.

Business event processing for the *right-now* business is a 21st-century development, and it is growing fast. It is a technology aimed at enabling an enterprise to take action *right now*, the instant information becomes available.

One of my motivations in writing this book was to raise the level of awareness of the basic concepts about events and the different ways event processing can be used in business operations. But the field is expanding and changing as different kinds of commercial applications of event processing keep appearing. So the book is really a work in progress about a field of activity that hasn't finished evolving.

The book was originally intended for people in business who wanted to know if there is anything of value in "event processing" that might be useful to them in running their businesses. But as it turned out, the book can be read by anyone who has some background in information technology (IT), and uses IT in their work. These days, everyone has a cell phone and is busy multitasking, so in fact all of us are using event processing quite heavily, whether we are conscious of it or not.

This is a much smaller book than the one I wrote in 2002. The field of event processing as we now know it didn't exist then, so the objective of *The Power of Events* was to lay out the principles of Complex Event Processing (CEP) that had been researched and developed at Stanford under DARPA contracts over the previous ten years. Its other goal was to encourage commercial development—in fact, I tried that myself, but it's another story!

Today, many businesses plan strategic initiatives under titles such as "Business Analytics and Optimization." Although they may not know it, CEP is usually a cornerstone of such initiatives. So another of my goals is to give the reader a good idea of the current marketplace for CEP and the kinds of businesses that are applying event processing and CEP in their operations. I have emphasized examples of event processing in use today in different kinds of businesses, including financial systems and services, transportation, security, fraud detection, health care, energy, and other sectors. And I have tried to make the book as nontechnical as I am able to, in writing about this subject.

CEP is fast becoming an enabling technology, hidden under the hood and forgotten except by the cognoscenti of the IT world. And I believe that is, in fact, the long-term future of CEP—to be forgotten just like the TCP/IP network protocols upon which our IT-driven lives depend.

The Power of Events contains a lot of event-processing techniques that have not yet seen commercial application. But I still think, as I did then, that these techniques will become part of commercial applications of event processing in the future. So I have included examples here of the use in business operations of such concepts as causal and timing relations between events and the organization of events into hierarchies.

The final chapter is a personal vision of some of the different roles that event processing technology will play in our information society in the future. This is my pet topic, and the chapter could have been a lot longer. Readers will no doubt think of other applications that are not included here, and indeed I hope they do! In this way, the book may contribute to the further development of event processing.

There are nine chapters. Here's what's in them:

Chapter 1: What event processing is and why might it be important to a business

Chapter 2: Four different event processing technologies that have developed over the past sixty years

Chapter 3: Basic concepts of event processing and CEP

Chapter 4: Stages in the development of modern event processing in business and government

Chapter 5: The marketplace for CEP, who's using event processing, and the kinds of business problems to which it is being applied

Chapter 6: More event processing concepts, such as patterns of multiple events, timing of events, and causality between events (understanding these concepts is important if you're interested in investing in event processing technology for your business, as they enable you to judge what you're being sold!)

Chapter 7: Strategies for applying CEP in a business

Chapter 8: Organizing events for different role players in the enterprise
Chapter 9: How the future of event processing and CEP may turn out

There is also an Appendix containing a glossary of event processing terminology.

DAVID LUCKHAM
Palo Alto, California
November 2011

Acknowledgments

I owe thanks to several friends and colleagues who have helped me with various drafts of this book. They gave their time generously to reading, correcting, and commenting on different versions, and alerting me to omissions and new material. Their comments have been influential throughout.

I am happy to thank:

Roy Schulte of Gartner Corp.
John Bates of Progress Software
Leendert Weinhofen of the Norwegian State University
Scott Fingerhut of Informatica, Inc.
Opher Etzion of IBM Research Lab, Haifa, and chairman of the Event
    Processing Technical Society

They have helped me greatly. Of course, any remaining errors or flaws are entirely of my own making.

I must also thank the Event Processing Technical Society (EPTS) for permission to include the EPTS Glossary of Event Processing Terminology (version 2.0) as an appendix. In an embryonic technology such as CEP, there is a lot of fuzzy undefined talk, especially at trade shows and meetings and in brochures for event processing products. I hope that including the Glossary will contribute to improving our terminology and discussions, putting all of us on the same page, so to speak.

There is a saying that "books are never published, they are abandoned." That is certainly the case with this one. I could have gone on improving it and adding more detail to it for another year. But I may not live that long! There comes a time to abandon a book to the publisher. So, having told you that, I do hope you'll find this little book useful.

CHAPTER 1

Event Processing and the Survival of the Modern Enterprise

All the world's information is at your fingertips—but can you make use of it?

—Vinton Cerf, 2005

You probably think that every twenty-first-century enterprise uses events and event processing in its business operations. That would seem obvious, given our information-driven world, which is inundated with sources of events from just about everywhere. But you would be wrong! The truth is that a lot of businesses think they use event processing. And, yes, a lot of them do—in their network management and communications. A few businesses go further and use event processing to drive some of their operations, such as supply chain management or consumer relations. And then there are the electronic stock trading and online gaming industries, both of which are totally event driven, but those are niche markets for event processing.

Many times, it turns out on closer inspection that businesses could make much greater use of the events already at their disposal in their business operations and planning. They could do a lot more with today's event processing technology than they currently do to improve the running of the enterprise, their awareness of the business environment, and consequently their business decision making—and it would benefit them greatly in terms of their competitiveness and profitability if they did. Indeed, for some of them, adopting the latest event processing technology in their intelligence gathering and business planning may become a matter of survival.

This book has four goals:

- Firstly, to explain the concepts of event processing and to answer basic questions such as "what do you mean by an *event?*"
- Secondly, to describe strategies for applying event processing in business and enterprise management, not only to run business operations but also as a tool for business intelligence and a basis for planning
- Thirdly, to describe the progress and probable limitations of commercial event processing technology
- Finally, to explore some of the future trends in event processing and its pervasive supporting role in very large–scale information systems

We include a short survey of how event processing has been a basis for different technology areas from discrete event simulation to business process management over the past sixty years. This gives some background about the multiple roles event processing is playing nowadays in everything from weather forecasting to operating a business or running a government.

The final chapter outlines some of the longer-term developments in event processing technology and the roles it will eventually play in the information infrastructure of our society. Many future applications are quite easily predicted now, and the only surprises are in finding out how long they will take to actually happen!

Four Basic Questions about Events

Here are four questions that every CIO, CTO, and business manager should have an answer to:

1. What are events and which ones are important?
2. Why invest in event processing?
3. What are the main concepts in event processing?
4. What kinds of enterprises have bought into event processing technology so far?

These are pretty basic questions—but they're the kinds of first questions people often ask when they're wondering if event processing has anything to offer them or their business.

What Are Events and Which Ones Are Important?

An event is simply something that happens. That's the common sense meaning, the one in the dictionary. We'll deal with the technical computer processing meaning later. Of course there are many indicators of events. Anything like a message on a news wire service, an email, a sensor signal, a text message, or a newspaper report can indicate an event that has happened.

Events come in all sizes. Some are small events, like getting a text message on cell phone, and others are very big events, like World War II. Historians tend to write about big events, but we live day to day by small events!

Business events are the events that affect our businesses. Those are the kinds of events that concern us here. Now, there is great disagreement as to which events *are* business events, and even more disagreement as to which events are the most important. To illustrate the contentious nature of business events, here is the top ten in *TheStreet.com's* list of the top 100 U.S. business events in the twentieth century, published in May 1999:[1]

1. Eisenhower creates the interstates: June 29, 1956.
2. Intel invents the single-chip microprocessor: 1971.
3. The Federal Reserve is formed: 1913.
4. The Great Crash of 1929: October 24–29, 1929.
5. Equal pay for equal work: June 10, 1963.
6. Ford introduces the assembly line: 1913.
7. Kaiser's World War II shipyards surpass all expectations of production: 1942.
8. The first Wal-Mart opens: 1962.
9. The current bull market begins: August 1982.
10. Carrier Engineering is founded, beginning the commercialization of air conditioning: 1915.

And, just in case you agree with all of these top ten, which is very doubtful, try to guess number eleven (don't look!).[2] Obviously, an event remains an event, something that happened. But its importance can vary over time, because importance is a subjective measure and relative to what else happens. For example, number 9, "The current bull market begins: August 1982," would have to be reworded nowadays as "the 1980s bull market," because that bull market was replaced by a recession, and

---

[1] www.thestreet.com/story/747965/the-basics-of-business-history-top-100-events-at-a-glance.html

[2] "11. Reagan is elected: 1980." (TheStreet.com)

then another market about which the experts disagree. Perhaps "the 1980s bull market" would no longer make the top hundred!

Events have *attributes*, such as the time at which they happened, how long they took to happen, and which events caused which other events. Attributes (such as timing) and relationships between events (such as causality) are important clues used in processing events to judge which ones are most important "right now" for the business. We'll deal with attributes and event relationships in Chapter 3.

To illustrate how an event's effects, such as causing other events, can increase its importance, consider for a moment this event from *TheStreet. com*'s top 100 U.S. business events:

42. *The Jungle* is published: 1906.

Why on earth is the publication of a novel by Upton Sinclair considered an important event in U.S. business?

Well, Sinclair wrote this novel to highlight the plight of the working class and to remove from obscurity the corruption of the American meat-packing industry in Chicago during the early twentieth century:

> Upton Sinclair originally intended to expose "the inferno of exploitation [of the typical American factory worker at the turn of the 20th Century]," but the reading public instead fixated on food safety as the novel's most pressing issue. In fact, Sinclair bitterly admitted his celebrity rose, "not because the public cared anything about the workers, but simply because the public did not want to eat tubercular beef." Their efforts, coupled with the public outcry, led to the passage of the Meat Inspection Act (1906, amended, 1967) and the Pure Food and Drug Act of 1906, which established the Bureau of Chemistry that would become in 1930, the Food and Drug Administration.[3]

So, event number 42, the publication of a novel, had far-reaching and permanent effects upon American society and the regulation of its businesses by the government.

However, Figure 1.1 illustrates that an event's causal effects can be temporary or may be superseded by later events. Of course, looking back at an event's causal effects is interesting, but for a modern business it is much more important to predict likely causal effects in the future of events—maybe several events—that are happening now! More on this later.

---

[3] Mark Sullivan, *Our Times* (New York: Scribner, 1996), 222.

"Up three points? My Gawd, I jumped too soon!"

FIGURE 1.1 "Up three points," by Frank Hanley, January 10, 1930
Source: www.archelaus-cards.com/blog/2009/01/12/the-great-depression-in-cartoons-part-1-1929-30/

Why Invest in Event Processing?

Events are carriers of *instant information*. And event processing is about having the ability to take *instant action*. Sometimes the usefulness of the information events carry is short lived. Putting events in databases for action tomorrow is yesterday's mode of doing business.

Events are arriving all the time from a multitude of sources. This is the era of the *real-time event*.[4] Our businesses, our transportation systems, and our government agencies depend upon all manner of events. Some examples are:

- Internet messages
- Stock market feeds
- Online reports from the company's departments
- Customer orders and enquiries on the business's website or by phone
- Cell phone text messages
- GPS tracking updates from a delivery truck fleet
- RFID tag readings from sensors in inventory and shipping
- Satellite-based location feeds from aircraft navigation systems

and many hundreds of other sources of events. All kinds of events are arriving continuously and driving our businesses. Often a business must react immediately to the events it receives just to keep the daily operations moving. So why not explore other ways to make use of them?

Events run our personal lives too! When we go home after a hard day's business there are all the traffic events that we have to put up with. We process those events right then—when they happen—to decide which route to take going home. And at home there's the evening news, weather reports, and even more events. Moreover, these events depend upon other event sources. Weather reports, for example, depend upon satellite communications, radio signals from deep ocean buoys, automated weather stations, and much else. It's an event-active world that we live in.

Whatever the business, many different kinds of events happening "right now" have an impact on it. There are so many events and so many sources of events out there that *the event cloud* is a term that is often used to describe our business environment.

It's an Event Driven World

Just consider a few numbers from the Technology market research organizations:

- There are 5 billion mobile phones worldwide and counting.[5] Many of them are smartphones, and 15 percent are Internet enabled (September 2010).

---

[4] *Real time* is a much overused term. What we usually mean by it in business processing is *right now*. And that means *this instant, immediately*, or *taking as little time as makes no difference*.

[5] The number of mobile phones in use worldwide has topped 5.0 billion, boosted by soaring demand in emerging markets India and China, according to a study by Swedish telecoms giant Ericsson in July 2010.

- In December 2009, texting was being used at the rate of 152.7 billion text messages per month—and that's just in the United States.
- The Internet has 2 billion users, as of June 2010.
- We are also seeing all manner of new kinds of event-enabled twenty-first-century business models: eBay, Amazon, Dell, Google, Yahoo, MSN, AOL, iTunes, Twitter, Facebook, Skype . . . a lot of them are very successful!
- Skype has around 560 million registered users and 8.1 million paying users. People spend an average of 520 million minutes every day talking on Skype.
- Facebook has more than 500 million users.
- Global collaborative communities, some social and some scientific, are springing up: Social Networks, OLPC, Google Earth, the large Hadron Collider, and the like. Some of these will be business-oriented. And their business potentials are being explored, as we speak.[6]

All of this event-enabled stuff represents a new way of doing business. It has been emerging for some time. And now it's here!

The obvious conclusion is that we have to use events. And the real question is how to make the best use of them.

The fact is a lot of us are already using event processing in our businesses. But I'll bet we could do more! Maximizing the use of the information carried by events can be of paramount importance, both from an offensive and a defensive viewpoint. Businesses should try to maximize their use of the events they already receive. And then plan to use more sources of events, ones they don't normally deal with. The question is how.

Let's start by discussing the ways in which events can be useful at the higher management levels of a business. Later in the book, we'll explain how to do it with modern event processing technology.

As we said before, we can think of an event as a message together with additional data. The added data are about who sent the event, where it came from, its duration and the time it was sent, how it got to us, and how it is related to some other events. That extra data, by the way, are very useful when it comes to building event processing systems. It is crucial in helping to figure out things about the events you're receiving, such as whether you should look at some other events at the same time, or whether they're coming from sources you normally trust and rely upon or sources that might be erroneous or corrupted in transit.

---

[6]Adam Shell, "Wall Street traders mine tweets to gain a trading edge," *USA Today*, May 4, 2011. www.usatoday.com/money/perfi/stocks/2011-05-03-wall-street-traders-mine-tweets_n.htm

You do have to be careful when you use events. But that's a fact of doing any kind of business today, and the beauty of event processing technology is that it gives you the means to do exactly that—be careful!

Patterns of Events

Each event might carry only a little piece of information. To make sense of that information, one may need to look at some other events as well, ones that are related in some ways to the original event. Events tend to arrive in patterns, mixed up with unrelated events.

When some patterns, perhaps containing several events, are looked at together and their total information is analyzed, they can often tell us what is happening or going to happen, where it is happening, and why. It might be a pattern containing only one event that's significant at a given moment. Or it might be a pattern containing hundreds of events, arriving in a millisecond or maybe spread out over days or weeks. We may not know in advance how long the pattern will take to happen. But event processing technology can help us detect the patterns we want to know about.

Also, event sources can be globally distributed and intended for a large number of users; or they may be local, company-specific and confidential to the company. We will deal later with sources of events and which sources may be relevant to a business or enterprise manager.

In the running of an enterprise, *patterns of events* can often play a critical role in providing vital information for taking action *right now*.

Principle 1: Patterns of Events Add Up to Actionable Information

Each event may carry only a little piece of information, but when the information in a pattern of multiple events is aggregated with the contexts in which each of the events happens, some patterns will yield intelligence upon which a business or enterprise must act.

Even so, many enterprises are asleep at the wheel. You will find that event feeds from the sales department, or inventory, or suppliers, or the company's website, drive its operations. The company reacts to these events as they arrive in various ways, sending out products, reordering stock, answering enquiries, scheduling services, and so on.

But this is *reactive* behavior to the events it receives, simply to keep its normal operations in motion. This reactive behavior is the equivalent of driving a car along the road on automatic while daydreaming, or even worse, dozing off at the wheel. Most enterprises are not making the maximal use of the available events and event processing techniques.

Here are three activities in which detecting and analyzing patterns of events can be an aid to higher level business operations. These are areas where it can really pay off to invest in real-time event processing to maximize the information you extract from the events that are available to you. The same event processing technology can be applied in all three areas:

1. *Knowing* how well your enterprise is performing in relation to your expectations and the competition[7]
2. *Detecting when* what you need to know happens, and then using that knowledge—quickly!
3. *Extracting the information you want* from the cloud of events available to you

But I hear the warning bells already ringing! What's it going to cost? Well, it doesn't need to be a lot of expensive software just to get started or put a toe in the water. We'll get back to that later. And one of the points we're making is that you're probably already using some event processing—it's a matter of going a little further with the events and the software you've got. When you see the payoff, you'll want to analyze whether it is worth investing in more technology.

Know How Well You're Doing

"No man is an island, entire of itself."[8]

A primary reason to invest in event processing is to keep tabs on how well your business is doing. To be sure, you're already using events to drive some of your business processes. Going beyond that normal everyday operation, events can be used to provide an up-to-the-minute understanding of the performance of the business.

Start by using events to track how well your business is doing and to give a *right now* picture of the competitive environment in which you

---

[7]Corporate performance management is often considered as part of *business intelligence* or BI.

[8]John Donne, "Meditation XVII," 1623.

are operating. Make better use of the events you're already using in your business. For example:

- The events you normally use to drive your business processes
- The events those processes create
- Events you receive everyday from the business environment

Just as importantly, these events can be used to detect *exceptions*—situations where you receive events you don't expect, or don't receive events you do expect—and take appropriate action.

Use All Event Sources

You should aim to gradually extend the business intelligence application of event processing towards the goal of monitoring the information in all your available sources of events. Of course this can't be done in one big installation of new technology. You will need to prioritize which sources you monitor first, second, third, and so on. An event monitoring facility is built up gradually—and is never finished!

You will start by monitoring the events in your own operations within the business. And then extend that monitoring to your interactions with customers through sales, orders, response to advertising, and so on. After that, you might attempt to monitor other event sources, such as the activities of your suppliers, customers, and your competitors. Consider Example 1.1.

Example 1.1

A company plans to introduce a new product. But while production is starting up, some of the company's event sources deliver information that may require changing production plans: (1) unusual back orders causing delays at some parts suppliers, (2) problems hiring skilled personnel at a subsidiary's assembly plant, and (3) transportation workers on some supply routes rumored to be about to strike.

Each of these events happening in isolation may signify a need to modify the company's production or marketing plans. We call them *actionable events*.

But there is another lesson here. When actionable events from different event sources happen together within small time windows, say within a week, the aggregation of those events must be considered, not just each event by itself. Higher levels of business planning and policy may be affected.

In most companies today, this kind of monitoring of multiple event sources is either not done at all or it is done in a very haphazard manner, and the results may not be aggregated. But there are already some industries where it is state-of-practice. News services and financial services are prime examples.

When monitoring of event sources is done properly, it is done using level-wise techniques for efficiency. For example, in the news industry, the first level of incoming raw event traffic is filtered by automated methods for the presence of keywords such as names of companies, newsworthy people, countries, weather events, stocks, and many other topics. One interesting keyword topic that is the subject of experimental use is a lexicon of sentiments that tend to crop up in news items such as "surprising," "hopeful," "unbelievable," "encouraging," "disappointing," and so on. Each sentiment is assigned a positive or negative value that is factored into the total newsworthiness of the posting. This kind of event processing is also being applied in stock trading algorithms.

The traffic that is caught at the first level by the automated filters then goes through a second level analysis for business relevance. This analysis is performed by humans with the aid of various predictive analysis tools. As Example 1.1 shows, this second level may involve aggregating patterns of events from several sources—a typical event processing operation, which can be applied using many of the tools currently on the market. The results go to a third level, which is a second level of human decision makers. It is here that the company uses event inputs to make business decisions and take actions—*right now.*

Automated monitoring of the sources of business events—possibly with humans in the loop—is essential to ensuring that a business is agile and capable of changing plans to save costs or to take advantage of opportunities in a competitive environment. It's not only about running the company efficiently; it's also about instant awareness of changes in the business environment—and what the competition is doing.

Note: Automated monitoring of all sources of business event inputs to an enterprise goes well beyond the kinds of media monitoring offered by some specialty companies. But if you do decide to hire someone to do your business event monitoring for you, then you must be able to judge how good a job they're doing.

Detect When What You Need to Know Happens

A second use of event processing in your business, and a big reason for making some investment in this technology, is to avoid the business being blindsided.

The goals of this activity are different from keeping track of your company's performance and the competitive environment—but you'll use the same technology to do it. The goals are more about keeping up to date with technical and product information than about running the business operations. Example 1.2 illustrates this usage.

Example 1.2

The company in Example 1.1 must deal with another situation during its introduction of the new product. A number of events that it has received, taken together, indicate that a competitor is planning an advertising campaign to publicize an improved technology for a similar product. The competing product will perform faster and cost less than the company's own product.

Obviously the company should have known about the technology improvements as early as the competition did. It should have known about the competitor's plans too. And there's a good chance it could have found the information in the sources of events it had access to but didn't monitor, or didn't monitor for information beyond what was needed to run its business. Learning about it now is probably going to be costly.

The old way of dealing with these kinds of issues was to use industrial spies. But today we use automated event monitoring technology to do some of our spying. And in doing this, sources such as social network sites can be useful. Let's call this process *information detection and gathering*.

A business must keep aware of new technical developments or product-marketing information within its sphere of activity that may affect its planning.

Today, news can happen in seconds. And quite often that information might be right under the company's own nose, contained in the cloud of events coming from the event sources that it either routinely processes to run its business or could use for business intelligence if it chose to do so. Being aware is a problem that event processing can help to solve.

Continuous Watch for Information

This second area of activity, *detecting when what you need to know happens*, is effectively a *continuous search problem*. That is, *being aware* is best implemented by a *continuous search* that never stops until you tell it to!

Being aware of new developments is complicated by the fact that there's lots of information out there that might affect the business, but we never know all of it—only parts. We might only have a few clues about this new information we should know about, such as the topics, possible sources, probable timing, who the likely competition is, or where our business is most vulnerable.

But it is also true that a successful business usually has a pretty good idea of what to watch for, based upon previous experience. One can approach the awareness problem by first taking steps to raise the level of watchfulness within the company. Start by making *watchlists* of the clues the company should look for about what's likely to happen. Use these lists to direct attention toward the events you should know about.

Personnel should be encouraged to use the watchlists.

However, a company, or a government for that matter, cannot rely only on its personnel.[9] A level of automated watching must be considered. If the company decides to invest in event processing technology, the watch lists will be useful input to an application for continuously monitoring sources of incoming events for technology and product information. But beware the limitations displayed in Example 1.3.

Example 1.3: The Lesson of Too-Late Information

The case of the 2009 Christmas day bomber illustrates the lesson of too-late information. The bomber traveled from East Africa to Amsterdam for the explicitly stated purpose of committing an act of terrorism on the United States. His father had given a U.S. consulate in Africa this information about his son. By the time the bomber arrived in Amsterdam, his name had been placed on airport watchlists. However, the process of updating watchlists made revised lists available only once per day. The bomber was able to board a United States–bound airliner because the Amsterdam watchlist had not yet been updated that day.

---

[9]For example, four days after the Christmas day 2009 bombing attempt, President Obama said publicly that Abdulmutallab's ability to board the aircraft was the result of a systemic failure that included an inadequate sharing of information among United States and foreign government agencies. He called the situation "totally unacceptable" (BBC News, "US President Obama notes 'systemic failure' on jet bomb," December 30, 2009. http://news.bbc.co.uk/2/hi/americas/8434275.stm)

Principle 2: Use It Right Now!

Businesses must design their processes to make the fastest use of actionable knowledge when it arrives. Event processing is about taking immediate action *right now.*

But first of all we must find that information.

Investing in search technology requires careful research by the technology officers of the company. Here are a few observations about *search* and *continuous search* technology.

Continuous search is part of the modern Internet-based way of doing business, an essential business intelligence technology. Everyone uses it with varying degrees of effectiveness, from individuals, to companies, to political organizations, to governments.

Secondly, at the moment we're stuck with far-from-perfect search tools. A useful Internet search engine led to the rise of the modern business world's most successful twenty-first-century enterprise, Google.[10] But let it be said that Google does not have anywhere near a perfect solution today—and won't for a long time to come.

All we have at the moment are rather simplistic kinds of searching tools that will answer only simple questions, deliver a lot of irrelevant answers, and sometimes will not find an answer at all. There's plenty of room for improvement. In fact, a lot of work is going on, usually in secret, to develop more sophisticated search engines based upon using the semantics of data to deliver intelligent answers to searches.

Thirdly, the *continuous search* problem requires a technical leap forward from what Google search can do at the moment. You can build a rather crude continuous search on top of Google. But to do it well, so that you can have confidence in the results, requires new event processing technology. There are two reasons for this:

1. Much of the information that needs to be searched is dynamic, like stock market trading feeds or the Internet. Its usefulness is often short lived. Putting real-time event feeds into a database to be searched later

---

[10]Google was created by Larry Page and Sergey Brin when they were Ph.D. students at Stanford University as a research project to create a better form of search. The domain Google.com was not actually registered until September 15, 1997, and the company Google, Inc. was incorporated on September 4, 1998.

is too slow—unless it is done very cleverly with in-memory databases, it will lose any advantage of being useful for *right now* action.

2. The information we need is often contained in patterns of many events, not simply single individual events. So we need an *event pattern* technology as the basis for continuous search, which means employing event processing engines in the searching process.

There are some encouraging developments in automated methods of detecting what you need to know as it happens. First, the new search technology we're talking about is beginning to appear, for example, in the form of Internet protocols like the Extensible Messaging and Presence Protocol, XMPP,[11] which can help to build information systems that receive the data they want whenever that data become available.

Secondly, the same event processing technology and principles that are employed in monitoring the company operations and business environment—how well we're doing—should be adaptable to work when the goals of the event monitoring are widened to continuously searching for technical product information. A single investment in event monitoring technology may well solve both problems.

Principle 3: Level-wise Watch for Actionable Information

Event sources should be subject to different levels of monitoring corresponding to the different goals of the enterprise—for example, (1) to know how the company is performing and (2) to detect information on technology and market developments. The goals of monitoring are separated into levels so you don't slow the system by taking the monolithic approach and doing everything at once.

What to Watch

There's another dimension to both the search and continuous search problems that is becoming increasingly important. Much business information is now *real-time*—which for business purposes means *right now* time. That information is increasingly carried in events in various kinds of networks, news media, and messaging systems, which we will call simply

---

[11] For more information on XMPP, the XMPP Standards Foundation website has an excellent introduction: http://xmpp.org/about-xmpp

event media. New events are arriving all the time. And new information media never stop appearing.

Keeping up with changes in the media that carry event traffic is taking on a dynamic component. Search engines must be able to deal with this challenge. To do this—to direct the searchlight on the latest information sources—event processing techniques will be employed. That's another reason to watch what's going on in event processing technology!

Event Media

All electronic sources of events, such as the Internet, messaging networks, cell phone text messages, newswire and news aggregation services, social websites, and emergency warning services, are examples of today's sources of events.

Event media are constantly changing and evolving, perhaps at a slower pace than the information they carry, but they are changing nonetheless. At the same time, the need to access that information as it becomes available—*right now*—has become an imperative for all enterprises. That is why "detecting it *when* it happens" requires a new kind of continuous search based upon event processing.

Principle 4: The Constant Evolution of Event Information and Event Media

The world's event information, and the media that carry those events, are constantly evolving and changing. The correctness and usefulness of the information is often short-lived. And new media are always appearing.

Event Processing in Use

Here are some short examples to illustrate how event processing—and more accurately, *Complex Event Processing (CEP)*[12]—is being used in solving real-time problems. CEP is a key technology in building event detection and reaction capabilities. We describe situations that develop and require solution within various time windows. And then we describe patterns of events

---

[12]We place the term CEP in its historical context in Chapter 2 and define it precisely in Chapter 3.

that might be used in event monitoring systems to detect these situations as they happen:

1. A problem in the baggage handling system of an airline (30 seconds— 1 minute).
2. The unexpected spread of an infectious disease, indicating a need to trigger national public health control measures (1 week–1 month).
3. Weather conditions cause delays in a company's supply chain, and the company must reorganize the schedules of the sales force in the field (8 hours).
4. Unauthorized message traffic on the company's internal networks indicating the possibility of a spyware installation (variable time windows, anywhere from 5 seconds–4 weeks).
5. A credit card company detects suspicious use of the cards of some of its reliable customers (1–12 hours).
6. A rogue nation or terrorist organization is accumulating the know-how and materials to build and deliver dirty atomic bombs (detection and reaction period may be several years and requires a very wide span of different event sources).

What kinds of events would indicate these kinds of situations? Stop reading for a moment and have a guess! Usually, it will be a pattern of several events, not just one event. Also, detection systems for these kinds of problems will monitor for many different event patterns at the same time.

Much the same event processing technology would be used to detect patterns of events through monitoring the event sources in all of these examples. It would be part of the operating processes being employed in these situations. Here are some possible event pattern detection scenarios:

1. Baggage in an airline baggage handling system is tagged with RFID tags at the ticket counter. Scanners are placed at various positions on the pathways that the baggage takes from the ticket counters to the flights. There are scanners on conveyors and at places where baggage is loaded on and off moving equipment. A scanner emits a tag reading (an event) as it "sees" each tag. This reading contains the scanner's position together with the information on a tag. All the readings are processed by a monitoring system. A pattern of readings such as:

   20 tags read at scanner A in last 10 seconds **and**
   no readings from scanner B in last 10 seconds

   might indicate a problem in the handling system, such as baggage piling up somewhere between A and B.

Different event patterns would be used to detect other kinds of problems, such as some bags being directed to the wrong flights. For example:

Bag destined for Los Angeles loaded on Flight F **and**
Flight F destined non-stop for New York **and**
Los Angeles /= New York
raise ERROR

Similar event pattern monitoring is used to detect problems in many other kinds of processing lines and factory assembly lines.

2. A national public health electronic reporting system receives events from several sources, including electronic reports from hospital admissions and emergency room visits, physician's offices, local health agencies, and sales of prescription items at pharmacies. One target for automated monitoring of this flow of report events would be to detect possible disease outbreaks. Human-in-the-loop epidemic monitoring systems have sometimes proved too slow in the past.[13] Monitoring would use levels of event patterns, so that the system would not be slowed by a monolithic number of patterns to be tested all at once. The first-level event patterns might detect increasing numbers of reports for the same disease on a week-by-week basis for a specified number of weeks. For example:

Number reports of A last week < number reports of A next week
during past four successive weeks

A match of this pattern might then trigger a second level of monitoring. The event data would be run through other patterns that match location data in the reports to detect concentrations of each reported disease in a geographical area or population concentration. For example:

Number reports of A in area X last week > 5 * 25 year weekly average

If the actual numbers are deemed high enough, the pattern matching system would trigger both human interaction and third-level actions, such as feeding the report data to predictive models. Models of propagation for the disease may predict an area outbreak or a

---

[13] The Canadian GPHIN system is credited with uncovering SARS in 1998 when the Chinese attempted to hide it. www.phac-aspc.gc.ca/media/nr-rp/2004/2004_gphin-rmispbk-eng.php#4

potential for a national outbreak, indicating the need to trigger public health controls.

3. A retailer with a national network of retail outlets and a supply chain system installs event monitors on a variety of different event sources. Interestingly, there may be several different event monitoring systems within a large company, each run by different departments. Separation of event monitoring systems can be a problem, because it is important for the separate systems to cooperate. One system might monitor the supply chain events (e.g., inventory levels and sales figures from the outlets, customer orders, and the company's orders to its suppliers and their responses). For example:

> **if** supply orders for item X < outstanding customer orders
> **then** send warning to supply chain manager

Another system might track the events in its distribution system such the status of its warehouses, distribution schedules and real-time data radioed from GPS systems on its delivery trucks. For example:

truck A is 30 mins late at scheduled delivery point B

This second system might also monitor outside event sources, such as national and local weather reports, traffic reports, driver availability, and other sources.

Situations can happen in which the two event monitoring systems must cooperate by combining their processing results. Suppose the first system receives low inventory level warnings from some outlets, and in the same time window, the second system receives events such as truck breakdowns and weather reports indicating delays in the delivery system. If these events all arrive within a short time window, say eight hours, then cooperation between the systems could trigger various actions, such as advisory warnings to be issued to some outlets, and the rerouting of some supplies.

> **if** low inventory warning at time T **then**
> **if** delivery delay warning received within T + 1 day
> **then** request reroute supplies

4. Message traffic on a company's internal network to an unknown outside Internet address may indicate the presence of spyware or a compromised database and the theft of confidential information. Patterns of events may indicate that spying is in progress or that stolen data are being transferred outside. Such patterns of events can happen

very quickly after data have already been stolen and stored locally. However, the theft activity can go on slowly for weeks "under the radar" if the company does not monitor its IT systems adequately. The company security system could monitor for patterns of attempted data transfers and absence of recent transfer authorizations like this:

> **if** data transfer attempted outside network **and**
> **no** outside transfer authorized **within** last 15 mins
> **then** send warning to security

Notice this example contains two patterns and the second pattern is the absence of an *authorize* event. We'll describe how the absence of events can be detected later.

5. Credit card companies have libraries of event patterns indicating possible use of stolen credit card information. They are usually not very sophisticated patterns, depending upon geographic locations, known centers of card fraud, and very simple patterns of fraudulent use.

   For example, if the card holder lives in the United States and her card suddenly starts being used from locations in Eastern Europe, the card company's monitoring system will create an alert. Usage patterns that involve using a card in different geographic locations within a short period of time will trigger alerts. Any card use outside the holder's residential area may trigger an alert, particularly for foreign travel. Some card company alert patterns trigger high numbers of false warnings and consequently produce lots of irate customers. For example, an immediate card block when a card is used in a jewelry or electronics store or an art gallery without prior notice. Event patterns used in credit card monitoring are sometimes totally simplistic, because the card monitoring systems are built without any general event pattern-matching capability and inadequate memory of recent prior use (state knowledge). They simply test large numbers of use cases.

6. Homeland Security and other national intelligence organizations use a lot of event pattern detection—and they could use a lot more, particularly in coordinating detection across different agencies.

   Security is an area where the critical indicator events come from many different sources and may be spread across separate and competing government departments. The detection processes for security event patterns can be long lived, taking years to match completely. It is a problem that is compounded by false reports and erroneous events. Event pattern detection demands collaborative efforts among organizations that do not normally collaborate very well. Automation of event pattern detection is an obvious direction toward a solution to this long-term global-scale monitoring problem. An example of a possible event pattern in this area would be:

if Classification of person A **is** terrorist threat **and**
report R received of A traveled to location B **and**
report R passes credibility test **and**
Flight F from B to USA **is** in progress **then**
alert homeland security **about** A onboard F

Each of the four events triggering an alert event in this hypothetical example would result from the aggregation of other, simpler events.

The time taken for the information content of several events to "add up" to an actionable situation varies greatly with the area of activity. But once the information is deemed credible, the enterprise must react—no matter whether it is a small business, a global enterprise, or a government. The ability to immediately detect and recognize patterns of events that have implications for decision making within the enterprise, *as and when they happen*, can sometimes be a matter of survival. And certainly, it is always a competitive advantage. Every enterprise today should possess these kinds of event-processing capabilities.

Principle 5: Constant Vigilance

Every enterprise should be capable of monitoring 24/7 those event media, both internal and external, that carry information likely to indicate the need for changes in its business processes, strategies, or organization.

The Human Element and Other Sources of Errors

No discussion of event processing systems can be complete without a word of warning about the human element. Human errors, including very often the error of omission or the error of lack of coordination between actors, are some of the strongest arguments in favor of adopting automated event monitoring technology. A case in point is the previously mentioned mishandling of information in the Christmas 2009 airline bomber case.

Automated systems do go wrong. But when one looks at the reasons why, they often turn out to be due to error by their human users. For example, incorrect event patterns—patterns that do not contribute to detecting the intended situation—can be input to an automated monitoring system.

Another common source of errors is due to noise in the event sources themselves (e.g., RFID readers can give blurred and incorrect results). The information carried by events can be corrupted, thus misleading the event monitoring. Networks that transport our information deal with this by building confirmation processes into their communication protocols.

Guards against errors will be built into event monitoring systems. Error checking should be part of event processing technology—the ability to go backward and find the history of high-level events. Whenever a result of event monitoring and processing comes to a management decision level and involves financial or other resource expenditure, there must be an automated process of double checking.

Processes and methods of reducing errors in automated event processors and in their use must be adopted. Error detection has to be done in *right now* time.

There are many approaches to this issue. Any event-processing system will have the usual event logs and will support their use to retrace the history of processing that led to a questionable decision and also to do retrospective analysis after the fact. There will be various kinds of checking that can be turned on or off in the event processors. In normal use, these checking systems will probably be turned off for speed and efficiency. But an important event processing result will be rechecked (e.g., for errors in event pattern matching).

Extract What You Want to Know

The third reason to use event processing, *extracting what you want to know from the cloud of events available to you,* is all about how to cope with the cloud of too much information. It is related to the other problems we have discussed and can be considered as a necessary part of solving them.

Event feeds come from everywhere, and many of them are unstructured and unfocused. They simply carry events. Some of the events are unreliable, a lot of the events are unrelated to what the enterprise needs to know, and other events are relevant or even vital. It is an interesting area for development of new event processing techniques, somewhat akin to news service analysis or sentiment analysis in financial news reports. It presents a challenge both to commercial enterprises and to governments. Some examples follow:

1. An international package distribution company operates fleets of airplanes and trucks and a network of distribution centers. Its business processes are intensely event driven and clocked. Timing is all-important to remaining on schedule and honoring service level agreements (e.g., overnight delivery). Its operations receive events from many sources, including its own fleets and distribution centers. Sources outside of the company are also tracked. These include traffic and travel advisories, labor disputes, and weather reports, much of which may turn out to be irrelevant. But all of those event sources must be monitored to extract any information that could indicate an impact on the company's operations. The potential impact on its schedules must be predicted and the affected operations replanned. The company has also to evaluate every situation that it considers for false alarms, because they are costly.

2. With more than 2 billion people traveling by air every year, an outbreak or epidemic in one part of the world is only a few hours away from becoming an imminent threat elsewhere. Worldwide epidemic warning systems must be improved so that the time lag between detecting the incubation of a possible epidemic anywhere in the world and alerting public health organizations is much shorter—on the order of days. Present reaction times in government-sponsored medical networks are sometimes on the order of weeks or months. The systems include human experts in making analysis and decisions. Also, these systems are hierarchical and involve time-delaying decisions at various levels, from local to regional to national. We must build event-monitoring warning systems that can detect epidemic threats while making minimal use of humans in the loop.

   For example, new systems are being developed based upon SMS cell phone reports from local field agents in rural areas of Southeast Asia. These systems also leverage popular social networking traffic. Rumors and hearsay have proved to be the earliest indicators of emerging epidemics, far earlier than medical reports in fact! websites such as Twitter are being monitored for indications of emerging diseases. Techniques include detecting increased use of disease and illness keywords in tweets. Lexicons of keywords are being developed and refined.

   The reason to use social interaction websites is to detect possible emerging epidemics as early as possible. Cell phone use has exploded in areas where some of the most infectious diseases incubate (SARS, swine flu, West Nile valley fever, malaria, etc.). Many rural areas in Asia and Africa have little recourse to medical networks, but they have a rapidly expanding use of cheap cell phones.

But there are problems to be solved. The cell phone traffic is in multiple languages and will obviously include data of varying degrees of accuracy and focus. The data must be filtered, translated, and analyzed for relevance to a disease outbreak, geographic location, and frequency. Voice-to-text transformation technology would add greatly to usefulness of the earliest sources, especially in third-world countries. Automated methods must be used in all of the early processing phases to allow high-traffic volumes. The resulting events must be correlated and summarized for the decision makers.[14]

And above all else, false alarms of an epidemic outbreak must be avoided at all costs, because they can result in disastrous global economic consequences.

3. Homeland security is a paradigm example in which information needs to be extracted from a large variety of sources and aggregated into actionable intelligence. Its operations receive event feeds from direct sources, such as INS passport and visa entry point data, as well as from U.S. government departments, foreign governments, airlines, and so on. There are also many indirect sources. At the other end of the scale is intelligence gleaned by monitoring the daily activities of sets of individuals already resident in the country. Phone traffic may be taken into account. The sources vary in their reliability.

The scale of the event input is one aspect of this detection problem. Another is time. Any single investigation may involve monitoring event inputs over long time periods. And intelligence has to be recognized from fragments of data that may appear at first to be unrelated or may be widely separated by both source and time. False alerts are expensive, but failures may be catastrophic.

As we previously mentioned, reaction times may be very different in each situation. For government agencies, both local and national, the situation may require alerting emergency services to meet a natural disaster within 24 hours, or averting a national medical crisis within a few weeks of the first indicators, or defending against a cyber attack on the power grid within seconds.

Commercial businesses must also uncover and evaluate the information in the event cloud in a timely manner. This will often have a direct

---

[14]The legality of this kind of monitoring is beyond the scope of this book but might involve exceptions for both governmental agencies and NGAs.

influence on the company's bottom line, maybe not immediately, but a few months or a year later. Again, reaction times from receipt of information to action may vary widely. Financial trading requires decisions in milliseconds. On the other hand, patterns of business events can take weeks or months to add up to information that forces adjustments in various managerial issues, such as marketing and sales strategies, or changes in the supply chain organization, inventory order schedules, stock investments, and so on.

Similar situations to the ones illustrated in these examples are happening all the time. Event pattern detection will play a key role in detecting actionable situations in large volumes of event inputs.

There is another factor to consider. The commercial offerings in this technology are improving rapidly. There's a continuous war of event processing technology going on. Enterprises that already have event processing in their business systems should keep their event processing capabilities up to date. And for those who don't—now's the time to start! The technology officers in the company should know what is going on in real-time event processing. This is not just about databases any more.

Principle 6: Keep Your Event Processing Technology Current

Event processing technology is evolving and improving. Enterprises must keep their event processing technology up to date and capable of coping with the changing problems they face.

This principle is about operating in the event driven world. There is a gap between the latest theories of event processing, such as Complex Event Processing (CEP), and the existing commercial event processing products in the marketplace. Commercial CEP technology is not static; it is evolving and improving all the time. Improvements are driven by competitive pressures and by financial incentives to solve new event processing problems.

Getting Started

We've described three of the more advanced reasons to add event processing technology to your business operations—*knowing, detecting,* and *extracting* various aspects of business intelligence. But there are many day-to-day reasons to add event processing too—just to make your operations run smoother and faster, for example.

You will find a lot more on event processing technology in the later chapters. Also, Chapter 5 is a broad survey of the different business applications of event processing and the markets for it—essentially, this chapter answers our fourth question: *What kinds of enterprises have bought into event processing technology so far?*

Now let's suppose you decide to experiment and introduce event monitoring and processing into your company. What technology do you need? And what about the cost? Event monitoring is going to require investing in a lot of expensive software, isn't it?

Not necessarily! A lot of event monitoring can be done with quite simple software that'll run on the usual computers in your business. In fact, you might well have the software you need already deployed for other applications within your company—you're just not using its event monitoring capabilities. Or the new software you need might be easy to add on to what you've already got. A database with a graphical interface would do to get started. But you have to set it up in a way that doesn't lose too much of the *right now* aspect of your event processing.

When the company gets serious about applying event monitoring to its operations, some technical knowledge on the part of some personnel in the company will be needed.

What do they have to know? The basic concepts in event processing and complex event processing. A couple of technically minded personnel will get you started. In these times of personal digital assistants (PDAs) and smartphones, event processing is almost a natural language.

The concepts in complex event processing play a major role in building applications of event processing. Sooner or later, one gets into the "build it or buy it" decision. Some CEP technology out there today is freeware. But you have to fit that freeware into your IT systems to use it effectively. That's where the two or three technical people for a few weeks are needed.

Eventually, you may come to think it's worth investing in commercial CEP products and the vendor's consulting on their use. You can do what we're talking about in this book with an investment that will certainly yield a positive return—if you understand just a little bit about CEP. We'll come back to this topic when we've covered some of the basic CEP concepts. So, read on!

CHAPTER 2

Sixty Years of Event Processing

Event processing technologies over the past sixty years up to today and likely developments in the future:

- Discrete event simulation
- Networks
- Active databases
- Middleware, SOA, and the enterprise service bus
- Event driven architectures

Event processing in one form or another is not new. It has been going on for the past sixty years or more. If we look at the history of event processing, we can see a natural development from the use of events in earlier applications to the twenty-first-century uses of events in communications, information processing, and enterprise management. History gives us a perspective on the origins of Complex Event Processing (CEP) and how the CEP techniques evolved and will evolve in the future.

This chapter gives a brief review on how event processing has been a basis for developing various technologies over the past sixty years. These developments happened very rapidly, one after the other, and they are all established technologies today—big business, as it happens! Chapters 5 and 9 describe a longer-term view of future developments in event processing.

Four technology movements have arisen during the past sixty years, all of them based upon processing different types of events and for very different purposes. They are *Discrete Event Simulation, Networks, Databases* (among which *Active Databases* made explicit use of event processing in their design), and the *Middleware* movement—which includes many developments such as event driven service-oriented architectures (SOA), enterprise service buses (ESBs), and event driven architectures (EDAs). And the ascent of newer event-based ideas continues with business processes, business intelligence systems, and the like. Figure 2.1 shows the timeline over which these technologies developed.[1] So modern event processing as we know it in the business world is not new. But there are some new ideas and concepts in its application to the management of enterprises; among them are (1) the types of events being processed, (2) the concepts and techniques being used, and (3) the objectives and goals. Some of those new ideas and concepts are CEP.

We should clarify the meaning of *event* here. There are two meanings. First, an event is *something that happens*. That's the dictionary definition.

But there's a second meaning. In using computers to process events with various kinds of analysis and predictions, we represent events as data (sometimes called "objects") in the computer. We refer to those data

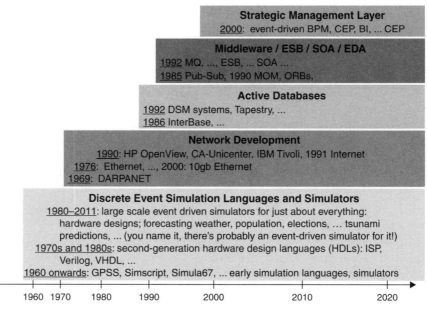

FIGURE 2.1 The Rise of Event Driven Technologies over the Past 60 Years

---

[1]The timeline in Figure 2.1 is not linear. More event processing developments took place in later years.

as *events*, also. So essentially, *event* has a second meaning, the *data representing the things that happen*.[2]

We use the word *event* in both meanings. But we can always tell from the context which meaning of the word we are using. Programmers call words with two meanings *overloaded*—so we're going to overload the word *event*!

There's another distinction that is perhaps worthy of mention. A terminology that is sometimes used is the distinction between *actual* events and *virtual* events. It is a distinction that is made in the world of modeling and computer simulation to distinguish between events in an actual system and their simulations in the computer model.

An example of a virtual event is an event that is *thought of as happening*—like using your imagination to visualize the events that will happen if you don't stop at a red light. Suppose, for example, there's a car crossing on green, and you imagine a crash! But since you stopped at the red light, those events didn't happen—you imagined them as virtual events. And you used them in decision making.

Event Driven Simulation

Event driven simulation refers to the use of events to drive the steps in computing with models to predict the behavior of systems—anything from a design for a controller for traffic lights, or a model for a manufacturing line, to a plan for battlefield operations. This is one of the earliest uses of events and event driven computing. Rooted in World War II, this area of computer programming took off in the 1950s. People started to use computers—a recent invention at the time—to predict how designs of devices such as controllers would behave before they were actually manufactured. The idea was to save costs involved in letting mistakes in designs go forward to the manufacture of the design and also to shorten the time taken in the design-to-manufacture cycle.

Computer simulation started out very simply as a haphazard activity in which people wrote programs, usually in machine code, to predict the behavior of a design or model. The activity quickly expanded to other things, such as predicting how the operations of a company could be improved to grow sales, and later on to much more ambitious undertakings like forecasting the weather.[3]

---

[2] We give definitions of both meanings of *event* in Chapter 3, "What Is an Event?".

[3] Robin Stewart, "Computers Meet Weather Forecasting," *Weather Forecasting by Computer*, October 1, 2008. www.robinstewart.com/personal/learn/wfbc/computers.html

During the 1950s, the techniques for building computer simulations quickly became understood and formalized. The core idea is to use a computer program that models—or mimics—an actual system. The system could be anything from a factory production line to a company's sales plans to voter behavior in an election. Simulation refers to executing the model on input data. It turned out that many simulations used events as a way to organize their computations. The *event driven* method is now widely adopted.

This became known as *discrete event simulation*, because events are used to control the progress of the computation that is simulating the system and to move that computation forward one step at a time (see Figures 2.2 and 2.3). Each step involves running the model on data representing the current state of the system—a discrete step. Events containing data are input to the next step. As a result, the model is run on those data and produces a new set of output events that contain data defining a new state. These events are input to the next step, and so on. So an event driven simulation produces a step-by-step succession of sets of events that represent states of the system being simulated.

A discrete event simulator is often structured into cooperating simulators for specific parts of the system being modeled. The whole simulation is driven by events. For example, weather simulators are commonly made up of a grid of three-dimensional cells. Each cell is a simulator for the weather in a specific small area, usually covering a surface area less than fifty kilometers square and going up to several thousand feet. A cell takes events from neighboring cells as inputs, uses those data to compute a change of state for the component as a function of the inputs, and outputs its results to its neighboring cells. In such a simulator, a cell is an event processing finite state machine. Figure 2.2 shows a single cell. It waits

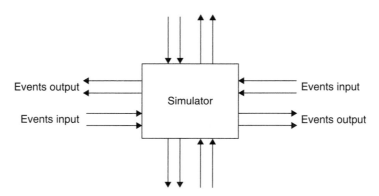

FIGURE 2.2 Event Driven Simulation Cell

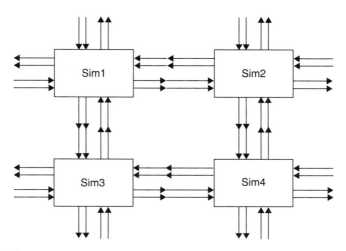

FIGURE 2.3 A Simulation Grid Showing Event Flows between the Cells

and does nothing until it receives input events, so it is essentially "driven by events."

The outputs from each cell are communicated as inputs to its immediate neighboring cells, and so on. The overall simulator is made up of a grid of cells (see Figure 2.3), each one driven by events from its neighbors and computing continuously as new inputs arrive. So events are flowing continuously in and out of the cells of the simulation. Each cell will have a different function and state from the other cells.

Figure 2.4 shows a grid structure for a simulator for weather forecasts over the Austrian Alps. Each cell will encode the unique geographic characteristics of its locality.

In general, event driven simulators use various scheduling methods to run each component of the simulation. A round robin scheduler is often used to ensure fair scheduling, so that each cell gets to run. As event driven simulation developed, many different types of events were used in simulations; in some cases they contained complex data, timing information, and details concerning their origin and destination.

Commercial companies began to see the potential of discrete event simulation. This activity escalated as the production cost benefits became obvious.

By the 1960s, most large manufacturing or aerospace companies had their own internal event driven simulation languages. Some of the better known early simulation languages are listed in Figure 2.1. Simula67 is perhaps the best known of them, notably because it was not only a simulation language but became known in the 1980s for its object-oriented use of modules— the programming language analogy of simulation cells.

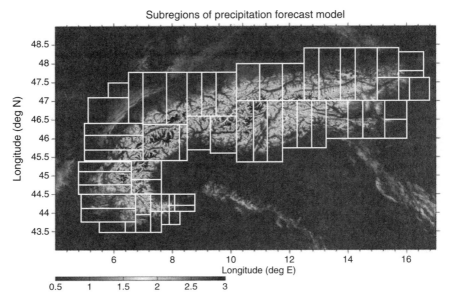

FIGURE 2.4 Grid Use in Simulating Alpine Weather Conditions over Austria

Today, event driven simulation is big business. The design of almost any product is subjected to some kind of simulation before it is produced. For example, designs for a new computer chip are subjected to CPU years of simulation at every design level, from the instruction set level to the gate level, before they reach the production phase. Indeed, the further along the production sequence of "design—simulate—prototype—test—manufacture" an error survives, the more expensive it is to correct. And today in many other technology areas we can find the use of large-scale event driven simulations, from weather forecasting to the petroleum industry's use of simulations in oil field exploration.

Some of the techniques in CEP were first developed to aid in analyzing the output from event driven simulations at Stanford University. This included the use of *event patterns* and *event abstraction*. At that time event driven simulators produced a single stream of events ordered by the time at which they were computed by the simulator. Many of the simulators did not show which events actually happened simultaneously in the actual system, and none of the simulators showed which events caused others in the system being modeled. The viewer had to figure all of that out!

The Stanford simulation analyzer did something new. Instead of letting the user try to analyze manually a simulation output stream of low-level events, all jumbled together, CEP techniques were first applied to organize the events in the stream. The stream was analyzed for patterns of low-level events that signified more meaningful higher-level events. This was used to produce a corresponding output stream of higher-level events.

The higher-level events were much easier to understand. These events were much closer to the concepts humans would use to design or talk about the systems being simulated—for example, CPU instructions rather than gate-level events. Also there were far fewer of them, which made them easier to analyze. The number of events produced by a simulation decreases exponentially as the level of the events increase. Errors tended to be magnified in the higher-level events and, therefore, much easier to detect. For example, a CPU instruction fails to complete. The corresponding design error at the gate level could be a single wrong connection among all the connections between two sets of 128 terminal pins, much more difficult to detect.

It was quickly realized at Stanford that these event processing techniques had wide application outside of the simulation area.

Networks

Event processing technology was also developed as a fundamental part of *networking*, starting with the ARPANET in 1969. But there was no recognition in the early days that there was such a thing as an event processing technology within networking. It was just there, as a part of networking. Of course, this was a very different kind of event processing from what goes on in discrete event simulation.

The emphasis was on using very simple types of events to build communications between computers over unreliable transmission lines. Communication was by means of *packets*. A packet is essentially a sequence of bits that encode a small amount of data, together with the packet's origin and destination in the network. Computers communicate by sending packets to each other over the transmission line. The sending and receiving of packets are events—things that happen. To ensure that a packet arrives at the other end, the computers engage in a protocol of acknowledging receipt of each packet or resending it if an acknowledgement is not received within a time limit. If a packet is lost during transmission, it will be resent until it does arrive. The communication protocols are methods of processing events to ensure certain properties (e.g., reliability of communication). Note that there may be several "hops" between the sender and receiver, that is, intermediate computers that pass the packet onward.

At the lowest level, then, *event processing* in a communications network is essentially very small message processing. To send a human communication—say an email—the message is broken down into a set of packets, each packet is transmitted using the protocol, and the set is reassembled at the other end. One can imagine a continuous activity in the network consisting of events involved in sending and receiving lots of packets. This activity obeys standard communications protocols such as TCP/IP (the Internet Transmission Control Protocol Suite, http://www.yale.edu/pclt/COMM/TCPIP.HTM). The standards definitions for network protocols are layered into hierarchies of functions, such as the Open Systems Interconnection (OSI) seven-layer model.[4] These functions define how an operation such as email is built up out of processing low-level events involving packets.

The concept of an *event hierarchy* is central to CEP, where the idea is taken further than the messaging standards by requiring that a means of computing events at one level of the hierarchy from sets of events at a lower level must be part of the event hierarchy definition. So whenever activity in a network results in a sequence of low-level events, the hierarchy definition can be used to compute the corresponding sequence of higher-level events. This gives the capability to view network activity in terms of more understandable higher-level events.

We will deal with computable event hierarchies in a later chapter. It will show how different computable hierarchies can be used to define more than one kind of higher-level event resulting from the same lower level events in a system. We call these higher level events *views*. For example, events in networks can be viewed at a higher level in terms of security concerns or performance concerns. Activity in financial trading systems can be viewed in terms of compliance to regulations, or in terms of profit and loss or economic impact. And an airline's day-to-day operations can be viewed as equipment utilization events, as airplane load factor events, or as profitability events. The applications of the event hierarchy concept to systems that are essentially event driven in nature are very far reaching.

It is likely that these event based ideas, pioneered in the Stanford CEP project of the 1990s, will become part of new standards definitions for networks and other event driven systems in the future. Standards definitions should be executable by anyone who has a simulator and wants to see how a standard works in a given case. One has only to consider recent developments and issues.

Networks that developed in the 1960s and 1970s expanded rapidly, first as research networks, such as the ARPANET, and later into public networks and finally the Internet. Today these networks play the role of information highways fundamental to the running of our society. They now include dynamic networks in which the member elements vary at any time, such as the newer satellite-based networks that support mobile

---

[4]Rachelle Miller, "The OSI Model: An Overview." SANS Institute Reading Room. www.sans.org/reading_room/whitepapers/standards/osi-model-overview_543

devices such as cell phones. The variety of protocols used in processing the communications (e.g., CDMA, GSM, 3G, 4G, etc.) has exploded in number, so new ones appear frequently. The communication activity results in events at many different levels of viewing. These are all event driven systems to which event hierarchy definitions can be applied.

Today, society depends upon the event processing that goes on in the Internet and mobile satellite networks. This event processing has become extremely complicated; in fact, it is not well understood. There are so many levels of issues involved that the event traffic has probably taken on a life of its own. What started out in the ARPANET as an experiment in network messaging to control and direct event traffic has been compounded with many other concerns, such as levels and quality of service, security, theft and hijacking of events, cyber attacks, and so on. In the early days, people didn't think of such things. Now the question is how to redesign the Internet to deal with all the modern concerns! It would seem that CEP facilities must be built into next generation networks to enable real-time event pattern analysis of the traffic. As for the mobile networks, one can only wait to see what scams arise in both the administration and the misuse of event processing there.

Active Databases

Event processing technology was also developed in the use of databases in the 1980s. Traditional databases are passive, in the sense that they wait for queries and respond to them. Active databases are capable of invoking other applications in response to a query. For example, an active inventory database might initiate an action with an inventory control system to reorder an item if the database detects that the inventory level of that item has fallen below a specified level.

Active databases extend traditional databases with a layer of event processing rules called event-condition-action (E-C-A) rules together with event detection mechanisms. An E-C-A rule has the form

    on event **if** Boolean-condition **then** action

It responds to the event, called its trigger, by evaluating the Boolean condition and executing the action if the condition is true. An event can be specified as a state change of interest—for example, a change in an inventory, in which case the condition would be the inventory level being below a specified level.

Active databases are another use of event processing. In this case, the idea was to extend the capabilities of the standard databases of the 1980s to bring them in line with the increasing use of real-time technology. One cannot say that they involve the kinds of volumes of event activity that occur in simulations or networking, but a part of their activity is driven by events. Also, they are of interest in building rule-based event processing systems because they had general problems, particularly with consistency of the sets of E-C-A rules, and race conditions between rules that might negate each other's state updates. Approaches to dealing with these problems apply to building and executing sets of E-C-A rules in general. So active databases are one of the precursors to the modern event processing that we shall be dealing with.

The use of E-C-A rules can be found in many applications of CEP. But the notion of a single event trigger has been extended to the use of event patterns containing several events. The complete pattern must match in order to trigger the rule. Of course, a single event trigger is a special case.

Example 2.1: Detecting Possible Misuse of Credit Cards

If credit card C **is used** at Location L at time T
and then C **is used** at Location L1 **at** time T1
and Travel **between** L **and** L1 **takes more than** T1 − T
then alert C **maybe stolen**.

Example 2.1 illustrates an E-C-A rule in which the trigger is a pattern containing two card use events and a condition on the locations of use. The action when the trigger is true is to issue an alert.

Middleware

Middleware technology started in the late 1980s and exploded in a variety of directions in the 1990s and 2000s. It started as an attempt to modularize the network layers and messaging protocols that were becoming the critical infrastructure that wired business applications together. The idea was to hide the messy details of the events and the various event transmission protocols by means of which messages flowed back and forth between users or between users and business applications. Middleware attempted to hide the events at the level of message transmission by providing higher-level communication functions in an application programming Interface or API. The users need not know anything about how their communications and requests were handled.

Thus the development of middleware can be regarded as containing the roots of a hierarchical approach to events and event processing. But there was a long way yet to go!

The perceived advantage of middleware in the beginning was that users no longer needed to worry about how their interactions were implemented in terms of message flows in the underlying network. Businesses could use middleware easily to link applications such as payroll, sales, accounting, inventory, and databases together across multiple geographic locations. Interactions between users and applications could be distributed across the enterprise, perhaps on a worldwide scale.

As middleware applications broadened, a variety of problems arose such as lower quality of service, loss of information, time lags, and the like, which led to many diverse server architectures being developed under the middleware cover to solve these problems. The event processing could involve many different levels of events, from heartbeats to message delivery protocols, but none of this concerns us. Today the use of middleware spans diverse areas from wireless networks to health care to business.

Two main categories of middleware were developed in the early days: synchronous communication, based upon remote procedure call (RPC), and asynchronous communication, based upon messages, called message-oriented middleware or MOM.

The synchronous API gave the ability to send a request for a service (the remote call) and wait until a reply was received (the service answer). This procedure call paradigm was distributed across the enterprise, and it fit right in with the object-oriented programming ideas prevalent at the time. A registry of services was also provided, along with ability to register a service. The classic example of this is Common Object Request Broker Architecture, or CORBA.[5] Although the RPC paradigm could be viewed as event communication in terms of function call (one event) and function response (another event), one of the main criticisms was that it was too slow and cumbersome.

Perhaps the simplest form of the asynchronous MOM middleware was the publish/subscribe paradigm, often called *pub-sub*. Applications can act as publishers, as subscribers, or indeed as both. A middleware product that implements pub-sub provides an API that lets an application publish a message on a particular *topic*. Other applications can receive messages on this topic by simply subscribing to the topic through the API. Applications that have subscribed to a topic will receive all the messages that are

---

[5]Ciaran McHale, "Corba Explained Simply." www.ciaranmchale.com/corba-explained-simply

published on that topic. This is a form of *one-to-many* communication. It is intrinsically asynchronous, because a publisher does not wait to get responses from subscribers, and subscribers can be doing other things while messages on their subscribed topics list are being published.

The event flow in pub-sub middleware can be viewed abstractly as flowing directly from a publisher to all the subscribers to that topic. In actual fact, messages are sent first to servers hidden somewhere in the middleware, and from there to the subscribers. Other common middleware paradigms for transporting events include point-to-point event transmission and message queuing.

The choice between them boils down to the particular cost/performance details of the kind of high-level event processing that will be hosted upon that choice. Each of these three kinds of middleware can emulate the other two kinds.

Middleware concepts did not really contribute to CEP. But middleware provided a fertile ground for CEP applications—to ensure correct functioning of the middleware, perhaps under imperfect conditions—and functioned as a medium that encouraged applications of CEP. For example, *content-based routing* of messages was an early application of some of the first principles in CEP. This is the routing of messages on middleware using both the content of the message (e.g., keywords within the message) and the history of patterns of activity in the messaging. It was an early application of event patterns. So in fact, middleware acted as an early application area for CEP, and as middleware morphed into more highfalutin' products such as ESBs, SOAs, and EDAs, the opportunities for CEP continued to expand.

The Enterprise Service Bus

Middleware is often synonymous with the concept of an enterprise service bus (ESB). There is considerable variation in the philosophy of what an ESB actually is or contains. Obviously, the spirit is that an ESB is a high-level application-to-application communications bus, analogous to the hardware bus that carries signals between hardware components in a computer. Alternative views are that it is middleware, based upon de facto standards such as J2EE or .NET, that encapsulates and hides network details and offers services such as document routing. Some philosophies claim that ESBs contain software products for business activity monitoring (BAM) and for building service-oriented architectures (SOAs). So a commercial ESB may bundle together a lot of event driven messaging, often including Web services, SOAP, and XML messaging. Some ESBs go as far as to say they offer CEP in the form of event interpretation, correlation and pattern matching. Much of this is playing into the currently fashionable market for SOA, with a trend toward EDA.[6]

However, if we ignore the marketing hype, the upshot is that various flavors of middleware now represent a fourth technology development involving event processing. An ESB is based upon event driven network communications at a lower level that is hidden from application programmers. It provides a messaging interface that makes it easier to connect applications into distributed message-driven communicating architectures and to allow such application architectures to evolve as new applications enter the enterprise.

Chaos in the Marketing of Information Systems

Different approaches to designing, building, and managing information systems have proliferated over the past fifteen years, so much so that a new collection of techno-marketing jargon now presents a confusion of competing and overlapping categories or products. It is a minefield of marketing banners to the uninitiated buyer of information technology. There are no guidelines or standards that products in these various categories must satisfy, not for the features they provide, nor the problems they solve, nor how they perform.

Some marketing banners specifically target event processing. And each of the other banners has been "souped up" at some point in time with the addition of event processing. So we'll review each marketing banner briefly and point out how and where event processing might apply.

First, there is the SOA arena (service oriented architectures), the BPM arena (business process management), and more recent arrivals in the area of event processing, including event driven architectures (EDA). There is much marketing hype associated with each of these three-letter acronyms.

SOA and EDA have often been presented as competing or conflicting, and religious wars have threatened to break out from time to time.[7] However, the truth is that at the conceptual level they are complementary, and they all have a role to play in design and management of IT systems. And recently, complex event processing (CEP) has been added to these areas.

---

[6]A survey of 125 banks and other financial institutions published by Gartner in August 2010 found that 40 percent identify SOA+EDA as their primary architectural approach for new applications, whereas 26 percent identify SOA, 10 percent as EDA, 18 percent as three-tier, and 6 percent as monolithic.

[7]Do a Google search for "SOA 2.0" for a recent view of this.

Service Oriented Architecture

SOA is an outgrowth of the object-oriented programming movement of the 1990s. The basic idea is to modularize sets of related services—the business analogy to functions in object-oriented (O-O) programming—into separate modules. For example, a pizza business would be a module that provided sets of services for customers, such as menu browsing, ordering, paying, and delivery tracking.

SOA did not start out having anything to do with event processing. It was a movement toward structuring enterprise software systems. But commercial opportunities helped proliferate the specialized kinds of services that could be included in SOA, and consequently many different flavors of SOA appeared on the marketplace, including event driven SOA. Today, it is a total minefield to the newcomer.

Those who wish to navigate the SOA minefield in the hope of finding a solution to their enterprise IT problems had better start by first mastering the simple ideas that are at the root of this marketing nightmare. And simple they are!

SOA has three top-level defining concepts, *services*, *modularity*, and *remote access*.

What is a *service*? Think of it as something you want to use: a weather report or a credit rating. Send the weather service your ZIP code and you get back a report for your local area. In its purest and oldest form, a service is a function—you call it, requesting data, and you get an answer.

Modularity deals with the organization of related services into a single-server module. Sets of related services are grouped into server modules. A server module consists of two parts: (1) an interface that specifies the services that are provided and contains metadata defining how they behave, and (2) a separate implementation of those services. An implementation (or module body) can be anything from, say, pure Java code to an adapter that maps the services in the interface to other services provided in other modules or even on the Internet.

An interface containing metadata tells a user what the services do and how to use them. The interface is the users' (i.e., the consumers') view of the services. On the other hand, the separate implementation is hidden from users and can be changed without the users knowing. So, one of the goals of SOA is that users of services don't have to understand how they work, which is pretty much the way drivers of cars operate these days. Of course, the implementation has to be truthful to the interface metadata (i.e., when you step on the brake pedal, the car should stop).

Consistency between an interface and its implementation is something that is ignored in most SOA presentations. In practice, if you purchase an SOA system, inconsistencies can be a source of surprises for the user—but that's nothing new in software, is it?

Actually, a modern interface design should contain other information not normally required in SOA. It should also specify which services are *required* by the server module itself—that is, the services that may be used to implement the services that are provided. The reason for required service specifications has to do with architectural design issues that are beyond the scope of our book. Think of them as a privacy statement— "when you use one of our provided services, we will only send your data to these required services."[8]

In the early years, a SOA module interface was an object written in a programming language like Java, but these days it is likely to be the user interface of a website. For example, services related to using stock market feeds, such as computing various averages and statistics over time windows (e.g., VWAP) are provided by a market feed website.

The *remote access* principle of SOA requires that services should operate in a distributed computing environment. SOA must therefore provide users with an ability to access services remotely. The remote access principle has different paradigms. Access in traditional SOA[9] was by remote procedure call (RPC), also called request/reply (R/R). Figure 2.5

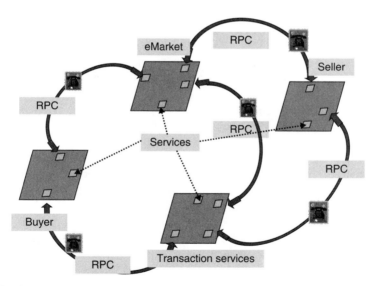

FIGURE 2.5 An SOA Containing Various Services for Stock Trading

---

[8]The motivation for required service specifications is to enable implementations to be changed without introducing inconsistencies, so called plug-and-play—see Luckham, *The Power of Events* (Boston: Addison-Wesley), 2002, Section 4.6.1.

[9]By *traditional SOA*, we refer to the state of SOA thinking about the time of the initial release of CORBA in 1991.

is a schematic view of a traditional SOA containing interfaces for eMarketplace services, users (buyers and sellers) and access to services by RPC.

RPC involves a synchronizing handshake between user and service. A user sends data to a service (e.g., the remote call to a function) and blocks, waiting for a reply (e.g., the value of the function on those data). One can regard the call and reply as two events. But the user is not free to do anything else until the reply.

An everyday example of RPC is the telephone call. This may be a little more conversational that a straight request/reply call, but it is a remote access and requires synchronization. And as we all know, phone calls can often waste a lot of the caller's time. We've all had the experience of phoning an airline for a service such as booking a flight and first having to deal with an automated menu of services we don't want before reaching a human who can provide the service or answer the question we do want. A lot of that time is wasted time for the user. Nice for the airline who can employ fewer humans, at the expense of the user!

Event processing (EP) at the level of business events now enters the picture with a new conceptual paradigm for remote access. A user no longer needs to access a service by RPC. Instead, a user can access services by sending and receiving events, asynchronously.

The upside of event driven service access is that it is much more versatile and efficient than RPC. It allows all actors—users and services—to multi-task. Instead of a phone call, you send an event—let's say over the Internet. In an event driven SOA, a call to an airline is executed by the user sending a request event, "Need Service." A protocol reply is, "Here is the menu of services." The user chooses to send the event answer, "Human contact needed, callback number N." Response event: "Your wait time will be exactly 15 minutes; make sure your callback number is free in 15 minutes. You will receive only one callback event." Now the user is free to use the 15-minute wait time to do other things instead of hanging on the end of a phone line.

Perhaps it is true that communications have been driven by events since the earliest days of networks. First, there were network protocols like TCP. Then the level of events in communications gradually rose with the advent of pub-sub middleware, message queues, and so on. Nowadays, the communication between users and services in SOA can always be by means of events. This gives us event driven SOA (ED-SOA). This is depicted schematically in Figure 2.6.

Event driven communication decouples the handshake by using events and protocols. So event driven SOA is an evolution of traditional SOA in which the communication between users and services is by events instead of RPC. Services are triggered by, and react to, events instead of procedure calls. Usually, the implementations of services use communication standards such as WSDL, SOAP, and HTTP for remote access.

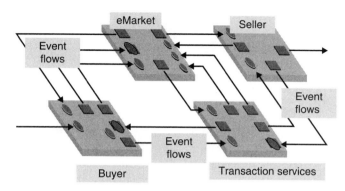

FIGURE 2.6 SOA with Asynchronous Event Driven Services

There is always a downside, of course. The increased versatility has magnified opportunities for everyone—users, services and, of course, crooks. Scalability has become another issue. We're talking about real-time operations with, in some cases, very large numbers of events (e.g., 200,000 trading events per second in stock market operations). The management and business intelligence issues are becoming more and more challenging. This is where BPM and CEP come into play.

Now, beware! The next idea is to organize the service modules and access to them into *architectures*. The simple programming ideas quickly got complicated by the need to add new dimensions to the original three concepts, such as distributed architecture. And then came the smoke-screen of commercial interests.

When you read further in the SOA literature, you may be told that "service component architectures (SCA) are part of SOA," or "a SOA must use protocol standards like XML and WSDL and SOAP," or "SOA is really just Web Services," or "SOA must contain load balancing and central service catalogues," or . . .

Indeed, these are all good and useful things that can play their part in various implementation approaches to organizing and building SOAs.[10] But, at the conceptual level, there are only three principal concepts in SOA: *services, modularity,* and *remote access.* The rest are packaging and implementation details. The concept "architecture" itself does not yet have

---

[10]Although I have never had complete confidence in Wikipedia, the entries on SOA as of 2009 were as good a documentation of the state-of-concept chaos in the SOA implementation world as I have found.

a widely accepted definition. And despite efforts toward architectures for SOA,[11] there is no widely accepted reference architecture for SOA.[12]

Event Driven Architecture

Figure 2.6 is an illustration of a typical event driven architecture (EDA). Its architecture is a set of interfaces defining the provided and required various services and the communication between those interfaces using their services. The communication is by means of sending and receiving events. The communications are variously called pathways, connections, and channels. These terms all have definitions that vary in complexity and have not been accepted universally within the event processing community. We can think of them simply as event flows. The activity in the architecture is driven by events.

Event driven architecture (EDA) and SOA are related in two ways.

First, event driven access to services is an *implementation paradigm* for SOA—not a competing technology. ED-SOA is a very good way to organize distributed services over any kind of IT infrastructure. And we're talking real-time use. Pretty much any modern enterprise's IT operations are organized as an ED-SOA, especially if they use the Internet or commercial networks such as SWIFT. This includes financial services, stock markets, cellular service providers, automated supply chains and inventory systems, on-demand manufacturing, Supervisory Control and Data Acquisition (SCADA) control systems (e.g., for power stations, dams), banking, and retailing—the list is endless. In fact, it is difficult to think of anything that isn't event driven, completely or in parts, these days. Of course, there's legacy in most IT infrastructures, so in practice what you see in most system architectures is a mix of event driven and request/reply.

And the EDA field is expanding. New event driven communication protocols are being developed all the time to support new applications, such as mobile ad hoc wireless networking to enable wireless mesh computing (e.g., the OLPC project). These technology developments are all event driven.

Secondly, SOA can be taken as a *design paradigm* for event driven applications. In software systems we've seen this happening, first in the middleware products and more recently in the enterprise service bus offerings. But SOA designs of event driven systems have been around for nearly fifty years in hardware designs—long before SOA, in fact! That is why

---

[11]www.oasis-open.org/committees/tc_home.php?wg_abbrev=soa-rm

[12]"Service-Oriented Architecture," *Wikipedia*, as of August 2009. http://en.wikipedia.org/wiki/Service-oriented_architecture

I have used a hardware diagram in Figure 2.6. Typically, all the components in a hardware architecture have interfaces that present services, that is, input events that request a service and output events that deliver the service. And their implementations are hidden. An adder requires two input events and then delivers sum-and-carry output events (i.e., its service). Registers, ALUs, and so on all define similar services with interfaces presenting their services (inputs and outputs). And the communication between the interfaces of these components is by triggering events flowing down the connecting wires, timed by a controller. That is, the architecture is a wiring up of the interfaces of the components. It is simple, it is SOA, it is disciplined design, and it is much less error-prone than software. Indeed, one might well ask, why can't software be more like hardware!

To summarize thus far, SOA and EDA are complementary. EDA is the paradigm for communications in SOAs, and SOA is the design methodology for EDAs. In the future, we would like to be able to define EDA as follows:

Principle 7

An event driven architecture (EDA) is a distributed service-oriented architecture (SOA) in which all communication is by events and all services are independent, concurrent, reactive event driven processes (i.e., they react to input events and produce output events).

Many systems out there today cannot conform to this standard, since many of their components are not event driven[13] and they were not designed with SOA principles in mind. Which brings up another question: Is there a test for whether a system is SOA or EDA? This seems to be about as difficult as asking if a system has a good design or not. Some systems are clearly SOA (e.g., built in Java using OO techniques and JMS). Others are clearly not SOA at all (e.g., lumps of COBOL code). But there's a large space of systems in between. Perhaps someone might design a questionnaire for users: "Is the system you are using SOA/EDA?" It might contain questions like (with a scale of satisfaction from 1 to 10):

- Do you find services are organized in logical groups?
- Is their documentation easy to understand?
- Do the results from services agree with their documentation?
- Do you need to understand how services are implemented in order to use them?
- Can you find the service you're looking for easily?

---

[13]See the definition of EDA in this book's Glossary of Terminology

- Are you happy with your service response time?
- Do you get surprising results when you request a service?

Finally, the proposed definition of EDA above has to be viewed as a philosophy for the future. The spirit of the philosophy is this: "think hardware designs. Then think hardware designs in which the numbers of components and the pathways connecting them can vary at runtime. And then, think multilayered designs." That kind of thinking leads us to dynamic, multilayered, event driven architectures.

Summary: Event Processing, 1950–2010

We have outlined four different event processing technologies that developed during the period 1950–2010. Most of these areas are continuing to develop and expand today. Each of these technologies, discrete event simulation, networks, active databases and middleware, use different types of events from each other, they use events in different ways, and their purposes and goals are completely different. But each of them led to problems that provided a demand for solutions involving CEP concepts

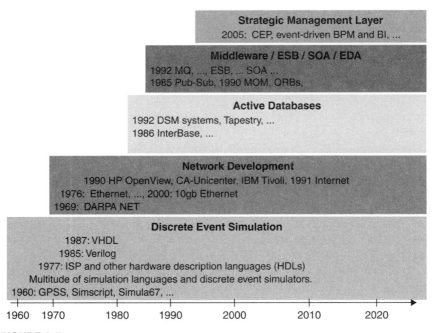

FIGURE 2.7 Historical and Future Developments of Event Processing Technologies

and applications. Some of the most important requirements were for new kinds of real-time analysis tools and more sophisticated triggering and real-time control logic in enterprise business processes.

As a result of the explosion in use of electronic communications, a new layer of event processing technology centered around enterprise management has been developing, the *strategic management layer*, as illustrated in Figure 2.7. This latest layer is still developing, and we will have to see what it contains in the future. It contains a new category of event processing products and event analysis tools that are now coming into play. They are targeted to the strategic enterprise management. This event processing technology for management uses CEP as an enabling technology, one of many technologies employed in managing the enterprise. As the event processing problems to be dealt with increase in complexity, more and more CEP techniques will be needed. Not the least of the issues these tools will be needed to tackle is security.

The rest of this book is about the strategic management layer and the roles of CEP.

CHAPTER 3

First Concepts in Event Processing

This chapter introduces some of the most basic concepts in event processing:

- Events
- Event clouds
- Layers of events
- Event streams
- Three terms in event processing: EP, ESP, and CEP
- Patterns of events
- Event hierarchies
- Complex event processing

Complex event processing (CEP) is the logical and obvious next step in the applications of event processing that are described in Chapter 2 and illustrated in Figure 2.7. CEP is a set of concepts and principles for processing high-level events—business events, for example. It describes the kind of modern event processing that is needed to support the management levels of today's business enterprise. There are many different ways to implement these concepts by means of tools and applications.

This chapter is about some of the basic concepts of CEP, how they were first used in the early commercial applications, and examples of how they are being applied commercially today. We also introduce two other common terms used in referring to the processing of events today, EP and ESP.

New Technology Begets New Problems

By the late 1980s, communication by higher-level events had become the basis for running enterprises everywhere—in business, in government, and in the military. Any large enterprise had linked its applications across the networks from office to office, sometimes around the globe. It now operated on top of what was referred to as "the IT layer"—a layered system of software and hardware for transporting communications at the level of business operations while hiding its underlying details from its users. Business and management level events (e.g., trading orders, sales reports, inventory updates, schedules changes, or just plain email) were entering the IT layer of the enterprise from all corners of the globe, from external sources as well as from its own internal offices, and in all the different formats used by the business software applications of the time.

Today, enterprises are no longer processing a simple stream of events—a single one-after-the-other sequence of events ordered by their time of arrival. This has become a cell-phone world! In some cases, businesses are now dealing with hundreds or thousands of event feeds simultaneously, coming from many different sources and all jumbled together. Essentially the modern information-driven enterprise is operating in a veritable *cloud* of higher-level events, some of which are relevant to business decision making.

As the use of information technology has increased, new concerns have begun to appear. Not only did one need to keep the enterprise IT layer running smoothly, but one was faced with trying to understand what was happening in it. The event cloud obviously contained a lot of information—called *business intelligence*—that would be useful in managing the enterprise. But the cloud did not come with any explanation; events simply arrived! And in some applications, say in arbitrage trading across multiple markets, events arrived at rates of many thousands of trading events per second. Prior to CEP, attempts to extract business intelligence from the event cloud amounted to storing the events in data warehouses and later on trying to do data mining, thus losing any ability to take *right-now* action!

What kinds of information might one try to extract from the cloud of events flowing thorough the IT layer of an enterprise? Here are a few examples of the kinds of questions a real-time enterprise might want to answer:

1. Are our business processes running correctly and on time? This question might apply, for example, to supply chain operations or online retail websites or airline operations, or various areas of trading and finance where time is critical.

2. How will the current weather conditions in the southeastern United States impact our flight schedules in Chicago during the next 48 hours?
3. Is our information at risk? Has someone installed spyware on our IT layer? Is anyone trying to steal data from us?
4. Are our financial traders violating their permissions?[1]
5. Are our accounting processes complying with government regulations?
6. Is there an opportunity developing right now between different financial markets for our trading programs to make a profit?
7. Are our trucks making deliveries and pickups within today's target schedule limits? If not, can we reschedule some deliveries or pickups right now to catch up?
8. Are our call centers servicing our customer requests in good time? How are our customers reacting?

Every business has questions similar to these that it would love to have answers to. They range across many different aspects of business, from managing the enterprise to detecting market opportunities as they happen, to protecting the enterprise or ensuring that its processes conform to policies. All kinds of possible uses of the information in the event cloud have arisen. And the emphasis is on *right now*—getting the answers as the events cross the IT layer.

These are the kinds of problems that created a market for CEP.

The most basic concept in CEP is the *event*. So we start by asking the obvious question.

What Is an Event?

We already mentioned that there are two definitions of the word *event*, and we use both of them in most of our discussions about event processing. So let's clear this up once and for all by going over it in detail.

First there is the everyday use that is found in a dictionary:

Definition 1

An *event* is anything that happens or is thought of as happening.

---

[1]Carrick Mollenkamp and David Gauthier-Villars, "France to Fault Société Generale's Controls in Report" *Wall Street Journal* (Eastern Edition), February 4, 2008, A3. For more information on Jérôme Kerviel, see Nicola Clark, "Rogue Trader at Société Générale Gets 3 Years," *The New York Times*, October 5, 2010. www.nytimes.com/2010/10/06/business/global/06bank.html?partner=rss& emc=rss

Examples:

- A key stroke
- A stock trade
- A simulated event using a model of a system
- A crash landing in a flight simulator
- A dream or imagined happening
- A natural occurrence such as an earthquake
- A social or historical happening such as the abolition of slavery, the battle of Waterloo, the Russian revolution, or the 1929 stock market crash

The dictionary definition is quite subtle because, as we discussed before, it not only allows that an event can be something that actually happens in the real world, but also that it can be imaginary and does not really happen. Our example is driving a car and approaching a red light. You might well imagine the events that would happen if you didn't stop! But since you do stop, the events you imagined don't happen. Those events were imagined as happening, but never did actually happen. Nonetheless, they are events. In the simulation world these kinds of events are called *virtual events*.[2]

Definition 2

An *event* is an *object* that represents or records an activity that happens, or is thought of as happening.

Examples:

- A weather prediction output by a weather simulator
- A purchase confirmation that records a purchase
- A signal resulting from a computer mouse click
- Stock ticker message that reports a stock trade
- An RFID sensor reading

This second meaning, *an event object*, describes events that are processed in computer systems. Computer systems such as simulations use event objects to represent or record events (activities) that happen or could happen. Often the purpose of this kind of event processing is to predict what might happen in the real world. As our examples show, these objects can be any kind of data structure from binary strings to records and other complex data types.

---

[2]See also the terminology "virtual reality," http://en.wikipedia.org/wiki/Virtual_reality

For example, a weather prediction is an object that can be read, shared with others, or input into a travel scheduler. It represents an event that may or may not happen. A computer operating system reacts to events such as a mouse click or a keyboard stroke. Clicking a mouse results in an event internal to the computer that is processed by the operating system. And a sensor reacting to an RFID tag results in an event object that is a set of electrical signals from the sensor.

Now, we have a choice to make about how we talk about events. We could choose to talk about both *events* and *event objects*—that is, we can distinguish between an activity that takes place and an object that represents that activity by always calling the first "an event" and the second "an event object." But this quickly gets tiresome. So we will use the word "event" in both meanings and rely upon the context to make clear which meaning is intended. Programmers would say that we *overload* the word *event*. But occasionally, for absolute clarity, we'll use "event object" where needed.

Events are not just messages—a popular misconception! Yes, one form of an event might look like a message. But it contains additional information. An event describes not only the activity it represents, but when it happened, how long it took, and how it is related to other activities. So an event describes an activity together with its timing and causal relationships to other activities. We speak of events as being related in the same way as the activities they represent.

An event has a time associated with it—called its time stamp—that is the time at which the activity happened. If the activity took some time to happen, then an event that represents it will have a time interval associated with it—its *start time* and its *end time*. And some events may cause other events, if their activities cause one another. So events may be related by causality, time, and other relationships.

Note that in practice, some event processing systems may not include time stamps in their events. We would think of such systems as being deficient.

We will describe data structures of events and how their causal and timing relationships are represented in a later chapter. For now, here are some examples.

Example 3.1

Event1: I send you an email at 13.00 Pacific standard time.
Event2: You send me a reply at 17.00 Eastern standard time.
Event1 **causes** Event2.
In fact, we could be more precise by giving the times of the events according to pacific standard time as well as their relationship:
Event1 **at** 13.00 PST **causes** Event2 **at** 14.00 PST.

Example 3.2

Event1: A black car approaches a traffic light as it turns from green to yellow and decides to enter the intersection anyway.
Event2: At the same time, a white car approaches the red light on the cross street decides not to stop as the light turns from red to green.
Event3: The two cars collide in the intersection.
Event4: Both drivers report not being injured.
Event1 **and** Event2 **cause** Event3.

Well, we said it was an event-driven world! The point in Example 3.2 is that the first two events, taken to together, caused the third event. A *pattern* of two events caused the collision. Patterns of events, and how to specify them, are one of the fundamental concepts in CEP. Again, we can be precise by giving the event times, since it is crucial that event1 and event2 happened very close together in time.

But what caused event4? Some would say it has no cause, since it is a report of the absence of other events, namely injuries! Others would say that event3 caused event4 because the report of no injuries would only have been given because of the collision. I'll leave it to you to decide. Causality between events is not always cut and dried. It is sometimes debatable and sometimes unknown.

Definition 3

Event Processing (EP) is any processing by computer of event objects.

Event processing (EP) is a very general term. It may refer to event-driven simulation—say, to make weather forecasts—or to the scanning of event feeds from airports and other entry points to the United States by Homeland Security to detect the entry of possible terrorists, or indeed any other kind of processing of event objects.

Complex Event Processing (CEP) is a subset of EP. We will describe the concepts of CEP later in this chapter.

Event Clouds

What kind of event environment does today's enterprise have to deal with? Well, nowadays most "wired-in" enterprises are using the Internet, cell phones, private networks, and other sources of events to do business, so they have to deal with a veritable cloud of events, as illustrated in Example 3.3.

Example 3.3: The Global Event Cloud

The term *global event cloud*[3] is often used to refer to the set of all the events entering an enterprise, together with the timing, causality, and other relationships between those events. The event cloud enters the enterprise through its own IT layers and communications as well as through a lot of outside sources that the enterprise is using to conduct business.

Figure 3.1 shows an event cloud of the customer actions on an online banking website. Each linear sequence of events represents a customer's actions in accessing an account and making various banking transactions in the order they were done.

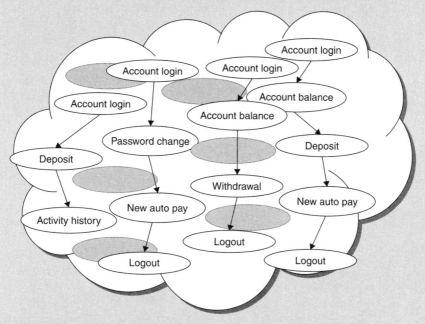

FIGURE 3.1 An Event Clous in an Online Banking Website

---

[3]This terminology was coined in *The Power of Events*, section 2.1.2, p. 28.

Example 3.3 assumes that a customer must perform banking actions one at a time. There may be hundreds of customers on the website at any one time. Example 3.4 illustrates how monitoring the event cloud can help.

Example 3.4: Detecting Patterns of Suspicious Activity in the Event Cloud

Figure 3.2 shows a result of monitoring the event cloud from the online banking website for patterns of events that might result from unusual activity. One of the event sequences involves an *account login*, a *password change*, and then the installation of a new *automatic payment order* to transfer money out of the account, all happening within a short period of time—under ten minutes.

Each of these events by itself is normal. But the order in the sequence is suspicious. Why change the password just before withdrawing money? If the action is fraudulent, it will deny the legitimate account holder access, making him or her unable to see what has happened and stop the transfer of money from the account. Detecting this pattern of events in the website might trigger an alert, which could itself trigger other rules to take further action, such as contacting the account holder or temporarily blocking the account from further activity.

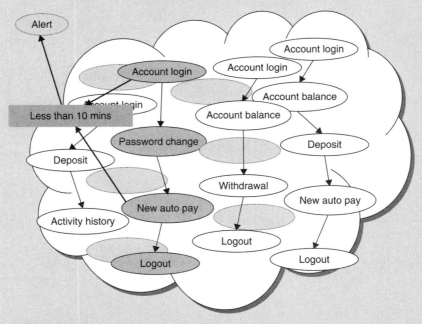

FIGURE 3.2 A Pattern of Unusual Account Activity

Fraud detection is an expanding market area for commercial applications of event pattern processing today. Unfortunately, it turns out that the methods of detection being employed at the moment are often clumsily hardwired—e.g., some are little more than very long conditional branches of computer code that test all the various special cases of fraud that have been experienced. This makes the detection system inflexible and difficult to change, and of course, subject to inefficiencies and errors. Inflexibility is the friend of the crook! Adoption of high-level event pattern languages supported by event processing rules engines makes fraud detection systems much more flexible and easier to update as new scams appear.

Levels of Events and Event Analysis

Clouds of events form the operating environment of every modern business enterprise today. Although one might think of the cloud of events on the IT layer as one big jumbled mass, it turns out that the events can be organized into some very simple structures. One way to organize events is by *layers* or *levels.*

The layering idea goes back to the earlier use of event layers in defining industry standards for communication over networks by means of events. The messaging standards, for example, define six or seven separate layers of events.[4] The lowest level is the physical electrical media that actually transport events called packets. Packets are just sequences of binary bits encoding the data and network information. There are lots of packets corresponding to one higher level event—like, say, sending an email message.

Levels of events are also used extensively in design methods, such as designing hardware chips, and in discrete event simulation of hardware designs.

The idea of levels of events has applications to business events too. It gives us one way to break down high-level business events into component lower-level events. One example is a very high-level business event, like a merger of two companies. That event will depend upon lots of lower-level business events: arranging financing and settling with stockholders, merging departments, eliminating jobs, unifying product lines, organizing marketing and sales strategies, and so on. The breakdown into lower-level component events is essential to scheduling and carrying out the high-level event, as well as to tracking the progress of the merger and keeping it on schedule.

---

[4]Actually, these standards define services (functions) at each level. But operationally, calls to implementations of these functions would result in layers of events.

There are lots of other reasons for using layers in structuring everyday business events. A business transaction such as a sale or trade will be broken down into lower-level events used to execute that sale or trade, such as the delegation of contracting and accounting and financing. And these events in turn involve lower-level events, such as the use of various business software applications. There are even lower-level events, most of which are IT events rather than business events. Some of the typical layers in processing business events are shown in Figure 3.3—note that this is a small sample; there are other levels in between the ones shown.

Event layers are useful in building analysis tools that help us to track the steps in our business processes as they are running. We can see with the help of graphical interfaces how a business transaction depends upon lower-level operations. Business process analysis tools work just like the network management tools of earlier times. They can show us how different transactions that are being executed at the same time might be competing for resources, or what we can do to improve the times required for those transactions and identify which lower-level operations might be causing errors. We can get the statistical breakdown of events at each level, as well.

Figure 3.4 shows business events and lower-level events at each of the levels.

A high-level business *transaction* executed using application software tools breaks down into a series of process steps, such as a *market search* followed by a *negotiation* followed by setting up *financing* and finalized by negotiating a *contract* (see Figure 3.5). These events are all at the business process level in our hierarchy.

Each of the business process level events is again composed of sets of lower-level events signifying the use of various applications. Market search

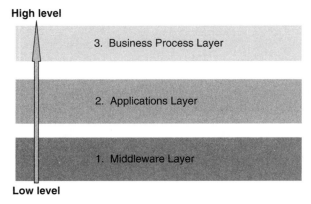

High level

3. Business Process Layer

2. Applications Layer

1. Middleware Layer

Low level

FIGURE 3.3 Some of the Typical Layers of Events in Business Processing

might involve several catalogue searches, for example. A negotiation may be composed of requests for quotes, bids, counterbids, and finally acceptance of an offer. Financing may involve a lot of accounting operations, use of spreadsheets, and so on. Figure 3.5 illustrates a few of the possible dependencies between events at each of the three levels in our illustrations.

Level-wise breakdown of business process events lets us analyze the steps involved in creating any high-level event, perhaps to see how we could have done it better or to see what might have caused a process to hang up or go wrong. Also, if we have defined the dependencies between events at different levels, we have the ability to track and analyze our processes right down to the use of individual software applications, databases, and perhaps lower-level events corresponding to distributed communications as well, if necessary—perhaps if something goes wrong.

For example, if a transaction fails for something as mundane as a message going astray and not being answered, knowing how the levelwise breakdown is done is crucial in finding out the causes of the error. Analysis using this levelwise breakdown of higher events into sets

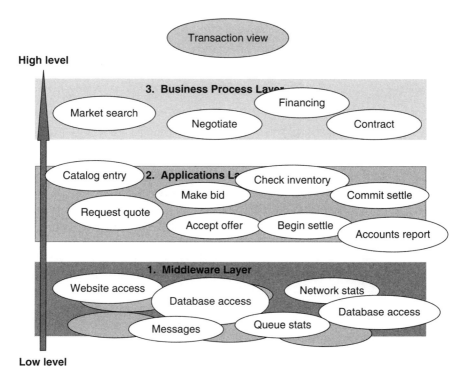

FIGURE 3.4 Layers of Business Events and Lower-Level Component Events

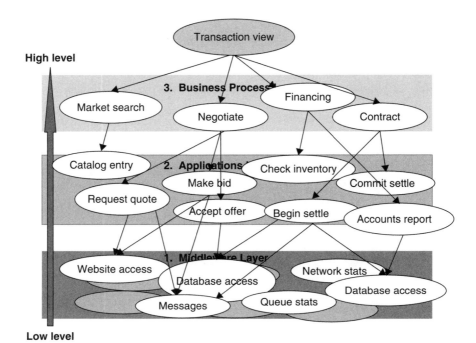

High level

Low level

FIGURE 3.5 Dependencies between Events Created by Business Processes and Lower-Level Events Resulting from Actions by the Processes

of lower events was one of the first applications of event processing analytical tools.

Of course, business managers are interested mainly in the events at the business process layer. And if it is necessary to analyze what happened at the lower-level events, that task is handed off to the IT department! But the breakdown is there for everyone to use.

While there are several examples of industrial standards for event hierarchies—for example, in defining messaging protocol standards—very little has been done to define business event hierarchies. Business event hierarchies can be defined by sets of rules that specify the breakdown of higher-level events into sets of lower-level events.

Remark on Standards for Business Events

The need to have precisely defined standards for business and management-level event processing will be one of the next challenges that commercial event processing software will have to face.

Standardization of event representations, event processing terminology, and eventually, event hierarchies will become a necessity in the future for specific business areas. Doubtless, it will be a somewhat chaotic activity focused on narrow areas of business activity, with localized standards between groups of companies gradually becoming more widely accepted.

There will be a variety of driving forces behind such efforts. One will be a need to integrate different event-driven business systems to facilitate collaborative business agreements, mergers and acquisitions, and so on. Another might be standards efforts arising among consumers of event processing products. Additionally, the event processing vendors might agree on some standards for event processing in specific markets. There is also a distinct possibility of mergers and acquisitions in the vendor space resulting in a few large vendors of event processing, which would certainly lead to partial de facto standardization.

We hazard a guess that event processing standards defining layers of events will be seen in the next ten years in such areas as stock market analysis and trading, real-time inventory control for specific markets, retail stores management, consumer relations, airline operations, manufacturing, online retailing and marketing, to name a few possibilities.

Many areas of opportunity will develop in which event processing standards will be beneficial to all of the actors. This much is obvious. What is not clear is how and from where the standards efforts will come—the vendors, the consumers, or all of the parties. Such efforts, when resulting from collaborations, are known to be arduous and time-consuming, and they always deliver less than one would hope. Nevertheless, they are worthwhile, particularly when one considers the alternative of complete chaos.

The glossary of event processing terminology provided at the back of this book can be considered a small start in the direction of business event processing standards.

Event Streams

Some of the first commercially successful CEP applications processed streams of events. They did not use information about how the events were related, such as which events caused others or whether some events were higher level than others. Only data contained in the events were used. So events such as stock trades were used simply as messages.

These CEP applications were stock trading applications. They processed events in the order in which they arrived in the event feeds. They may have been receiving events from several different markets at the same time, so some events were clearly unrelated, while others may have had close trade relationships. The advantage was simplicity of implementing the event processing. It allowed high volumes of events to be processed in near real time. The disadvantage was that sometimes information that could be used to advantage in trading was lost, such as which pairs of events tended to occur together in small time windows.

Definition: An *event stream* is a linearly ordered sequence of events occurring within a specified time.

Note: The concept of *event cloud* includes the concept of an *event stream* as a special case in which the events fall nicely into a linear order, one after the other. The time between each of the events in order for the events to be considered a stream is left open (i.e., to be determined by the observer). Event clouds and event streams can be finite.

Common examples of an event stream are a stream of readings from a sensor or a ticker tape of stock market news. These kinds of event feeds are a sequence of events that arrive at a processor one event at a time. This is called the *order of arrival* ordering.

When events are processed in their order of arrival, this is called *event streams processing (ESP)*. Typically, stock trading feeds or sensor data are processed in their order of arrival. For example, stock trading feeds reporting buy, offer, bid, or sale trades in stocks are the result of merging lots of events from different exchanges into a single stream. Figure 3.6 shows a stock market feed of trading events. The events are ordered by when they were entered into the feed. This is necessarily not the order in which the trades were executed.

Early trading algorithms processed trades in order of arrival. These event processors had to deal with high numbers of events in a short time window, say ten minutes. They had to make computations on the data in the events and produce a stream of results. Some trading algorithms were programmed to react in milliseconds when they detected trading situations indicated by patterns of events that had been defined beforehand.

So in these early financial trading applications, one of the requirements was that the event processor could handle the rate at which events arrived in stock trading feeds. Thus a name for a subset of EP and of CEP was coined: *event streams processing* (ESP). The intention was to infer that a tool that did ESP could handle high-speed event feeds.

There was another reason for the appearance of the acronym ESP. Some of the event processing vendors' marketeers feared that the "complex"

FIGURE 3.6 A Stream of Stock Market Trading Events

in CEP would arouse fears in their customers, associated with the idea of impenetrable and faulty software. This is quite understandable, one must say! So some vendors used the term ESP as a marketing ploy for a year or two. But they soon began to realize that they needed to explore other markets where the event clouds were, perhaps more complex than streams.

There are many event processing applications, outside of stock trading, where orderings of events, such as their creation order or their causal order, are not taken into account, even though the processing could be more efficient and yield more accurate results if they were. This is because the implementations of event processing are not as sophisticated as they should be. Consider Example 3.5.

Example 3.5: Event Streams Processing

A common component in stock market event processing is the Volume Weighted Average Price (VWAP) computation. Figure 3.7 shows a typical event feed as a sequence of stock trade events where each event contains data such as the stock symbol, the number of shares of that stock traded, the price, and the time. As events arrive, they are processed during a time window that may be a few minutes up to perhaps an hour. The VWAP computation shows two feeds being processed simultaneously.

First, a filtering operation is applied to split the two feeds into a set of streams of trade report events, one for each stock symbol. This is a basic event processing operation. These streams of report events for trades in each stock symbol are sent to two functions. One computes total dollar amounts over a time window, while the other just adds up the total volume of the trades in the same time window. The results are a stream of dollar amounts and a stream of share volumes for each stock symbol. These two streams are fed into a third computation that divides the dollar amounts by the share volumes. The result is a stream of complex events giving the VWAP for each symbol. Only simple techniques of event processing are involved: filtering stock feeds by symbol and moving events between computations. The complexity of the algorithm lies in the functions that are applied to the events. So the real "smarts" are in the computations performed on the data in the events. The events themselves are treated simply as carriers of data. Actual financial trading applications will involve networks of such

(continued)

like computations in which VWAP is just one node, but the event processing is still very simple.

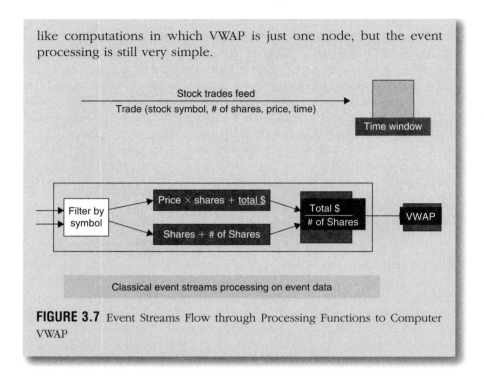

Classical event streams processing on event data

FIGURE 3.7 Event Streams Flow through Processing Functions to Computer VWAP

In a later chapter we will discuss another way to look at the VWAP events—as higher level abstractions of time windows of stock trade events.

Today, algorithmic trading is an increasingly important market for event processing applications. This is particularly true in arbitrage trading on electronic markets, in which the execution of trading orders is automated because the times involved are on the order of milliseconds. The algorithms used at trading companies are often closely guarded secrets.

Processing the Event Cloud

In general, an enterprise has to deal with many event streams simultaneously, and the events in these streams can be connected or related in many ways. Events in the same stream are related by their arrival time in that stream. They may have different timing relationships as well—their creation time, for example, which is not necessarily the same as their order in the stream. Events in different streams may also be related; some of the events in one stream may be the causes of events in other streams.

If knowing how events are related is important for the kind of event processing that needs to be done, then the streams cannot be treated separately, or shuffled into a single stream. The processing must deal with the event cloud and the event relationships that exist in the cloud, such as timing and causality.

The order of arrival of events can be misleading for many applications. It may not be the order in which events were created, or happened. The time at which an event was created is called its *creation time*. An event A can be created earlier than another event B according to the local times[5] in which they were both created, but B can arrive at the processor before A does.

Consider, for example, medical reports of incidents of a disease that may be suspected as a precursor to an epidemic outbreak. These may be coming from doctor's offices all over the country. Some reports are made at the same time—in parallel, so to speak. And the reports from different offices are independent because there is no relationship between the doctors or the patients. The reports arrive at the Health Department as an *event cloud*. They may be shuffled into one big stream at the Department's information office, but the timing information in the reports would not be ignored, and it certainly isn't the time at which the reports arrived.

Many industrial event processing problems cannot be simplified by treating the incoming events as a stream ordered by their time of arrival. Common relationships between events are usually not linear. For example their creation time is often "all over the place"—that is, it is not a nice orderly sequence. Some events can happen at the same time, while others happen hours apart. The times of some events may need to be adjusted to a common time zone because they happened in widely separate locations.

Causality between events is usually nonsequential too. Take your email folder as an example. A message in it caused another message, if the second one is a reply to the first one. You can get causal chains, message M1 caused Message M2, which caused M3, and the like—that is, a reply to a reply to a message. But your message folder is not likely to be one single long chain. It is far more likely to contain lots of short chains of three or four messages and replies.

---

[5] Comparing creation times of events may require adjustments for differences between the timers or clocks local to where those events were created.

Example 3.6: Airline Baggage Handling

One industry that was an early adopter of event processing was the airline industry and, more generally, the transportation sector, which includes railways and shipping. Adoption within a company is not a single decision, since it usually involved substantial investment not only in the event processing software but also in integrating the new technology into the company's operational structure.

Adoption usually starts with a toe-in-the-water proof of concept experiment.

One of the early proof of concept experiments was in airline baggage handling. This is both an airport as well as an airline responsibility. The airport starts with the problem, but at certain points the airline should take over.

The motivation, of course was money—quite simply, the cost to the airline of a misdirected bag. More than 42 million items of baggage were mishandled or delayed in 2007, an increase of 25 percent on the previous year, costing airlines and airports an estimated $3.8 billion.[6] The biggest cause was baggage being mishandled when passengers transferred flights. The next major cause was failure to load baggage (16 percent), followed by ticketing error, passenger bag switch, security, and "other," which together accounted for 14 percent of the total.

Ideally, an event monitoring system to tackle this problem needs to process many different event feeds resulting from diverse monitoring sources. These include (1) the various pathways that the baggage takes through an airport to be loaded onto the flights and its subsequent handling at connection points and at the final destination; (2) the progress of passengers through the airport, security checkpoints, and final boarding on the flights, as well as at changes of flights; and (3) the progress of the flights. Essentially, such a system is operating in a cloud of airport and airline events, not a simple event stream.

The input-event feeds shown in Figure 3.8 include the baggage tag readers at curbside, ticket counter, and at various points on the pathway transporting baggage from the counter to flight. Similar feeds could be positioned at passenger check-in gates and so on. In total, the events from the input streams form a cloud. Events in different streams

---

[6]The figures come from the fourth annual SITA Baggage Report compiled by specialist baggage tracking company SITA, whose technology is used by 400 airlines and ground handling companies around the world. www.sita.aero/about-sita

are related by time and by common data elements such as passenger names. The information in the input cloud should be checked for consistency—but currently, it is not! A prime example is consistency between the routing of baggage and the routing of a passenger from the ticket counter to the gateway to board a flight. A passenger and a bag are linked together at the ticket counter. At that point the system should know, if it has enough smarts, which flight both should be on. But inconsistencies can and do occur en route through the airport.

Typically, a bag can get lost for different reasons—for example, simply falling off a conveyor and failing to arrive, or being misdirected and arriving at an incorrect flight. A passenger can fail to board a flight or get rerouted or delayed by security. The system should detect these situations and issue notifications. More advanced systems might replan baggage handling according to changes in the passenger schedule.

In practice, current baggage handling systems handle only some of these event streams and detect just a few of the situations we have mentioned. Modern airport systems use handheld RFID scanners at points along the baggage routes. But a passenger can disappear into a black hole of security checks or simply get distracted by shopping.

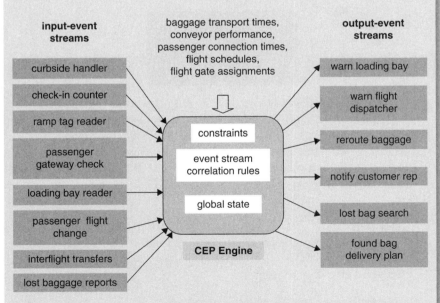

FIGURE 3.8 Input- and Output-Event Streams and State Data in Event Processing for Baggage Handling

Detecting simple mishandling errors is the first issue. But heading off errors before they occur requires detecting patterns of baggage mishandling in the input-event cloud as they are happening. Patterns of events can be used to detect situations where the handling of a bag is likely to result in an error.

Example 3.6 and Figure 3.8 show an idealized view of an event processing system for airline baggage handling. It is getting lots of input streams from the left. The system contains an event pattern rules engine— that is, a CEP engine. It also has smarts about airport operations, such as baggage transport times within the airport, how the conveyors are performing, flight schedules and schedule updates, gate assignments, and so on. And it outputs various notifications and warnings on the right in Figure 3.8. Examples of some of the outputs are to warn airline flight dispatchers about late baggage, put out advisories to plan re routing baggage, notify airline customer reps that baggage has missed a flight, and plan delivery of found baggage that had been lost.

Some examples of simple event pattern monitoring rules in baggage handling systems are:

Counter checks:

if bag.tag.flight_number $=N$ **and** N.destination $=$ passenger_ticket. destination
then accept bag
else raise error **and reject** bag.
if flight.departure_time − passenger.check_in_time < bag.transit_time
action notify (passenger, "insufficient time")

The counter checks are aids to airline counter agents who deal with passengers and baggage. They are real-time event monitoring rules. The first rule compares the destination of the flight on a baggage tag with the destination on the passenger's ticket when it is issued at the ticket counter. The second is a rule that will warn passengers that their bags may not reach their flight in time to be loaded.

Trolley loading check:

if bag.tag.flight_number $=$ trolley.destination.flight_number
then load bag
else send bag **to** rerouting

This is an example of a rule that could avoid some baggage handling errors. It could be applied at many points in an airport—for example, when bags are in transit between connecting flights. The event feeds could be generated by handheld RFID tag readers during unloading and loading.

Baggage handling systems using CEP rules have been in operation at some airports for a few years. The event processing in these systems can involve quite sophisticated CEP principles. They are being continually improved by updating the patterns of events that they use to monitor the event inputs.

We may expect to see proactive flight management event patterns like the following example in future systems:

Security bag loading check:

if bag.tag.passenger_name = X **and** loaded(bag) **and not** boarded (X) **and** gate.closed
=> **action set** flight.status = hold **until** unloaded(bag)

This rule would take a bag off a flight after it had been loaded if the passenger was a "no show."

More recently, event processing systems are also being employed to deal with other dimensions of airline operations such as crew scheduling and aircraft maintenance operations.

Complex Event Processing and Systems That Use It

Complex event processing (CEP) does *not* mean "very complicated processing of events." It is *simple processing* applied to events that might sometimes be very complex, but usually not as complex as some of the events we face in daily life!

The term CEP for complex event processing was coined in the late 1990s at Stanford to codify what was going on in the Stanford event processing project and to distinguish that work from research in networks and other areas. It entered the public domain of event processing terminology in 2002.[7] The acronym stuck as the name for products that process high-level events in business transactions and generally in many areas of enterprise management. Other terms such as "business event processing" and "real-time business intelligence" are also often used.

CEP refers to (1) a set of concepts and principles for processing events and (2) methods of implementing those concepts. Some concepts are well known from other kinds of software systems. Other concepts are

---

[7] With the publication of *The Power of Events*.

only just beginning to enter the state of general practice. For example, one of the key concept deals with how to specify patterns of events and the elements of computer languages needed for defining event patterns (i.e., the expressive power of pattern languages). Another is how to build efficient event pattern-detection engines. A third area of CEP deals with strategies for using event patterns in business event processing—for example, building systems of event pattern–triggered business processes and monitoring their execution and performance, both when they run correctly and when errors occur. Finally, there are concepts that deal with how to define and use hierarchical abstraction in processing multiple levels of events for different applications within the enterprise.

CEP is best understood in the context of how and where its concepts and techniques are used in an event-processing system.

Event processing systems involve many different technologies that include CEP. They usually deal with several event feeds concurrently from different sources and with different types of events. Event arrival rates from a feed can vary from a few events per hour to thousands of events per second. The techniques of processing that are applied vary widely depending upon its goals.

An event processing system may flow the events in a continuous stream through a variety of processing steps that apply various technologies. The processing time of each step is an important consideration.

The commonest first step is to apply very simple criteria to get rid of most of the uninteresting events (i.e., events that cannot contribute to the goals of the processing). This is called *filtering*. For example, events might be filtered by whether they contain names on some list (say names of stocks), or by who sent them or their date of origin. These criteria are called *filters*. The main requirements of filters are that they take very little time to execute and that they will not eliminate events that might be relevant.

The remaining events after filtering are processed by more complicated techniques. In stock trading, as an example, a next step might be to apply various statistical algorithms to the data in the events. Another processing step, say in medical systems, might be to group events together by some commonality, such as "all reports of malaria cases from West Africa," and then to apply summarization methods over time windows, say week by week over the past eight weeks. These kinds of steps will result in new events being created that contain the summary data.

One of the cardinal principles of an event processing system is that events are *immutable* (see the following discussion). They may be copied or they may be ignored in all processing steps.

One of the first CEP concepts that may be applied at the earlier processing steps is *event pattern detection*. Patterns of events are critical to many areas of event processing, from stock trading and sales analysis to fraud detection and security. We will have a lot more to say about event patterns and how to specify them!

Another CEP concept is *event abstraction*. Event-abstraction methods allow us to build systems that can analyze vast numbers of low-level events and create high-level events that summarize—or abstract—information contained in those events. There are far smaller numbers of higher-level events resulting from first round methods. These high-level events are called *aggregated events, enriched events*, or *abstract events*, depending upon the kinds of techniques that are used. The result is fewer events, but ones that provide views of the information contained in the event sources that are meaningful to humans. High-level events are more suitable for specialized analysis that may draw on technologies such as:

- Artificial intelligence and heuristic programming
- Statistics and probability theory
- Game theory and decision analysis
- Event driven simulation
- Semantic analysis
- Other technologies

A processing system may cycle many times between applying CEP and applying other technologies, so all of the technologies are interwoven, so to speak.

Here's a brief outline of some of the main concepts of CEP. Some of them will be quite familiar, since they have been common elements of many software systems. Other CEP concepts are new and need explaining which will be done in later chapters.

- *Immutability of events.* In CEP all events are immutable. An event cannot be altered or deleted. It can be dropped from any further consideration in an event-processing system, which in effect is the same as deletion (e.g., as a result of filtering). But if an event makes any contribution to the processing, then that original event must always be retrievable if needed. Copies can be created that include changes to data contents or other attributes. Such modified copies are new events. There are strong reasons for immutability. See the discussion following this list.
- *Adaptation.* The input events are transformed into formats required by an event processing system. This is a preprocessing step that is in general use in any event processing system. Adaptation is often nontrivial, since some event processing systems require many different adaptors to cope with the different types of event input.

- *Filtering.* Filtering out irrelevant events is a first step toward reducing incoming events to manageable proportions. It should be a fast, small computation step. Criteria for irrelevancy are often decided in advance. But a CEP processor should be flexible enough that the criteria can be adjusted at runtime. Filtering criteria depend upon the goals of the event processing. Filtering is often combined with adaptation. The simplest CEP techniques are used in recognizing irrelevant events or sets of events. There may be several different filtering steps applied in sequence. Many irrelevant events still get through, because filters are usually configured to err on the side of letting through anything that might be useful.

- *Prioritization.* Prioritization of events as they arrive is an important early step. High-priority events are the ones that require immediate response from the business. They are usually delivered on reserved or private networks and media specially set up to carry the critical operational information. In fact, prioritization may be set up to take place before or after filtering, or sometimes the two operations are applied alternately on the input-event feeds. High-priority events must be dealt with first.

- *Computation on event data.* The data contained in events are used in computations. This step may involve computations carried out in parallel on the contents of the events. CEP allows any kind of algorithm to be applied at this step. In fact, a set of algorithms may be applied concurrently and the resulting new events put back into the event cloud for the next step.

- *Event pattern detection.* The event input is searched for the presence of patterns of events. An event pattern is a template that can match many different sets of multiple events, or, in a special case of single event patterns, it may match many different single events. It may require particular data to be present in events, or the events in a matching set to be related in various ways—for example some events may be required to be causes of other events in the set, or to happen within a specific time window. An event pattern may also require some types of events to be absent. CEP suggests minimal requirements on the power of expression of a pattern language.

- *Exception detection and handling.* The event processing may also result in the detection of errors and anomalies, called *exceptions*. In CEP exceptions are detected by the presence or absence of events and patterns of events—for example, absence of an event pattern is detected when that pattern fails to match within defined time bounds. When exceptions occur, they are handled by creating new events that signify the specific error that has happened. Note that the absence of an event or event pattern often indicates an error within the system that is the source of the event input.

- *Event pattern abstraction.* Whenever a pattern of events is detected, the processing may take the action of creating new events that contain properties of, and data in, the set of events that matched that pattern. For example, a new event may contain a summary of the important data contained in several of the events in the set, or it may be a report signifying that a match of the pattern happened. One purpose of the new events is to summarize the important details of the matching events and to filter out or omit what is not important. Another purpose is to make sense for humans of large numbers of low-level events. The new events *abstract* the matched set of events.

- *Event pattern–triggered processes.* Reactive processes triggered by patterns of events are used for automating the actions a business or enterprise must take in response to specified patterns of events. Business processes must be set up to react to expected patterns of events. Understanding the enterprise's operations is part of planning in advance and defining the reactive processes. This step requires planning for patterns of events that may happen and having solutions ready to take action. Typically, such systems are rule-based, each rule being an event pattern trigger and a business-process response to the trigger. It is important that the set of rules can be easily changed while the event processing system is operating.

- *Computable event hierarchies.* Events that happen in a particular kind of business operation or a specific technology usually fall into layers. Some events are low level, and some are higher-level events. The difference is that higher-level events are composed from sets of lower-level events. For example, a completed sale might consist of several events, such as negotiating a price, checking a customer's credit rating, processing a down payment, updating inventory, and so on. The sale is at a higher abstraction level than the steps in negotiating it. Events within a specific area of activity can often be categorized into several layers. Some of the goals of event hierarchies are (1) to focus information for individual users and (2) to reduce the number of events that need to be processed at higher levels.

There are several industry standard event hierarchies today, examples being the famous Open Systems Interconnection (OSI)[8] seven-layer hierarchy of messaging operations, or the six-layer TCP/IP network protocol.

---

[8]Rachelle Miller, "The OSI Model: An Overview," *SANS Institute Reading Room.* www.sans.org/reading_room/whitepapers/standards/osi-model-overview_543

Such classifications promote common terminology and interoperability of event processing systems, diagnostic systems, reuse of rule libraries, and so on. Event hierarchies are important in delivering relevant views of business operations to different role players in the enterprise, as we shall see.

In CEP, event hierarchies are *computable*. We'll explain what this term means and its uses later. It is true that, as yet, little has been done in exploring the use of hierarchical classifications in commercial CEP. This is a point at which CEP theory goes beyond current commercial practice.

Of course, there are interesting open questions where CEP concepts and techniques may need to be extended to process information in new types of event sources. One example is what kinds of event processing are needed to take advantage of public event sources such as social networks such as Twitter and Facebook (see Example 3.7). These sources are sometimes the carriers of unexpected and important information—for example, (1) how various items are selling, or are viewed by the public; and (2) rumors and early indications of possible epidemic illnesses and outbreaks or public health breakdowns. Another example of a potentially rich event source is cell phone communications.

To deal with event processing in new event sources as they continue to arise, we may need to apply CEP in ways that have not yet been explored. The definition and use of probabilistic event patterns is one area that is yet to be explored both in theory and in event processing systems. And of course, there are always questions of privacy that perhaps go beyond the domain of technology such as CEP.

Example 3.7: Beware of What You Tweet!

An individual with a good medical insurance plan from his workplace reported a serious back injury to the insurance company. He claimed it necessitated his taking leave from work, and thus he required insurance compensation for loss of wages and medical costs.

During the processing of these claims, an insurance company adjuster Googled the individual and discovered Facebook and Twitter accounts in the individual's name. The Twitter account revealed the claimant tweeting about his golf game during the time he was supposedly off work injured. Needless to say, the insurance company did not pay, and the individual was faced with fraud charges.

While this example resulted from a human-directed search, it may be expected that event processing applications in the area of fraud may do similar searches for information on the Web and other sources automatically in the future.

Discussion: Immutability of Events

Once an activity has happened, it is history. We cannot alter history, much as most of us would like to! An event object represents an activity that happened—it signifies that activity.

If we could alter the event object by changing its data parameters or its attributes, it would no longer signify that activity. It then becomes questionable as to what activity the altered event object would signify, if any at all. An altered event, therefore, has no known significance. And we cannot trace it back to anything that had significance, because that traceability to the original event is lost.

An event processor that alters the input events in situ is doing object processing. Not event processing. The objects resulting from the processing have no significance, real or imaginary.

On the other hand, if a processor creates a new event from its input event by changing some of the data parameters or attributes of the input, and maintains traceability to the original event, then the new event does have significance. It is the result of operations on an event with significance. If the operations signify real-world activities, then the new event will also signify an activity.

Example 3.8: Enriching Events for Record Tracking

Suppose event E1(M, S, C, T) signifies that I received an email M on a topic S from a correspondent C at time T. I may be interacting with several correspondents on the same topic, a back and forth of arguments and data and counterarguments. And I may want to keep track of the timeliness with which various correspondents respond. A trace of the previous email on topic S with correspondent C will be

(continued)

contained in M. So I have a tracking system that creates a new tracking event E2 from E1 by adding to the data contained in E1, say,

E2 = E1(M, S, C, Avrg, T, T + ΔT)

where Avrg is the average time it takes C to respond to all my emails on topic S using the email trace in M, and T + ΔT is the time at which E2 is created.

I use the E2 events described in Example 3.8 to decide which correspondent to interact with next, depending upon who is likely to respond the most quickly. E2 is created by enriching the data in E1. It is traceable back to E1 and related to it by an enrichment operation. E2 signifies the average response time of correspondent C to a particular topic S at a particular time of day T. Of course, it doesn't encode how much I agree or disagree with the correspondent, but I could add another enrichment parameter for that too!

The point of this example is that E2 is a different event from E1, created at a different time, and traceable back to E1. If, instead, I altered E1 by adding the Avrg to the parameters, it would cease to have any significance with the real world. It does not signify the email that C sent to me at time T. It is an event obliquely associated with that. I would be doing bookkeeping in situ. I can make sense of it, but I would need a dedicated event traceability system dependent upon what kinds of bookkeeping operations I was performing on events to make sense of the altered events.

Summary

This chapter describes basic concepts in event processing (EP) in general and outlines the concepts in complex event processing (CEP) in particular. It describes the concepts: event, event stream, event cloud, patterns of events, levels of events, and computable event hierarchies. The next chapter will outline the stages by which modern event processing happened.

But the reader may now be wondering, what is it all good for? Chapter 5 will deal with the current markets for CEP products and services, the size and growth of these markets, and how CEP is being applied. Later chapters deal with the basic concepts and strategies for their application in event processing in more depth. There is a final chapter (Chapter 9) on our vision of the future of event processing.

CHAPTER 4

The Rise of Commercial Event Processing

This chapter discusses   t
processing (CEP) have d   l
in the future through in

- Simple event proce
- Creeping CEP
- A CEP becomes rec
- CEP becomes ubiquitous and unseen

The explosion of event traffic over the past twenty years created a new set of demands from business enterprises. The IT layers (i.e., the company's networks, middleware, enterprise service bus, cell phones, and websites) of every sizable business were humming with this traffic, and people in every management role wanted to analyze it and understand its implications for their own roles in the organization. The demand to extract information from the IT layers, sometimes referred to as business intelligence, had increased dramatically. As we shall see, it is difficult to think of anything other than CEP that could have taken place in the processing of higher-level events at a particular point in time around 2000.

This chapter describes four stages of commercial development and adoption that CEP is going through and will go through in the future. As we shall argue in later chapters, the long-term outlook is for CEP to become a contributing technology under the hood of those global applications of real-time information systems that are essential to running our society.

We start with the situation facing event processing vendors at the beginning of the twenty-first century.

The Dawn of Complex Event Processing (CEP)

With the advent of networks came a host of network management tools[1] whose job it was to monitor network activity and display the results graphically. Some of these tools, such as HP Openview, CA UniCenter, IBM Tivoli NetView, and BMC Patrol, were some of the leading network management tools of their day. They were used to monitor events in networks and provide graphical views and statistics for network managers. They could be considered as the early precursors of business activity monitoring (BAM).

The application users wanted to know what was going on too, especially when the applications failed because of network problems. But users of applications understand higher-level events, not network-level activity. Sometimes, the tools could use composition rules to construct higher-level events from the network activity and conversely to drill down from higher-level events to the lower-level events that caused them. So by the mid-1990s, we could see the tip of the CEP iceberg! Whether the implementers of these tools had any explicit definition of CEP principles in mind may be open to doubt. But two things are worth mentioning.

These network management tools made graphical dashboards the main access medium (see Figure 4.1). The dashboard was developed to supply tables, graphs, and animations of the information delivered by the monitoring tools that were tracking the network traffic. So dashboards became the default interface for delivering insight to the user, or at least for kidding the user that insight was being achieved! We'll come back to dashboards and implied insight later.

Secondly, an astounding fact. The major IT suppliers of these early network management tools were slow to capitalize on the opportunity to extend their technology to the higher levels of events used in business processes and management operations. The technology implementing event pattern detection and simple kinds of event pattern abstraction was already buried in some of these tools. It is clear that such extensions of network monitoring could have been done far in advance of other entrants into the business event processing market.

But no commentator or student of event processing or business has a satisfactory answer to why the major IT suppliers failed to make such obvious extensions to the capabilities of their network analysis tools. Some guess that perhaps they were too focused on the existing network market

---

[1]See Chapter 2, Figure 2.1.

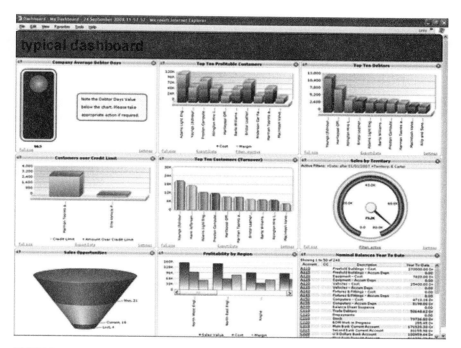

FIGURE 4.1 A Graphical Dashboard Attempting to Aid Human Understanding of Events and Data

and didn't really believe there was a market for higher-level business event processing. However, there can be no doubt that all the major IT vendors of the time missed an opportunity—and for that, the small start-up vendors in the BAM and CEP field today must be eternally grateful.

Of course, all of the large companies are in the business event management market now. Some of them have three or four competing products from different divisions within the same company! These larger companies are, in fact, busy buying up the smaller CEP vendors that pioneered the field. That's one way they are playing catch up. Today the market for higher-level event processing is a battleground for market share, and the smaller players are being assimilated into the large vendors.

Four Stages of CEP

CEP is about analyzing events at all levels, from the highest level of the business and management operations of the enterprise down to the network level, if necessary. And it is about supplying event processing capabilities in a general form that can be configured to apply to any types of events in different problem areas.

Following the developments in network management tools, the next step that needed to be taken in event processing was CEP. The commercial story of CEP begins around 2000, perhaps slightly earlier. In the beginning there were no clearly defined or published principles or concepts for the field. There were no publications, no presentations at meetings, no formal society devoted to event processing. CEP was a vague cloud of half-formed ideas in the heads of the more forward thinking people in business and academia. It was the subject of a few research projects in various places that could be counted on the fingers of one hand, perhaps without the thumb!

Ten years on, it can be seen clearly that there are four stages in the evolution of commercial technology based upon CEP concepts. There are no sharp distinguishing time points at which one stage ends and the next begins. In fact, each stage overlaps in time with the next. Figure 4.2 shows the approximate time intervals of these stages.

Each stage can be characterized by a set of technology indicators that summarize the CEP capabilities that were appearing in commercial tools and also the state of the marketplace of that time. As these technology indicators begin to appear, the previous stage begins to evolve into the next one.

The first stage, called *simple CEP*, was really a struggle to explore and develop markets, and to gain market traction, on the part of the early event processing vendors. The CEP concepts had not been published at the

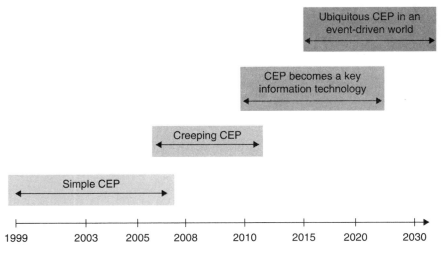

FIGURE 4.2 The Four Stages in the Evolution of Commercial CEP Applications

beginning of this stage. The ideas were evolving and being formulated. So the event processing implemented in the early tools was "simple," if not rudimentary to say the least, but still capable of answering some of the business intelligence questions of interest to potential customers.

The second stage, *creeping CEP*, is where we are today. CEP concepts were published during the simple CEP stage and began creeping into the tools. The present generation of tools on the market today has event processing capabilities that implement a lot of CEP concepts. And more CEP is creeping into the tools all the time.

The next stage is the *key information technology* stage, in which CEP becomes a recognized area of information technology and computer science. The more advanced concepts of CEP, such as event hierarchies, will be introduced into commercial applications, and standards for event processing will appear.

And the final stage, some way off in the future, is *ubiquitous CEP*. It is a stage where CEP technology simply disappears under the hood of event processing applications and is really no longer visible, or talked about by end users of the applications. It is an enabling technology that users don't see, but it is used everywhere!

Simple CEP (1999–2007)

Some event processing applications in the first years, say around 2003, claimed to provide CEP capabilities.[2] In fact, they implemented only a few of the simplest CEP ideas, if any. So I refer to this as the era of simple CEP, even though the *data* processing (as opposed to *event* processing) contained in these applications was often very sophisticated. In other words, the data in the events were being processed and might be subjected to complex algorithms, but only the simplest event pattern–processing techniques were used on the events themselves.

For example, event monitors could be installed on the IT layer to give business managers an online view of how the business was operating by displaying key performance indicators (KPIs) for business processes. But they allowed only a small number of predefined[3] conditions to trigger alerts. In the earliest KPI monitors, the triggers for alerts could only be single events. The use of trigger conditions containing several events in a specific pattern came later.

---

[2]See the list of CEP concepts in the section in Chapter 3 entitled "Complex Event Processing and Systems That Use It."

[3]"Predefined" is sometimes referred to as "out of the box."

The CEP technology indicators for this stage appeared gradually during this time span, mostly between 2000 and 2005:

- Adapters for translation between common event formats
- A small number of predefined event types in commercial tools
- Commercial tools capable of computing simple statistics on events, such as counting numbers of events of a specified type
- Extensive application of computations on the data content of events such as in stock trading algorithms
- User-defined alerts
- Alerting based upon single-event triggers
- Moderate event throughput in event processing, up to 1,000 events per second
- Playback and event storage
- Primitive dashboards for displaying results
- A small number of established commercial applications

Claims of higher event throughputs, sometimes in the range of 10,000 events per second, were made, but in these cases the tools were doing little more than simply reading the event inputs.

Building adapters for event formats was perhaps the first step that most CEP tool builders took. And a ready market for adapters appeared. They were needed, so that the tools could be configured to work on a customer's IT layer.

This was the era of single event triggering in the most advanced tools of this time. That is, users could define event-condition-action (E-C-A) rules, but the conditions to trigger them could only contain a single event template. So, if an event arrived that matched a condition, then the corresponding data computation or alert was triggered. Also, users were usually restricted to a fixed number of different types of events, all of them predefined in the tool. Event templates of these types could be used in conditions. Some tools had user features for specifying additional types of events beyond those predefined in the tool.

Many of the event processing applications at this time were simply devoted to computing statistics using the data in the events (e.g., computing the volume-weighted average price or VWAP of the trades in each stock on a list of stock symbols in the past hour). More advanced applications were warning systems applied to IT layers to monitor events and detect conditions defined by the user, for example:

- To monitor conformance to company policies of traffic accessing a secure database
- To monitor communication between the controllers in a chip fabrication line to ensure correct progress of the pallets of wafers through the processing steps

More complex alerts using patterns of events came later. The explanation for the rudimentary nature of the CEP implementations at this stage is simple enough: Implementations of event pattern detection for complex patterns were nonexistent. Only the simplest of event patterns, most often just single event templates, were all that could be handled at that time. The rates at which events could be processed were moderate by today's standards. Lastly, the first uses of graphical dashboards in general-purpose CEP products (as opposed to say, stock market trading tools) arrived in these early tools.

The next generation of KPI monitors around 2004 included a bit more CEP. They provided a limited facility for users to specify additional types of events and to use them in E-C-A rules. Triggers could be patterns containing multiple event templates. But the user features for defining event patterns were primitive, and complicated to use which is why many of the tools were more suited for use by software professionals than by business analysts. In cases where the monitors allowed users to define their own types of events, or event patterns and event-triggered rules, those definitions usually had to be coded in a version of Java script or an extension of SQL. Also, the event patterns that could be used were limited to simple Boolean combinations of event templates.

CEP versus Custom Coding

The first problem that vendors of CEP products encountered upon entering new markets such as financial trading was custom coding. Custom-coded event processing had been going on in a few areas such as stock trading since the mid-1990s. That was their biggest competitor. This was in the early days, around 2000–2005. CEP vendors would often complain, "Our biggest competition is from custom-coded solutions." What did that mean?

You might well think that it meant some machine-coded hackery. But in fact it simply meant that the competition was coded by the customer's own IT department and not purchased from an outside source. Often, a custom-coded solution was indeed a program that was focused on a single, specific problem and had an overly restricted range of applicability. Even so, it might apply principles of CEP, although the IT department may never have heard of CEP. And usually a custom-coded solution worked pretty well, because it had been working for some time before the CEP vendors entered the market. Also, the first-generation CEP solutions were far from perfect, and as we have said, most of them supplied only a little CEP.

However, when the potential customers wanted to extend their custom-coded solutions to other event processing tasks, even in the same problem domain, it usually turned out to be a labor-intensive and expensive process. And event processing packages and tools were becoming more commonplace. That led potential customers to re-evaluate the "build it or buy it" equation, and general-purpose CEP began to make inroads into these markets. This battle is still going on today!

Creeping CEP (2004–2012)

More and more CEP concepts began to creep into event processing products around 2004 and the years following. These were difficult times for most small CEP vendors. It was a time when business analysts talked about the need to "gain traction" in markets. A lot of the small pioneering vendors that had been first into the field were assimilated by larger companies, and others failed. But many continued to pioneer new markets while running at a loss. Belief, the stuff of innovation and enterprise, kept them going. Usually they had one or two proof-of-concept experiments with customers that paid enough to keep them in operation.

At this time the medium-size vendors of middleware products began to add CEP to their middleware and enterprise service bus (ESB) products. Meanwhile, the large players were sitting on the sidelines developing event-processing additions to their product suites and trying to decide if there was a business event processing market.

It was in this critical formative period that business activity monitoring (BAM) emerged as a market area for CEP. Educational material in event processing began to appear in the form of university courses and books. Graphical interfaces and computer languages for event processing made their way into CEP products—and the BAM dashboard arrived, as we will discuss in a moment. All of these were indicators that event processing was a growing and active area for computer applications in business areas.

The technology indicators for this stage were many improvements arriving in CEP tools during 2004–2009:

- Somewhat higher-level languages, allowing users to define event patterns; these included stream-SQL, Java language extensions to allow expressions with patterns of events, finite state machines, Petri Nets, and graphical input schemes
- Detection of user-defined event types and event patterns, such as Boolean combinations of event types, or regular expressions of event types
- Timing bounds in patterns of events
- Complex event patterns involving multiple-event templates as triggers for alerts and E-C-A rules
- Sophisticated graphical dashboards for displaying event pattern monitoring results, KPIs, and alerts, and for authoring E-C-A rules

Business Activity Monitoring

Business activity monitoring (BAM) was one of the most successful areas where CEP applications appeared early in this stage, alongside financial trading and services. This is the time of the "great creep forward" in commercial CEP!

While BAM started in the previous stage of *simple CEP*, it developed into a rallying cry for all the vendors during this stage of *creeping CEP*. It crosses our timelines.

The term BAM was first coined by Roy Schulte at Gartner[4] for business activity monitoring to classify the market that KPI event monitors and similar tools were targeting. This simple label had the effect of focusing attention on this new area and helping people understand in general terms what it was all about and what its goals were. True, three-letter acronyms have proliferated beyond all usefulness in the business applications area, but this particular one was worth its weight in gold!

BAM was a successful market category for the first generation of CEP products. As we have already discussed, only the simplest event processing technology was involved—that is, formatting events, categorizing and counting numbers of events in each category, computing various KPIs, and displaying the results as graphical meters. But the BAM market funded the next generation of commercial CEP products.

The first BAM tools were used to monitor business parameters and business processes. A period of gradual adoption took place. BAM tools were applied to real-time data in banking operations. An example is monitoring the progress of mortgage applications across a global network of cooperating financial institutions (see Figure 4.3). Each mortgage application progresses through various steps in a pipeline: for example, income review, credit checking, loan application risk analysis, background checking, and a final decision step that, if it has a positive outcome, leads to a funding approval process. Each step, executed by a different company in a collaborative network, might initiate a subprocess involving another series of steps. An income review, for example, might initiate concurrent steps to check income, bank accounts, ask for recommendations, and so on.

At any one time there might be several hundred applications at various stages in the pipeline. A BAM dashboard provided a central monitoring panel for statistics on the whole pipelined mortgage process and its subprocesses. Similar BAM dashboard monitoring of multiple stages of business

---

[4]D. McCoy, R. Schulte, F. Buytendijk, N. Rayner, and A. Tiedrich, "Business Activity Monitoring: The Promise and Reality," *Gartner's Marketing Knowledge and Technology Commentary* COM-13-9992, July 11, 2001. Can be viewed at www.gartner.com/gc/webletter/rok/issue2/issue2.pdf

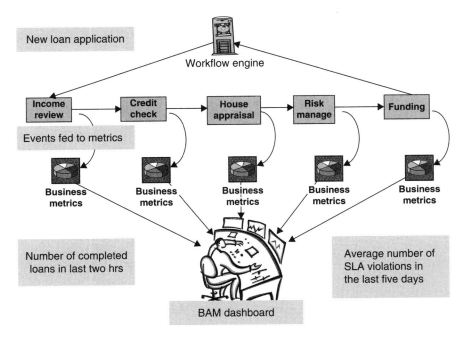

FIGURE 4.3 Event Monitors and Dashboard Display Applied to Monitoring Business Processes

processes can be found, for example, in the insurance underwriting business, where the risk analysis may involve several complex steps.

About the same time, more CEP applications were being added to the event processing tools already in capital market applications (e.g., in trading bonds, commodities, derivatives and foreign exchange). Here the event input contained market trading data from various sources, usually including several stock market feeds. Financial trading had a tradition of custom-coded tools, so CEP vendors found that event processing was already well understood in that field. In fact, as already mentioned, the biggest competitor with CEP products was, and still is, custom-coded solutions.

Elsewhere, vendors found that their most significant problem in penetrating new markets was educating the marketplace about event processing and its potential benefits. There was a lack of educational material, not only for customers but also for the vendor's sales force.

As the development of CEP tools progressed, graphical input tools were introduced to help users define event patterns. Graphics give a user a way to easily compose the outline and Boolean structure of an event pattern. Even so, at some lower level in specifying all the details, a user has to resort to writing program text in code (e.g., SQL or Java) to fully define an event pattern.

Awareness and Education in Event Processing

The early vendors of event processing entering into the CEP arena were faced with a new problem. It didn't matter if they were established vendors of middleware, business process management (BPM), and first-generation ESBs products; were already in the financial services market; or were new startups in CEP. The problem was the same: education! First they had to raise the level of awareness about CEP and the kinds of commercial problems it could be applied to. Educating both the customer and the company's sales force was a pressing need. And it was made worse by the fact that educational materials were lacking.

The only book on the topic at that time, and for many of the following years, was *The Power of Events,*[5] an outgrowth of ten years of research in event processing at Stanford together with experience in the startup marketplace. It contained a simple introduction to the concepts of CEP in Part I and a comprehensive overview of CEP principles and possible applications in Part II. Ideally, it should have been two books, and for many, Part II is a tough read, even today. Some marketing departments bought the book in volume and handed out free copies to potential customers—and their own sales force.

Languages for Event Processing

Gradually, the event processing tools progressed beyond simply monitoring the activity on the IT layer to compute KPIs. They added features that allowed users to define patterns of events. The monitors were supposed to detect instances of these patterns in the enterprise activity. The event patterns that could be defined became more sophisticated, and languages for defining event patterns began to appear. Timing conditions could be added to events in a pattern, but only very simple ones, such as "event E **at** time t."

The appearance of event pattern–definition languages was a step forward. Most of these were variants of SQL with one or two additions for defining events and patterns, such as Stream SQL (SSQL), and SQL

---

[5]David Luckham, *The Power of Events* (Boston: Addison-Wesley, 2002).

variants such as CQL.[6] These languages were targeted to defining event patterns in event streams such as stock market feeds—which were the target market for these tools. They could be applied to other kinds of event input, of course, but the pattern-detection capabilities would still treat the input as if it was an event stream.

One reason for the popularity of SQL variants as the event pattern definition language of choice was ease of implementation. The tool builders at this time were mostly from the database industry and were experienced in SQL, but not in event processing. Funnily enough, questions of correctness of implementations never seemed to arise. The other common justification was that SQL was what the customers understood. And also the sales force, one might add!

But some of the new event pattern–definition languages were not variations of SQL. They assumed that the event input was indeed a cloud of events. These pattern languages could specify event patterns that were regular expressions containing event templates. They were extensions of algorithmic computer languages such as Java and had been designed earlier in the 1990s. One language was an elegant extension of Java for parallel processing.[7] It allowed users to define classes of processes that could execute independently and concurrently, together with their interactions and communications. This language came out of Cambridge University in England and forms the basis for some commercial products today.

Another notable event processing language was *Rapide*, developed by the Stanford event processing project to support building event driven simulation models. It was a strongly typed algorithmic language, based upon the modular concepts of Simula67, Modula, Ada83, and VHDL, but with added constructs for defining concurrent threads of control called *tasks* and *architectures*. It is the only language with an ability to define different levels of events (say, management events and business-operations events). This gave users an ability to actually define management-level events in terms of the way they were composed out of lower-level events. One could define how management-level events were to be executed by means of *maps* between event layers. It was applied at that time to building simulations of multilevel systems, notably hardware designs.

Multiple levels of a system design could be simulated concurrently and the results compared automatically for consistency between the executions at each level. The results of comparative simulation of different levels of a CPU design (e.g., instruction set level, register transfer

---

[6]Arvind Arasu, Shivnath Babu, and Jennifer Widom, "The CQL Continuous Query Language: Semantic Foundations and Query Execution,"Technical Report, Stanford. http://ilpubs.stanford.edu:8090/758/

[7]The author was Dr. John Bates.

level, and gate level) were impressive.[8] Rapide is also the only computer language to record both the causal relationships between events and their timing in simulation results.

Rapide was also applied to event monitoring on commercial middleware and was used on various research projects at other universities. It has remained largely a research tool, probably because of the implementation challenges it poses. A few commercial implementations have been attempted by startups. And some are still in use.

The development of event processing languages is ongoing across the different development stages of commercial CEP.

Dashboards and Human-Computer Interfaces

The dashboard became the standard means of displaying the results of event monitoring applied to the enterprise IT layers (see Figure 4.1). Historically, the idea of using digital dashboards to convey information to humans comes from the 1970s decision-support systems. In the late 1990s, with the surge of the Web, digital dashboards as we know them today began appearing in more business applications. Many systems were developed in-house by organizations to consolidate and display data already being gathered in various information systems throughout the organization. Today, one can find dashboard templates and software for building dashboards in Web development toolkits and elsewhere. Most CEP vendors use dashboard-building tools and configured their own dashboards.

Every dashboard was different. KPIs and other statistics were computed from the input event cloud and displayed in all manner of meters, dials, and real-time graphs, and in all colors of the rainbow. They were impressive at first glance. But there were absolutely no standard for dashboards. And when one attempted to draw conclusions or insight upon which to base management decisions, one was often left at a loss. There was no aid to help a viewer draw conclusions from the pretty pictures and the statistical data that could be used at a level of management decision-making.

In fact, the situation in applying business event processing to enterprise management was quite similar to the situation in network management. The average network management operations room is filled with an impressive array of monitor consoles in all colors and configurations, from floor to ceiling and from end to end of the room. Every statistic imaginable is displayed in real time, as in Figure 4.1. The managers sit viewing this dazzling display and wondering what should be done.

---

[8]Rapide won the Design Automation Conference Best Paper Award in 1994.

In the more advanced dashboard products that contain CEP, one can define alerts that ring automatically when specified event patterns are matched by the event inputs over specified time windows. And one can construct E-C-A rules to be triggered when event pattern conditions are matched, thus taking some simple kinds of action to control the enterprise. Basic problems like load balancing of servers and power fluctuations in the network can be seen and addressed. But there is no automated reasoning from the meters and statistics. Network management situations that develop slowly beyond the time-window limits of the tool, like long-lived intrusions or thefts of secure data, are never seen on these dashboards. And distributed denial of service (DDOS) attacks usually arrive far too quickly for any actions.

Dashboards do not give insight into the enterprise's business situation, nor do they suggest management decisions. They do not tell you what is going to happen. The human has to sit and try to predict developing situations from what the dashboard displays. Usually the graphic representations of the event inputs can be helpful, but when everything suddenly goes red and bells begin to ring, it is generally too late. This was exactly what happened with those in control of the power grid during the great northeast United States electricity grid blackout of August 2003.[9] Indeed, the controllers' reactions during that situation were that their computers were under cyberattack and their dashboards were not believable!

There is no better example of both the strengths and the limitations of the dashboard than the United States Geological Survey Natural Hazards website (see Figure 4.4). This facility provides users (e.g., local government authorities, fire and police departments, first aid planners, and also the private individual) with an ability to see immediately, in near-real time, what kinds of weather and other environmental events might be happening in their area. It displays input from a multitude of sources: weather satellites and forecasts, ocean monitoring stations, earthquake sensors, hydrology monitors in rivers, local authority flood and mudslide warnings, and remote automated weather stations (RAWS) around the United States[10] and in some cases around the globe. The display is a dashboard with an interactive world map.

There are graphic tools for manipulating the map, such as zoom and focus, and for displaying location-specific information. For example, as a hurricane nears a shoreline, NHSS users can see its current location and

---

[9]U.S.-Canada Power System Outage Task Force, *Final Report on the August 14, 2003 Blackout in the United States and Canada: Causes and Recommendations*, April 2004. https://reports.energy.gov/BlackoutFinal-Web.pdf

[10]There are nearly 2,200 RAWS located throughout the United States (USGS, 2008).

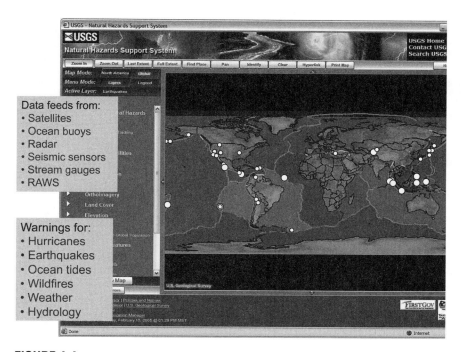

FIGURE 4.4 USGS Natural Hazards Dashboard

can click on the map to access real-time information on stream levels, wind speeds, and tide conditions. The website also stores historical data.

This is a powerful use of the dashboard concept. But as Figure 4.5 shows, it lacks any kind of reasoning capability. When querying activity at a location, one should be careful to query not only the predictions for that area but also the recent history within a time window. And then one is left entirely alone to draw conclusions.

For example, to investigate the possibility of mudslides or avalanches, one must take account of the geology as well as the weather forecasts and recent history. Taking the USGS NHSS system to the next step of informativeness is a challenging project, but very worthwhile and entirely feasible.

Human-Computer Interfaces

An amusing thought is that at some point, dashboards for businesses could morph into human-computer interfaces.

The term *interface* has been coined for the kinds of machine-human links that are being experimented with in research labs at the moment.

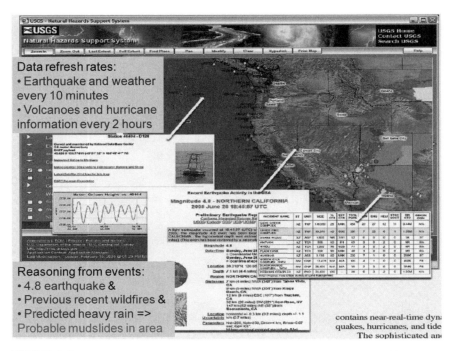

FIGURE 4.5 Reasoning from the Data on the USGS Natural Hazards Dashboard

An interface is a link between systems, equipment, or people that can be applied to virtually any engagement between humans and machines. The next-generation user interfaces will facilitate control with much greater intuitiveness derived from natural actions and behaviors. Improved integration between the human body and electronic devices should usher in the age of the organic user interface, whose potential implementations include biometric sensors, displays projected onto the user's skin, and eventually brain-computer interfaces.

It is claimed that human-computer interfaces could be used for vehicle control, emergency services dispatching, augmented reality, architectural design, telemedicine, and traffic flow modeling. So maybe they might find application to business intelligence gathering and managing businesses too? One potential use of future interfaces is eye tracking, which in passive applications can be employed for advertising and marketing feedback by collecting useful data about where a user's gaze is directed. In some interactive applications of the technology, eye tracking is already letting quadriplegics interface directly with computers, choosing letters and commands by fixing their gaze on the appropriate region of the screen. This form of interaction is expected to provide an input control mechanism for wearable computers.

CEP Becomes a Recognized Information Technology (2009–2020)

Stage 3 is where event processing becomes recognized as a technology area in computer science separate from any of its applications in simulation, networking, or other areas. Hopefully we are entering this stage now. It has been said that the applications in stage 2, *creeping CEP*, are about *chaos management* within the enterprise, whereas the applications in stage 3 are about *proactive management*. In truth, chaos management will probably be the mode of operation in businesses for a long time to come.

The technology indicators of stage 3 include:

- A much-expanded range of areas of applications in many different markets
- An established event processing community[11] sponsoring
  - Conferences
  - Publications
  - Standards
- Open source development of event-processing tools with CEP capabilities
- Next-generation high-level languages for specifying complex event patterns and pattern-triggered reactive rules
- Definition and commercial use of event abstraction hierarchies
- Event processing standards
- Libraries of event processing rules engines and event processing agents for building CEP solutions
- Tools for event driven applications, such as statistical analytics tools, simulation tools, and constraint-based optimization tools
- Funded academic research and teaching in event processing

The most important indicator that we are beginning to enter stage 3 is healthy and established markets. And the best measure of this is the diversity and number of areas where there are substantial commercial

---

[11]The Event Processing Technical Society, EPTS, www.ep-ts.com

applications. A second indicator is interest in CEP, not only among potential buyers but also on the part of technical people—the engineers and computer scientists who will design and build more capable CEP products in the future. This interest is manifesting itself in the formation of a society to sponsor meetings and publications addressing the subject of event processing. This activity started taking place in 2008. Chapter 5 deals with the market areas for event processing products and CEP in detail.

In stage 3, the more advanced concepts of CEP that were yet to be included in products at stage 2 will become understood well enough to find useful commercial applications. As a result, the technology in event processing products will support the use of more CEP concepts in building applications. This has begun to happen. Implementations of event pattern detection have improved considerably so that quite complex patterns are being deployed in applications in areas such as security and real-time fraud detection.

But CEP concepts such as event hierarchies have yet to see useful commercial applications.

Some industry observers say that people are often using event hierarchies implicitly in their event processing work without realizing it. But that if they had explicit hierarchy definitions to work with, they could achieve a lot more.

The basic idea is that businesses have a hierarchy in their operations and management. Correspondingly, the events created in running a business should also be organized in an analogous hierarchy. We should be able to view the events that correspond to any level of the business operations that we are interested in—as they happen, or post mortem.

Example 4.1: An Event Hierarchy in Factory Fabrication Line Operations

Here's an example of a CEP event hierarchy that could be featured at stage 3 in commercial tools for observing events in a particular kind of business operation. It is a *computable hierarchy of events*. It provides a framework for building tools for viewing events at different levels in the operations and analyzing the causes of an event at any level by retrieving the lower-level events that caused it.

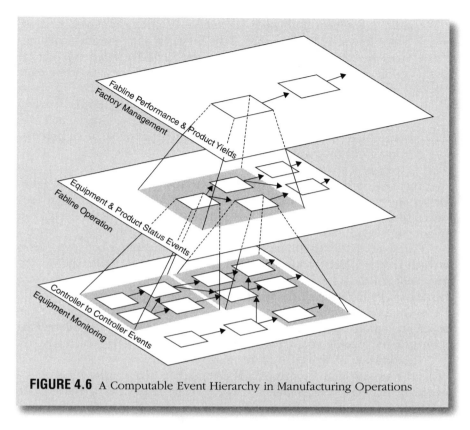

FIGURE 4.6 A Computable Event Hierarchy in Manufacturing Operations

In Example 4.1, the business is a manufacturing company. The event hierarchy defines relationships between events at three levels. Here is a small selection of the events at each level:

Level 3: Factory management–level events. Events at this level are measurement events used in decision making. They give fabrication line performance (e.g., equipment failure rates, maintenance times, etc.), product yields (e.g., wafer yields per pallet) and operating costs (e.g., energy consumption measures per machine per day, raw materials consumed per day, etc.).

Level 2: Fabrication line operations–level events. Events at this level are operational events from the fabrication line—for example, equipment status events for each machine (e.g., in service, idle, loading, operating, unloading, standby, in maintenance, in error status, etc.) and fabrication line movement events (e.g., number of pallets in process, pallet positions, pallet statuses, pallet throughput times, etc.).

Level 1: Equipment and controller communications-level events. These are low-level events that flow between the various machines on the fabrication line and the controllers that keep the fabrication process on schedule and measure the results from each machine—for example, communication events between machines and controllers (e.g., controller to machine polling events, instruction events) and machine-to-controller responses (e.g., machine state, temperature, gas density, operating phase, stage in processing, time to completion, etc.).

There are many thousands of level 1 events per minute in chip fabrication line (fabline) operations. The numbers of level 2 and level 3 events decrease exponentially with level (e.g., there are hundreds of events per minute at level 2, and perhaps as little as tens per hour at level 1).

Figure 4.6 illustrates the hierarchy levels and mappings between events at each level and sets of lower-level events. In the figure, a fabline operating event at level 2 has a shadow of level 1 communication events from the fabrication line. These are the level 1 events that lead to the level 2 operating event. For example, a *machine-loading event* (level 2) might result from several communication events between that machine and a controller telling it to enter the loading phase, together with the machine's responses.

This shadow is defined by a mapping between level 2 events and sets of level 1 events. And the mapping is computable. That is, given the level 2 event, the mapping will compute the level 1 events in its shadow that led to it.

Similarly, the management events at level 3 are mapped in the hierarchy to sets of events at level 2. For example, an equipment failure rate event, say a weekly level 3 measure of performance, will map to a set of level 2 error status events for machines over that week. A daily or hourly product yield event will map to a set of pallet status and pallet processing–time events at level 2.

A computable hierarchy has a number of applications. First, the cloud of level 1 events from a fabrication line can be fed to the hierarchy mappings. They in turn will compute and output the events at level 2 and then at level 3. So we automatically receive the level 2 events reporting the operations of the fabline, and then the level 3 factory-performance measures, all right now as they happen.

Second, the hierarchy helps in analyzing performance failures. If there is a problem, such as persistent equipment failures over time, we want to drill down the hierarchy to analyze the level 3 operating events that are related to the failure events. The reverse mappings from level 2 to level 1 let us do that.

Again, if there's a production problem at level 3, such as low yields, then we need to analyze intermediate level 2 events such as product yields and manufacturing times. If we find events at this level that indicate problems, we will want to drill down further to see the related level 1 events. Here we may find emerging problems such as a machine with parameters (e.g., temperature, gas density) that are near performance limits but not yet error status.

Events are being created in a continuous flow as the factory is running. Using the hierarchy maps we can see how higher-level events are caused by sets of lower-level events. If we are given a flow of level 1 events coming from running the fabrication line, we can compute the fabline status events at level 2 and then the factory performance events at level 3.

Note that hierarchies are an operational tool in event-driven systems. Sometimes maps will yield "don't know" results! One important advantage of event hierarchies is that the numbers of events decrease exponentially as their level increases. So operational errors that might not be detected at low levels sometimes become glaringly obvious at higher levels. For example, an expected high-level event is missing! The high-level event is missing because a lower level event that it depends upon is missing. But you might not notice that missing lower-level event, because there are too many low-level events.

Methods of defining computable hierarchies of events and maps between levels of events are given in Chapter 7.

Event Processing Standards

As CEP becomes a mature technology, we expect event standards to be developed during stage 3. In fact, some event standards, such as formats for events, are being reviewed in some of the standards committees. There are several drivers for standards, not the least being the need to develop modular libraries of CEP components analogous to Java Beans or JMS. One should be able to buy an off-the-shelf pattern-matching engine or rule-execution engine to build a solution using CEP. It would help to have shared libraries of various building blocks of the technology (e.g., rules engines, libraries of event patterns for specified application areas, and event processing agents that are special-purpose rules engines that perform specified tasks such as event filtering and aggregation). Some open source CEP rules engines have already appeared and are being used in various projects.

Another indicator that should happen during stage 3 is the development of standard event hierarchies for application areas, such as supply chain management or airline operations. These hierarchies of concepts would be analogous to the ISO seven-layer messaging standard, or the TCP six-layer event transportation hierarchy. Events at each level correspond to the concepts at that level. This is a step that must be taken toward spreading the use of event abstraction in applications of event processing, and toward standardizing both the terminology and the applications.

There are many other developments that may or may not happen during stage 3. One that is often talked about by some vendors is making CEP available as an Internet service. An approach would be selling computation time on clouds of CEP engines. It will not take long to find out whether these kinds of ideas come to fruition!

Ubiquitous CEP

In our final stage, CEP ceases to be a visible technology that is accessible to the average end user of an event processing system. Instead, it simply disappears under the hood of applications, rather like network protocols today, and becomes a tool of event processing specialists. The time at which this final stage begins is hard to determine. Some would say that we entered this stage in 2011; others would say not yet. But it is already the case that some very large-scale global event-driven applications are being developed in which CEP plays a supporting role.

Some of the indicators for *ubiquitous CEP* are:

- Complex event processing is a part of common event driven applications across the board, small and large, from household automation to real-time enterprise to national cyber defense.
- Event processing is used as an integration technology across market boundaries, unifying applications in different markets and event spaces.
- Holistic event processing becomes a reality. These are very large-scale applications of event processing, such as global environmental monitoring systems.
- Many systems that process events and use CEP concepts are built without the builders even knowing that they are using event processing or CEP, and without ever knowing anything about the concepts discussed in this book.

The wheel has been invented many times over history, and in many guises!

Holism (from Ὅλος, or *holos*, a Greek word meaning *all, entire, total*) is the idea that all the properties of a given system (e.g., biological, chemical, social, economic, mental, linguistic) cannot be determined or explained by the sum of its component parts alone. Instead, the system as a whole determines in an important way how the parts behave. The general principle of holism was concisely summarized by Aristotle in the *Metaphysics*: "The whole is more than the sum of its parts."

Two examples of holistic event processing systems are:

1. *Unified global air traffic control.* A unified international air traffic control system spanning all commercial air travel.
2. *Global pandemic watch systems.* A real-time global pandemic watch system based upon analyzing and correlating (1) multiple real-time news feeds in different languages from around the globe, (2) SMS messages from trained rural field agents in southeast Asia, Africa, and elsewhere, and (3) electronic reports from health authorities at every level, from local to regional to national and finally the WHO.

The development of holistic event processing applications is a final indicator that we are in stage 4. Chapter 9 will deal with *holistic event processing* and the future applications of CEP and event processing in general.

CHAPTER 5

Markets and Emerging Markets for CEP

This chapter provides a review of markets for complex event processing products and the purposes for which those products are bought.

Event processing is now a basic component in many different IT systems used in business and government. This often includes complex event processing, as explained in Chapter 3, and in particular the section in Chapter 3 entitled "Complex Event Processing and Systems That Use It." As a result, the number and size of markets for CEP applications is growing at a significant pace.

This chapter is a survey of market areas for commercial CEP products and the uses to which this technology is being put. Our purpose here is to give the reader a feel for the range of CEP applications that are in the field now— as well as future market areas where event processing is being tested experimentally at the moment. But we must add the caveat that this survey is not intended to be complete or exhaustive. It is simply a selection of CEP applications at a moment in 2011. Hopefully it will remain valid for a few years.

There have been a number of research studies of the size of markets in financial terms for CEP products and services. Estimates seemed to agree that the total market for 2009 was somewhere in the region of $190 million in sales of products and service contracts for their maintenance, and that the market rose to roughly $280 million for 2010. This was deemed by the market researchers to indicate "an emerging market in the early stage of development." Predictions are for an average growth rate of about 30 percent per year to around $580 million in 2013.[1]

---

[1]Based on private correspondence with Roy Schulte, Gartner Corp, and industry research reports.

One of the difficulties with these studies is separating event processing products that apply CEP technology[2] in some of their operations from those that do not use any CEP at all.

The CEP market studies have made strenuous efforts to specify the markets and have devoted much of their space to classifying the market areas, and mentioning by name the vendors, products, and sometimes consumers that have been included in the study.

In keeping with our guiding principle in this book, we do not mention names of companies making the studies, nor those that are subjects of the market studies. But these studies are easily accessible, possibly at a price, to readers who are interested in more details.

The event processing market in general is a multibillion dollar market—estimated at up to $5 billion in 2010. But a lot of conventional business event processing is for applications that deal with "business events" for recordkeeping and routine operational purposes such as accounting. They simply store events in a database and, later, employ data mining methods for business intelligence.

We exclude this kind of processing of events. We are dealing here with that part of the broad EP market that uses CEP techniques for *right now* applications. That leaves us with a much smaller market!

The only products that are counted in the estimated $280 million (2010) CEP market are the general-purpose event processing products in which the CEP technology can be configured to deal with different problems and is not hardwired for any particular business problem. These general-purpose products can deal with multiple types of events from diverse sources and can be applied to a wide variety of problems. They contain development tools that make it relatively easy for software developers and expert knowledge workers to create and modify CEP applications. Development facilities include event pattern languages and tools to test and debug systems of event pattern–triggered rules and to replay and analyze the performance of rule-based systems on event streams. The products typically also include adapters to connect to databases, external analytical tools, business dashboards, sensors, actuators, and a variety of event sources, such as messaging systems and market data feeds. Both end users and vendors use these general-purpose platforms to build many kinds of customized CEP applications.

We have excluded the market for hardwired event processing applications—that is, applications intended for a specific use or problem and not generally configurable for use on different problems—which is estimated at $5 billion by some research studies. These hardwired

---

[2]See the section entitled "Complex Event Processing and Systems That Use It" in Chapter 3.

special-purpose event processing applications are to be found among the systems used in supply-chain management, customer contact centers, network management tools, risk management, fraud detection, and manufacturing control systems. The CEP technology in these products is narrowly focused on solving a specific industry or business problem. Their use of events is usually relatively simple; the adapters are oriented toward only a few kinds of input and output; and the development tools are limited or nonexistent, because the buyer is not expected to modify the application by adding new event patterns or changing the configuration of event processing operations. Although such products implement CEP principles, their buyers and users do not typically think of them as CEP tools—they are known by their business purpose. These types of CEP applications are not counted in our market estimates.

Also excluded are CEP applications that compute offline. Generally, these are business intelligence (BI) tools used to generate business reports or answers to queries submitted by an analyst or manager. Virtually all BI tools perform computation on events *offline* in online analytical processing (OLAP) cubes or other forms of data warehouses in memory or on disk. In the course of their work, they perform many of the same kinds of operations found in the general-purpose event processing platforms. For example, they filter and correlate events, calculate aggregates (sum, average, rank top-k, and so forth) and detect instances of event patterns. These applications do involve CEP, if one uses a broad, academic definition of the term ("any computation involving complex events"). However, they are not considered part of the CEP market, and the term CEP is almost never used to describe their role because they work "after the fact" and not in *right now* time.

The reader of this chapter will be struck by the underlying similarity of event processing applications in vastly different areas. All of our examples are summaries of actual event processing applications, either fielded or under experimental testing. For example, applications in fraud detection and in, say, health care rely on the same templates for event triggered rules and the same rules engines. Of course, the actual rules are different in each case. The differences lie in the types of events being input and output, the event patterns that trigger the rules, the types of actions and alerts that the rules output when they are triggered, the rates at which events arrive or are output, and the states of the rule processors. But the event processors in each case could be the same rules engine.

We have written the examples so that a reader can skim through and get a good idea of the similarities in the event processing as well as the actual kinds of events and rules in use in each area. To emphasize the similarities, we give as much detail of the event processing in various examples as space will permit.

Market Areas

The overall CEP market can be divided into categories in a hundred different ways. None of them are really satisfactory, and any set of categories overlap. So, with that said, we'll simply choose one categorization. Our purpose is simply to manage a broad overview by breaking the market into application areas and dealing with some of the main subcategories within each area.

Here are some of the major areas for sales of CEP products and services, not in any significant order:

- Financial systems, operations, and services
- Fraud detection
- Security
- Transportation
- Health care
- Energy
- Consumer relations management (including online sales and marketing)
- Operational intelligence (in business and government)
- Location-based services
- Military applications

We won't be able to give details of applications in all of these areas, so we'll take the major ones that have the least overlap.

Financial Systems, Operations, and Services

Financial systems, operations, and services are the largest market for CEP in dollar terms, accounting for about 40 percent of the total revenue for general-purpose event processing platforms. This category covers a variety of application areas with different requirements for CEP processing. Typically, the high-performance event driven applications in terms of event throughputs and processing speeds are in the stock and financial instruments front-office trading sector. They involve processing multiple event feeds in *right now* time at event speeds on the order of tens of thousands of events per second required to make buy or sell decisions in hundredths of a second. But most of the other applications in the financial sector, such as middle- and back-office applications, involve lower event throughput rates.

Some of the main areas of financial systems, operations, and services are:

- *Stock (equity) trading* using market data feeds. Systems in this area simultaneously process several event feeds containing reports of stock trades in different markets. They use that information in milliseconds to create further trading events when conditions are judged to be favorable. This category of event processing includes completely autonomous trading systems in algorithmic trading and futures trading, as well as systems that have human traders in the loop.

Financial trading systems, whether human-in-the-loop or autonomous, mostly process the data carried by events in the feeds. The algorithms applied to the trading data are proprietary, although the trading strategies share many of the same fundamentals.

Both general-purpose event processing platforms and domain-specific trading platforms are used in exchanges and in virtually all large banks and other financial institutions that participate in capital markets. Usually, the event processing involves applying proprietary algorithms to streams of events in real time as the events arrive. Often the algorithms use of patterns of multiple events, and CEP techniques and pattern detection engines are creeping into these systems.

- *Arbitrage*, using secret sauces (algorithms). This involves either arbitrage between different exchanges trading in the same instrument or between the price of the same instrument at different times in the future at the same exchange. Again, these are very high-speed, multiple-feed event processors, and may involve some detection of patterns of multiple events—for example, tracking the behavior of predetermined sets of stocks over small sliding time windows on each of several markets. The detection of specified patterns triggers sets of trading orders in the markets being tracked, resulting in sell orders in some markets and buy orders in others.

- *Foreign currency trading* in multiple markets. Complex and proprietary algorithms are in use to detect favorable trading situations between multiple markets; favorable situations can happen and disappear in seconds, so these applications are often automated with the occasional intervention of human overseers.

- *Automated pricing of financial instruments*. Many types of securities, derivatives, mortgages, and so on are increasingly subject to real-time pricing that reflects minute-by-minute fluctuations in the markets, as well as demand by consumers. These systems employ event processing methods; some CEP is involved.

- *Dynamic credit risk computation and credit rate selection* for online credit services offered by banks. This area uses CEP to track customer behavior at ATMs and online banking and to compute customer's credit ratings in real time. This kind of event processing is used both when customers apply for loans, as well as to make unsolicited loan offers to those who qualify. Event patterns are used to detect behavior that might indicate the need for loans and to determine whether customers qualify for loans. These patterns are becoming more sophisticated as banks increase targeted marketing in this area while attempting to reduce risk.

- *Near-real-time (or "right now") profit and loss accounting.* Autonomous trading cannot be allowed to run wild! High-frequency autonomous trading has an increased risk of accumulating either profits or losses very rapidly. The use of automated trading systems has therefore been accompanied by the introduction of automated real-time monitoring of their profit and loss performance. This also enables feedback from the profit and loss system to the trading system to adjust the amount of capital available to trade. Trading systems can now adjust their strategies in real time to attempt to maximize trading profits or reduce risks of losses.

  For example, the more profit that is made with a given strategy, the more resources are made available to the trading system to use that strategy. The performance and risks of different strategies can be tracked in real time, and the balance between the strategies can be adjusted minute-to-minute within the trading system.

- *Compliance monitoring* for violations of company policies and government regulations in capital markets, health care, and many other industries. The activities of individual traders, workers, companies, and exchanges may be monitored across multiple markets and over time. Generally, very simple searches for violations of regulations and policies have been used in the past, and they have often been done by database searches at the day's close of business. But real-time CEP is arriving in compliance monitoring. This is in the form of event patterns to detect violations as they happen. Detecting a pattern of activity that adds up to a violation will trigger reporting and, sometimes, automatic enforcement of rules for corrective actions.

- *Fraud detection.* Amazingly simple-minded event processing has been used to detect fraud in many cases, perhaps because crooks are simple-minded too! However, there are some applications in fraud detection where event patterns, perhaps even patterns whose detection may require time windows of several weeks, are now being used.

Many types of companies are involved in the areas of activities listed above as users of event processing products and CEP. We will refer to them as "users of event processing." They include large investment banks, smaller hedge funds, savings and loan associations, bank branches, mortgage lenders, credit card issuers and servicers, and security services companies.

Business activity monitoring (BAM) within the financial services area now can encompass all branches of a company, whether it is large or small, in every community across the country. Generally speaking, the EP applications in the areas listed above employ only very simple kinds of event processing and CEP. For example, in the past one found that most of the time, only the data carried in the events were used in the trading algorithms and market opportunity analyses. If patterns of events were used at all, they tended to be looking for a few trades or quote events occurring together within a small time window of a few minutes.

But today there are an increasing number of exceptions to this. More sophisticated event pattern processing is being used involving a wider range of event types, including elementized news feeds, weather reports, and data about user or corporate changes. This is due in part to the improved capabilities of the available CEP products, and also to front-line experience in many areas that points to the need to detect complex patterns involving many events over time.

Example 5.1 illustrates the aggressive use of event processing by a bank in an area that is an aspect of "customer relations management." In

Example 5.1: Targeted Marketing to Banking Customers

A major international bank has installed an event driven transaction-processing system for its routine business operations. However, it is also using the CEP capabilities to analyze patterns of events flowing into its banking system from customer activities. The purpose is to target banking customers to make cross-selling and upselling offers of other banking products. The input events include ATM transactions, credit card purchases, home loans, insurance and mortgage purchases, automobile loans, etc. involving each customer. But there are also other events that the bank factors into the system, such as a large deposit of funds, or a change of address or change of employment, or a life event such as a marriage.

The bank's CEP system uses event pattern–triggered rules to create offers to customers. A principle behind this system is to make offers to qualified customers at *the right time*. Examples are:

- A credit card purchase of an airline ticket triggers an immediate offer of travel insurance
- A large deposit into a bank account triggers an immediate offer of personal financial counseling or of an investment opportunity to get higher returns for the customer—and the bank!
- Large credit card transactions trigger an offer to the customer of a flexible installment repayment plan

fact, the same system using different event triggering rules would be able to process customer complaints, loan defaults, and suspicious activity. It is thought that the use of *right now* event processing in marketing banking services, rather than traditional methods based upon data mining customer records, has an advantage in timeliness. The bank has determined from its customer data that this system seems to have improved sales of the services by about 20 percent.

But there are pitfalls with such systems, not the least being to ensure that customers are not put off by overly aggressive tracking of their activities or inundated with offers. So these systems have to have constraints on their marketing activities; for example: "Send an offer only if the customer has not received any offers in the past week."

Example 5.2 shows another area where CEP can be an asset.

Example 5.2: Dynamic Stock Portfolio Management

A stock portfolio must be managed so that the value of stocks in certain market sectors (e.g., utilities, drugs, health care, energy, capital goods, transportation, etc.) must remain within predefined bounds of a fixed percentage (i.e., asset allocation targets) of the overall value of the portfolio at the close of business every day.

As the market fluctuates, stocks in some sectors must be sold and replaced by stocks in other sectors. Obviously, maintaining this kind of invariance is very hard for a human trader to do, since the portfolio's total value fluctuates continually with the events of the minute. It is best achieved by automated algorithmic trading.

Many of the programs used in securities trading were built in-house by the users in the early days, around 2000–2005. The IT departments of large banks usually built their own applications. This was a prime instance of the "build it or buy it" equation that we discussed earlier. But as the CEP vendors improve the features and performance of their products, this aspect of the financial markets is changing in favor of the vendors. Several CEP vendors now rate financial services as their main customer base.

The area of *compliance monitoring* became a high profile issue with the arrival of government regulations such as Sarbanes-Oxley[3] in 2002 and

---

[3]PUBLIC LAW 107–204: The Sarbanes-Oxley Act, July 30, 2002. http://www.gpo .gov/fdsys/pkg/PLAW-107publ204/content-detail.html

the Basel Accords.[4] Large banks and stock market companies have always had their own in-house policy monitoring. Often this goes well beyond the government regulations and includes monitoring of all operations within the company for compliance to the corporation's policies. However, it is true to say that a lot of this work is simply database monitoring to determine compliance by the day's close of business, rather than real-time event monitoring. But this is also an area where practices are becoming more *right now*, because preventing errors from happening costs less than unwinding them after the fact. Consider the error described in Example 5.3.

Example 5.3: How One Very Naughty Algorithm Ruined Everyone's Day[5]

On May 6, 2010, a mutual fund in Kansas entered a rather large ($4.1 billion) sell order in E-mini S & P 500 futures contracts on the CME derivatives market. The order sparked a totally human panic on a day when fear was in the air and sentiment was leaning toward the bearish. The fire was then fueled and fanned by automated trading strategies and high-frequency trading, causing an unprecedented drop within minutes.

Regulators are examining what caused some shares to fall 90 percent or more that day as orders flowed to electronic platforms with few if any buyers. At the height of this activity, $860 billion was erased from U.S. equity values over 20 minutes. U.S. exchanges agreed on May 6 to break trades that were 60 percent or more away from their price at 2:40 p.m., when the sell off intensified. Transactions in 326 securities were canceled.

[5]Courtesy of John Bates, CTO, Progress Apama Inc.

This is an example in which existing event processing technology, using trading event patterns to monitor stock market behavior in *right now* time, could have monitored the markets for anomalous behavior and alerted the parties involved when it was detected. Had this technology

[4]Bryan J. Balin, "Basel I, Basel II, and Emerging Markets: A Nontechnical Analysis," The Johns Hopkins University School of Advanced International Studies, May 10, 2008. https://jscholarship.library.jhu.edu/bitstream/handle/1774.2/32826/Basel%20 I%2c%20Basel%20II%2c%20and%20Emerging%20Markets%20a%20Nontechnical%20 Analysis052008.pdf?sequence=1

been used, red alerts would have been going off, with real-time risk analytics highlighting impending problems. The regulators would have been able to see an "early warning" and respond from a central control market watch system.

In summary, the financial systems, operations, and services area involves very sophisticated *right now* processing of the data in events, often at very high throughput speeds, and, to a somewhat unquantified extent, also the use of event patterns and CEP. It is continuing to evolve as a major market for CEP vendors.

One of the major impediments to standardizing the use of CEP in financial services (e.g., by introducing off-the-shelf libraries of event processing rules and specialized event processing agents; that is, components of EP systems) is the secretive and proprietary nature of much of what goes on in this area. However, the building of CEP applications in financial services does get some help from the wide availability of libraries of commonly used basic functions such as weighted average computation, regression, and other statistical operations. Costs of EP products and services to consumers in this area can be expected to remain high. But then, they can usually afford it!

Fraud Detection

Monitoring real-time event activity for fraud is a second large market for event processing and CEP products. Many instances of fraud detection overlap with both financial operations and services, as well as with the security area, and can legitimately be classified as being in those areas of CEP applications. We describe some fraud applications separately here.

Some market estimates put fraud detection at more than $1 billion per year. But these include all manner of after-the-fact detection methods. We are interested only in *right now* applications of EP and CEP that are intended to catch fraud in the act, so the market is smaller than that. On the other hand, fraud detection spreads itself into many markets beyond capital markets—as we shall see.

Consumers of fraud detection products include the expected players, such as banks and credit card companies, and also government agencies such as Homeland Security. In addition, they also include all manner of other types of businesses—particularly energy, telcos, health care, insurance, online retailers and auction houses, and online gaming. Internet-based operations are big users of fraud detection.

Many fraud detection systems were homegrown within the user organizations. These systems evolved over time as fraudulent techniques appeared—fraud detection is very much an arms race between the good guys and the bad guys. Some systems have in fact gotten so unwieldy—not much more than very large sets of conditional rules codifying cases of actual fraud in a programming language such as Java—as to be in need of a complete redesign.

More recently, many of these systems have been augmented by CEP products. Fraud-detection systems using CEP are rule-based systems with rules triggered by patterns of events that signify possible fraudulent behavior.

Fraud can originate both in-house and outside a company. CEP products are used to track many different types of events within a company, including user network activity, file accesses, database accesses, authentication, and any other events that might add up to suspicious activity on the company's networks. Such activity can originate with employees, outside persons with access rights to the company's networks, or via various types of malware and spyware. Some estimates put the market for fraud-detection products within the credit card industry alone at more than $1 billion, with the caveat that a lot of it is not what we would call *right now* event processing.

Credit card companies are large consumers of EP and CEP products; Example 5.4 demonstrates why.

Example 5.4: Detecting Patterns of Fraudulent Use of Credit Cards

A credit card belonging to a holder resident in California is used in Czechoslovakia over the Internet. The holder has never traveled to that country and never uses a credit card for purchases less than $40. In this case the card number is first used for a charge of 2 cents over the Internet. Subsequently, after the first charge is processed, it is used for increasing charges of 10 cents, then $2, $10, and $100. Each charge is made after the previous one has cleared processing. This is a pattern of fraudulent card use that is well known to the card companies and is detected by automated monitoring within the card processing systems. Before the $100 charge was processed, an alert was created and the holder was contacted in California. Had the $100 charge cleared, the thieves would probably have gone for a bigger number next, perhaps $1,000.

Detection of event patterns that indicate the use of a stolen card is most effective if it is done in real time by automated event processing. One problem with automated systems is to reduce false positives.[6] The pattern in this example consisted of a timed sequence of card charges, with each charge increasing in value. It was obviously not the holder's normal pattern of use. And it is also easily codified for automated systems checking—a monotonically increasing set of charges over a small time window.

Surprisingly, the sets of event patterns in common use to detect credit card fraud are often overly simple-minded. Single events can trigger a card's closure. For example, fraud detectors for credit cards use the location and type of merchant processing the charge as primary triggers. Using a card in a jewelry store or an electronics store away from the card holder's home location is often enough to trigger a closure of the card.

The simplicity of these event pattern triggers contributes to false positives—so much so that it often leads to very annoyed and sometimes embarrassed customers! Adding in-memory state knowledge of the recent history of card use and location of use to these simple triggering rules would often help in this regard. For example, if the holder has recently used a credit card to settle hotel and restaurant bills in a location away from home, then perhaps use of that card in a jewelry store in the same geographic location should trigger an alert to contact the card holder—but not an immediate closure of the card account.

Credit card fraud often involves theft and use of card information without the actual theft of the card itself. This kind of fraud is enabled by card company policies that allow cards to be used over the telephone or Internet without any physical check that the user is in possession of the card— the three digit security code on the back of the card is usually required in Internet transactions nowadays, and therefore can be stolen just as easily as the card number on the front! As a result, there is a big business in some parts of the world—Eastern Europe is a well known example—in the sale of bundles of stolen credit card information.[7] There are websites that auction these card data bundles and even keep customer satisfaction profiles of the sellers. Card issuers consider this type of fraud to be a price of doing business, but they are willing to invest in people and software—typically software with a CEP component—to minimize the damage. Ultimately, however, the card holders pay indirectly in higher fees.

In summary, fraud detection is an expanding area of event processing applications. The currently fielded event processing systems can and should be improved with the introduction of rule-based CEP products. The field

---

[6]That is, uses of a card that are flagged as fraudulent but which turn out to be legitimate.

[7]See the case of Vladislav A. Horohorin, *New York Times*, August 24, 2010. www.nytimes.com/2010/08/24/business/global/24cyber.html?_r=1&scp=1&sq= horohorin&st=cse

is in a continual arms race with the fraudsters! Fraud-detection systems are often antiquated from an event processing viewpoint and are in a continual state of improvement. Secrecy on the part of the event processing users in fraud detection has a negative impact on any efforts to standardize the libraries of high-level CEP rules and reduce the costs of event processing systems for this market area. However, there is a positive trend toward building standard sets of CEP rules, which are being packaged and sold.

Transportation

The airlines, railways, trucking, and shipping industries are all using CEP products and event processing in running their operations.

Airlines

The airlines have been the most obvious and prominent early adopters of event processing products in various parts of their operations. Different airlines have tested and fielded CEP in different aspects of their operations.

Some airline companies use CEP systems to run their aircraft maintenance operations—for example, to schedule the routine maintenance of aircraft, monitor parts inventories, and trigger reordering of parts.

Other airlines are using EP and CEP products in flight operations systems that do real-time tracking of flights, coordination and transfer of passengers making connections, rebooking of passengers who have missed flights or missed connections, and of course baggage handling[8] and other aspects of customer services.

Also, there have been cooperative agreements between airlines, typically partnering in flight scheduling and sharing, that involve using CEP in the implementation of the agreements (see Example 5.5).

Example 5.5: A Monitoring and Alerting System in Airline Operations

A major airline is using a rule-based system in which rules are triggered by patterns of events to track airline operations and deliver *right now* alerts when something deviates from a preset plan. This

(continued)

---

[8] See Chapter 1, "Event Processing in Use."

system tracks a fleet of 500 airplanes operating a schedule of flights to and from about 50 airports. Input events include ground movements of each plane, such as taxi in, taxi out, turn into gate, as well as similar in-flight events of the planes when they are in the air. The system maintains an updated state that represents the current situation of each plane and its planned schedule. The state is a data structure that is continuously updated by rules triggered by patterns of incoming events. At present, the system contains two broad classes of rules:

- Rules that update the state of the system
- Rules that trigger alerts and corrective actions

It is hoped to evolve this system to encompass all aspects of the airline's operations, such as passenger handling, schedule changes, crew assignments, and aircraft maintenance. It will eventually replace several separate special-purpose systems currently used by the airline.

Railways

Over the past few years, railways have been using CEP to help monitor various aspects of their operations, such as the status of trains, freight cars, shipments, crews, and equipment. For example, CEP is used to help guide crew assignments to reduce the loss of work time due to safety requirements. It is also used in systems that control the scheduling, composition, and operation of the trains.

There is one overarching goal of using event processing systems, which has been summed up succinctly in a quotation by a senior industry official:

If we could increase our average speed by just one mile per hour, it would mean an additional $140 million to our budget.

This quotation was in relation to goods transportation by a national railroad company with operations spanning the United States.

CEP systems have since been deployed within day-to-day operations of some railway companies in the United States and Canada (see Example 5.6 for one company's experience). A good example of this use is the reduction of fuel costs. Fuel is the second largest cost, after labor, for railways. Using CEP, companies are able to calculate where and when to buy fuel for each train to minimize the prices paid, taxes paid, refueling time, and the cost of carrying extra fuel between places where fuel can be sourced. Airlines make even more intensive use of CEP in their operations to reduce fuel costs.

Example 5.6: From Tracking Trains for On-time Performance to Running Them on Time

One application of EP by a railway company keeps track of each of its trains using sensor events from instrumentation on the trains and from sensors on the tracks on which the trains run. This gives a *right now* view at the company control center of the position and on-time performance of each train. Currently, it is a simple BAM application, but the system is being evolved to incorporate other aspects of company operations, such as fuel usage, engine maintenance, crew assignments, and scheduling crew transit to meet trains and relieve other crews. These operations are subject to safety regulations and also to constraints on the numbers of trains various stretches of track can handle. The system must continuously check conformance to these constraints, expressed as event pattern rules.

There have been interesting event processing problems involved in train tracking. One is dealing with interference of the event transmissions from different trains in close proximity. Another is the security issues raised by safety requirements. One approach to these problems is to aggregate the events from a train or a stretch of track at local relay event processors and then transmit the aggregated events to the central control system. This means that the tracking system is using an event abstraction hierarchy to increase reliability.[9]

---

[9]See Chapter 8 on event abstraction.

Future planning is to upgrade the event processing in this train-tracking system so that it is capable of tracking not just the trains and freight cars, but each individual shipment within the freight cars. The advantages are in being able to schedule the movement of freight and the composition of each train in a single system that maintains consistency with operational constraints and cargo schedules over the whole of the railway's operations. Crew schedules will be created automatically to optimize crew workloads.

Trucking

Trucking is another transportation sector that is using CEP products in the running of operations. There are a few examples in this industry sector of the use of event processing systems, including rule-based CEP, in the management of trucking fleets (see Example 5.7).

Example 5.7: Long-Haul Truck Fleet Management

A national trucking fleet has satellite navigation systems and wireless-enabled controllers installed in all of its long-haul trucks. The objective is to reduce the costs of operations by improving the routing of trucks in progress, optimizing the assignments of cargo orders to trucks and the scheduling of drivers.

A truck's on-board system sends data by wireless about the condition of the truck to regional fleet control stations. The system communicates with the regional control center governing the truck's current position. This continuous feed of events from each truck includes a lot more than just its position. The on-board system monitors fuel level, temperatures in the engine and cargo compartments, vehicle speed, tire pressures, and other performance parameters. It also monitors trip data, such as the expected time to the next scheduled route stop, the driver's work schedule, and the truck's progress with its delivery and pickup schedules.

A regional control center monitors the event streams from each truck in its region. Each truck has a *trip plan* that has an associated set of constraints for that trip. The constraints are based on the type of truck, the cargo, load factors, delivery and pickup schedule, driver's schedule, and other parameters. The event stream from a truck is monitored for conformance to its constraints. A control center also has historic data on routes, traffic conditions, and current weather reports.

As a result of these event inputs, the event processing system at a regional center may trigger various alerts and instructions that are communicated back to the truck and driver. The intent is to keep a truck on its preassigned trip plan, conform to driver safety policies, and minimize costs such as fuel consumption.

The automated rule-based tracking of trucks also can help to optimize trip times.

For example, if a tanker truck is expected to pick up a load at a port that requires a special equipment setup, the regional center will give the port an arrival alert 15 minutes in advance. The alert allows the port crew to be ready to load the tanker instead of it idling while equipment setup takes place.

Regional control centers communicate events summarizing the current states of the trip plans in its region to a national control center. Events received at the national center are therefore aggregations of events at the regional centers. A hierarchy of status and control events for the whole trucking fleet in motion is thereby computed in real time.

The national control center has a view of the whole trucking operation in progress across the country. It may communicate instructions back to the regional centers on the management of the trucks in their region. These instructions might include reassignments of cargo pickups to different trucks, changes in truck routes, driver assignments, and so on. Planning of future assignments, maintenance, schedules, and long-term fleet planning is done at the national center.

Example 5.8 shows the use of a CEP rules engine in trucking operations to monitor and control a fleet of delivery vans within a large and congested metropolitan region.

Example 5.8: Monitoring and Controlling a Fleet of Delivery Vans[10]

A fleet of 400 delivery vans must be monitored and their schedules updated in *right now* time as they go about business in a large metropolitan city. There is a fleet supervisor operating from a graphical screen that receives input events from each van's radio and GPS. Figure 5.1 illustrates a fleet supervisor's control screen. The supervisor's system also receives inputs from customers, suppliers, traffic reports, weather, and other sources.

A van's schedule is created when it is assigned a work order. A work order specifies a cargo, a route, a pickup time and location, and a delivery schedule. Each van carries out between one and twenty work orders per day, depending upon the complexity of the work orders.

When a work order is assigned to a van, an average of twenty event pattern rules are created and sent to the CEP control system.

(continued)

The rules for two different work orders are instances of the same rule templates, differing only in parameters that depend upon the van, cargo, driver, routes, and pickup and delivery times in the work order. When a work order is completed those rules are deleted. At any one time the system may be monitoring about 8,000 similar rules for the different vans in the fleet.

The rate of flow of events from the vans to the CEP fleet control system is quite low. For example, each van probably contributes about one location report event every two minutes, which adds up to approximately 200 location events per minute from the whole fleet. But there are lots of other types of event inputs, too.

The function of the CEP control system is to automate much of the work of a fleet supervisor. It monitors incoming events from the vans for conformance to the rules created by the work orders. There are also rules that encode safety requirements.

---

[10]Based on private correspondence with Marco Seirio, Rulecore.

For example, the rules in the CEP fleet control system monitor:

1. That a van is following the planned route.
2. That it makes good progress (selected waypoints are passed at specified times).
3. That each van leaves a package pickup or delivery point within reasonable time.
4. That each delivery is at its destination on time.

There are work orders that allow a driver to choose any route. But there are general safety constraints. For example, there are a number of areas of the city that must be avoided, especially at night. The system alerts the fleet supervisor when a truck deviates from its work order, runs behind schedule, or is held up in traffic.

When a driver is approaching a destination, the system will trigger a "package delivery soon" alert to the customer waiting for the delivery. This prepares the customer to sign off on the delivery and shortens the time spent at delivery points.

Typical event pattern rules that are monitored for any work order are:

If a van diverts from its designated route **for more than** five minutes **then send** an alert to the supervisor.
If a van **is more than** 20 minutes between the waypoints

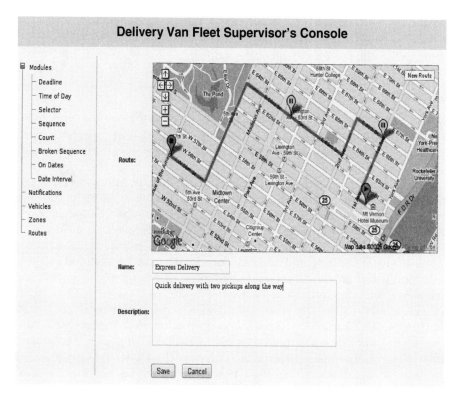

FIGURE 5.1 Simplified View of Van's Work Plan on the Fleet Supervisor's Control Screen

and it is a weekday
and it is **not** Friday between 4pm and 6pm
then send an alert to the supervisor.
If a van **does not** leave the starting point before 1pm **or**
If a van **does not** arrive at its planned final destination **before** 6pm
then send an alert to the supervisor.

These constraints operate as filters on the console input. They focus the operator's attention on patterns of behavior that violate company rules or workplan requirements.

The advantages for the delivery van company are that the number of supervisors needed has been reduced to one. Before the introduction of the CEP-based rule system, there was a small army of supervisors doing monitoring. Experience shows that there are only a few violations per hour, which show up as alerts to the supervisor on the control screen.

Instead of watching a map with lots of moving vehicles, the supervisor can spend the time trying to resolve violations. This work is more interesting than watching a map. Also, the system improves customer service, because violations are detected early and many times they can be corrected so the customer is not affected.

Shipping

Within this industry, container ship companies have been experimenting with event processing and CEP in the scheduling of ship trip plans. Here the goal, as with trucking, is to reduce costs by increasing the efficiency of overall operations.

A container ship trip plan is somewhat different from trucking. First of all, the size of modern vessels is overwhelming. Some measure 400 meters in length and can carry loads of up to 15,000 truck-size containers, each 20 feet in length. Most containers used today are bigger, and measure 40 feet (12 meters) in length. Loading a container ship is a complex scheduling task in itself. Safety and security constraints must be adhered to. Risk reduction is a prominent concern. Accidents at sea happen. Containers are lost at sea, and container ships have actually capsized.

A container ship's trip plan might well take several weeks, say across the Pacific, with cargo deliveries and pickup scheduled at ports along the way to the final destination. A trip plan may be changed at almost any time. New orders may come in at company headquarters, triggering a decision to reschedule a ship for a new stop. Or events on board a ship, such as bad weather or accidents, may also trigger changes.

A unique problem is the scheduling of the loading and unloading of containers. This scheduling must optimize the container positions on board the ship so that those to be unloaded earliest are scheduled to be loaded last. Since new orders for cargo transportation are coming in continuously, the shipping companies are experimenting with using real-time event processing as an approach toward monitoring and running all the company's trip plans. Decisions must be made concerning to which ship the cargo should be assigned. There are real-time delivery constraints to be maintained by the trip plan. As cargo is loaded, the status of a ship and its trip plan may change, as may the overall costs of operating the trip.

From an event processing viewpoint, a container ship trip plan is a continuous event processing engine with input events, operational state, and output events. The event throughput rates for high-level events dealing with cargo and ship operations are slow compared with, say, stock-trading systems. Event inputs to and from a single ship vary from, say, 100 events per hour during certain operations, such as loading and unloading cargo, to 100 events per day while at sea. The state of the trip plan must include all the constraints of the vessel itself, the current state of the load, and many other factors involving actual day-to-day operation. Output events can be updates on the status of operations, alerts about conflicts with cargo schedules, and even refusals to load particular containers.

This is one of many areas in which event processing technology is likely to become so influential as to change the way things are done. The use of event processing technology in the running of container ships will lead to a revolution in container ship operations. Specifically, we may expect changes in the way trips are planned, how trip plans are represented both for humans and automated tracking systems, and how humans interact with trip plans. Event driven technology will be used to construct trip plans and to drive container ship operations according to the trip plans. CEP is just the beginning!

In summary, the use of event processing systems and CEP in the transportation industry is still in its infancy. The potential for EP and CEP in *right now* operations is clear in every one of the industry sectors. This is another industry in which custom-coded applications were in place in many companies. As a result, CEP vendors have had to work hard to sell to this industry. Many of the current CEP applications are in an experimental proof of concept phase. But there are also many instances where EP and CEP technology is now part of day-to-day operations—in other words, EP and CEP have been adopted. And one may expect the market to open up more to the CEP products and vendors in the future.

Security and Command and Control

The security area is another large market for event processing, closely related to fraud detection. Security is about preventing problems from happening, in contrast to fraud detection which is about detecting problems as they happen or after they happen. Security is the first line of defense of the business—or the country—whereas fraud detection is a working tool, part of doing business. But truth is that similar systems are at work in both areas.

Computer security systems for most businesses used to be glorified firewalls. It was simply a matter of not letting anyone onto the IT system or the company database unless they had the right privileges. But this is changing, and systems that are categorized as security systems have multiple purposes.

Security systems these days do, or should do, a lot more than act as gatekeepers. They must assume that if anyone is allowed in, then those who shouldn't get in will (as demonstrated in Example 5.9)! So a security system must continuously monitor the event traffic on the company's networks for unusual or unauthorized traffic. Doing that requires knowledge of the event patterns that signify legitimate traffic, as well as the security constraints against illegitimate traffic. Violation of security constraints must be detected immediately.

Example 5.9: The Great Australian Sewage Disaster

A famous example of inadequate security in a Supervisory Control and Data Acquisition (SCADA) control system is the great Australian sewage disaster. This happened in 2002, but is indicative of what might happen today to our nuclear power stations, dams, and power grids.

A disgruntled ex-employee of a software company gained remote access to the control computers of a state-of-the-science sewage treatment plant outside of Brisbane on Australia's Sunshine Coast. The control system was produced by his ex-employer. So he sat in his car parked on a roadside outside the sewage plant with a laptop computer and a telemetry system. He gained access to the sewage control system by a wireless connection. By opening and closing the control gates he released millions of liters of raw sewage into a protected sea inlet, corrupting the local environment for many years to come and completely ruining a Hyatt Regency Hotel's grounds on the sea front.

He broke in 46 times over a period of two months before he was caught—and that was purely by luck. Police happened by and thought the parked car was in trouble, and went to help. Then they saw all the computers and telemetry equipment!

Until the miscreant's capture—during his 46th successful intrusion, for which he got two years in jail—the sewage plant's IT management didn't know how the spills were occurring. Somehow the system was leaking hundreds of thousands of gallons of putrid sludge into parks, rivers, and the manicured grounds of a Hyatt Regency hotel. Janelle Bryant of the Australian Environmental Protection Agency said "marine life died, the creek water turned black and the stench was unbearable for residents."[11] But they never detected events from a fake controller communicating with their control system by wireless.

Nearly identical control systems run oil and gas utilities and many manufacturing plants. But their most dangerous use is in the generation, transmission, and distribution of electrical power, because electricity has no substitute and every other key infrastructure depends on it. There have been other cases, sometimes unintentional, where outsiders, even schoolboys, have gained access to the control systems of energy resources such as dams.

The FBI's National Infrastructure Protection Center (NIPC) issued an advisory in the light of this disaster:

. . . control and telemetry systems should be monitored for possible trends that may evolve into malicious activity.[12]

But the advisory never said how to do that or what technology might be used!

---

[11]Barton Gellman, "Cyber-Attacks by Al Qaeda Feared," *Washington Post*, June 27, 2002. www.washingtonpost.com/wp-dyn/content/article/2006/06/12/AR2006061200711.html (p. 3)

[12]National Infrastructure Protection Center, "A publication providing information on infrastructure protection issues, with emphasis on computer and network security matters." www.iwar.org.uk/infocon/nipc-highlights/2002/highlight02-03.pdf (pg. 6).

Command and Control for Security

The security category is perhaps a bit stretched these days, in that some security systems are now fully fledged command-and-control systems that run the company's operations as well as protect the company. These kinds of security systems make extensive use of event processing and CEP. They are in use by national and local government agencies and by most large and medium-sized companies, no matter the business area. The Immigration and Naturalization Service (INS) and the national intelligence agencies such as the National Security Agency (NSA) and the Central Intelligence Agency (CIA) use these systems, as do large metropolitan police departments. In the business world, any company with intellectual property to protect, trade secrets, customer lists, or the like will employ an event driven security system as part of its operational IT infrastructure.

The use of CEP in security systems varies; some use a lot, others not so much. For example, some event processing systems in Homeland Security or the INS search for threats that may require detecting patterns of events across sets of very different types of event feeds over long periods of time.

As an illustration of event processing in command-and-control systems, we take an example from a large metropolitan police department's central operations system. Example 5.10 is a proposed future evolution from the system that is currently in operation. It has all the aspects of event processing for command and control and security.

The overall goal of this system is public safety—to keep the community secure. Crime prevention is a major part. As such, it is categorized as a security application. But a large segment of its application is in dealing with crime and emergencies in progress or that have already happened. As such it could equally well be categorized as command and control.

We are concerned here purely with the *right now* event processing involved in the system.

Example 5.10: Event Processing in the Operations Support System of a Large City Police Department[13]

The system has multiple goals:

1. Support ongoing police investigations
2. Detect major crimes that have happened, are happening now, and to predict crimes that may be about to happen
3. Share information with other authorities in receiving warnings of emergencies such as fires, medical emergencies, bomb threats, etc.
4. Initiate responses to emergencies from the appropriate authorities (other police departments, ambulance services, fire departments, port authorities)
5. Track terrorist activity, terrorist organizations, and terrorists, and assess and respond to terrorist threats
6. Track known criminals, recidivists, and wanted persons
7. Track and coordinate response to domestic violence incidents with appropriate authorities (police, child welfare, domestic court, etc.)
8. Track missing persons and stolen property
9. Provide early alerts on disease or pathogen outbreaks (e.g., anthrax)
10. Provide alerts in targeted metropolitan areas (e.g., parade routes, major sporting events)

Event inputs arrive from many diverse sources and at vastly different event arrival rates. Sources include 911 phone calls and other phone calls from everywhere, and reports, mostly email, from other police departments and from federal (e.g., INS, FBI), state, and local authorities. The system collaborates in sharing information with the port authority, fire, and emergency services, as well as other law enforcement authorities around the country and abroad.

Event input rates at the level of messages and phone calls are estimated at about 100 events per minute.

The system has a complex state that supports police operations by making recently acquired data available in *right now* time. It provides both data related to operations in progress and archival records that are distributed over other systems. It includes, for example, the personnel on duty and their current assignments and locations; the disposition of all police assets, such as patrol cars; the history trail of all investigations, fires, and emergencies in progress; and records of recent major crimes, criminals, wanted persons, and much else. The state is spread over several different IT systems, both within the operations center and at other authorities.

CEP features are being introduced to support predictive capabilities and alerts. For example, major crimes tend to occur in patterns, possibly due to a run of activity by a gang of criminals intent on hitting their targets quickly before disappearing. The system matches past crime event patterns in the metropolitan area against incoming crime reports. It also builds new crime event patterns.

Crime event patterns include types of crime, time intervals, target of the crime (person or commercial), modus operandi, description of perpetrators, means of flight (foot, car, subway, bus), and geographical locations. Matches of these patterns are used to predict possible further activity and to output crime alerts. For example, gas station robberies tend to occur in adjacent locations quickly, one after another. Crime prediction alerts are sent to the commanders on duty.

Output events have several functions:

1. To direct response to requests from the field
2. To give ongoing investigations up-to-date context
3. To supply relevant records to field officers proactively
4. To alert commanders to recent high-profile crime in their precincts
5. To assign and track police resources

As an example, a 911 call reporting domestic violence will result in the system sending an alert to a duty officer to initiate a response. But whereas current systems will provide little context, the future system will inform the responders of any criminal or past fire or drug activity associated with the address or persons to be investigated. So the responders will have the *right now* context they need. Similarly other departments, such as fire or emergency services, are sent the relevant context of any fire or emergency to which they are responding.

The future police security system as described in this example is expected to be operational within the next three years.

---

[13]Based on private correspondence with Gary A. Maio, Public Safety Practice, Data Vision Group, LLC, New Jersey.

In summary, many large businesses with *right now* time commitments have security systems with features similar to many of those in the example. Large international banks, leading transportation and delivery companies, and energy companies are some examples. As we commented before, security systems are encompassing more and more aspects of command-and-control systems that run the business in a secure manner.

Health Care

Health care is a growth area for event processing applications. Computers and information systems have been used for collecting patient data in health care for fifty years. But progress toward a unified national health care delivery system has been slow. Currently, many different specialized systems are employed, each with part of a patient's treatment record, and there is no central system with a complete history. As a result, a lot of relevant information is never included in evaluating a patient or a treatment plan. And costs of medical care have not been reduced. This situation obviously has to change.

A vision of the future is one system across all hospitals, all patients, all diseases and conditions and diagnostic tests. One goal of the vision is a system that automates the coordination and delivery of a patient's treatment over his entire lifetime history. Another is a system that enables remote medical diagnosis and treatment by consultants and specialists who may be far away from a patient's location. Everything must be done in *right now* time, and all relevant information must be immediately available to the medical staff who need it. These systems will be event driven.

There are also projects to develop medical event driven systems for the early detection of emerging epidemics across the world. We will discuss these systems later.

In general, progress has been slow. Most event processing applications in health care delivery so far are rather mundane event gathering operations for accounting and records. But there are examples of experimental systems that apply event processing and CEP principles in health care delivery, for example, in the monitoring of the treatment of patients in hospitals. Example 5.11 shows one such system for emergency room processes.

Example 5.11: Event Driven Processes in Emergency Room Operations[14]

Types of events input to the system include the status changes of medical personnel, medical tests, equipment and resources such as treatment rooms, stages in the processes of treating patients, and so on.

- Equipment status events, such as E in service busy, E in service available, E in maintenance, . . . where E might be an equipment or examination room
- Events such as accesses to medical IT systems, such as EMR (electronic medical record) access by X, RIS (Radiology Information System) access by X, Update to EMR, Update to RIS, . . . where X is a person with access privileges
- Medical tests and their status changes, such as blood test sent to lab, blood test results ready, patient record updated by test result, radiology report ready, examination report entered in EMR
- Events signifying changes in the status of doctors, such as signs on duty, is available, is unavailable, is assigned to task T, etc., where tasks (e.g., in conference, in operating room, in diagnosis, updating patient record) can vary in urgency and affect the doctor's availability (e.g., interruptible, not interruptible, . . .); similar for other types of medical staff
- Events tracking the status of patients, such as P entered into ER system, P assigned exam room, P under evaluation, P in radiology, P in OR (operating room) . . .

For a medium-sized university hospital, the event input rates to the electronic medical record systems would be on the order of 50 events per second, with a large variation for time of day. This includes events involving accesses to patient records and equipment tracking.

Types of events output by the system include events responding to requests (e.g., for patient records, test and radiology results) as well as events resulting from monitoring the hospital processes, such as events to keep those processes on track (e.g., patient treatment alerts, equipment and staff assignments, equipment maintenance orders, operating room cleaning, etc.).

The hope is that this kind of system will aid in the efficient use of medical staff and equipment, reduce errors (for example, in prescrib-

(continued)

ing drugs in treatment plans or in duplicating tests), and ultimately help to reduce the costs of health care.

CEP is also being used in fraud detection for medical insurance plans. Claims for reimbursement are analyzed for event patterns to detect which patients or health care providers demonstrate unusual levels of activity or suspicious combinations of claims.

---

[14]This example is based upon private correspondence with Leendert W. M. Wienhofen and Andreas D. Landmark of the Norwegian University of Science and Technology.

In summary, while information systems have been used in health care systems for many years, their use has been largely old-fashioned. The adoption of event driven architectures and CEP technology where it can obviously help has been slow. Privacy issues are a continuing concern and something of a brake on progress. There are, however, many ongoing experiments both in the United States and Europe introducing event processing methods for *right now* health care delivery, not only in running healthcare systems efficiently, but also as a support technology in new infrastructures for delivering medical treatment remotely (e.g., when the patient and physician are located in different parts of the country). Health care is a growth area for EP and CEP.

Energy

Control systems for the generation, trading, transmission, distribution, and consumption of energy are another area where the potential for *right now* business-event processing and CEP is obvious. Perhaps the investment at the moment is not as large as one might hope, but it is a good bet that this will become an important market. It holds many lessons for modern business infrastructures in general, and much can be learned about the kind of event driven technology that is needed from the past failures of these systems.

Control of electricity grids to keep the flow of electricity smooth and stable—so-called smart grids—is a prime example to be studied. This is where the business-event processing should occur. However, the energy area includes other infrastructure resources, such as dams and water supplies, oil and gas transmission lines, power plants and sewage plants. Again, it is difficult to quantify the investment in EP in this area, but there is no doubting the importance of energy systems in the infrastructure of our society. The quickest way for a terrorist to bring the country to a standstill would be to take down the electricity grid!

Not only are energy control systems event driven, but they need to become secure command-and-control systems, very much along the lines described in the security section. There are plenty of examples of what can happen when a control system for an energy resource has inadequate security. Perhaps the most famous of them is the Australian sewage disaster described in Example 5.9.

Electricity Grid Failures

Not so long ago. electricity grids both in the United States and Europe had catastrophic failures.

A notable failure was the great northeastern United States blackout of August 2003. At that time, portions of the grid in different states in that area of the United States were controlled by different ISO[15] companies. The grid failure resulted from a sequence of events starting with a simple broken transmission line, then a power generator tripping and going offline, and so on, over a period of four hours. Events cascaded in a domino effect. Final events were very large, such as power transmission reversing direction around Lake Erie. There was speculation among the grid controllers in the various ISO control rooms that the events they were seeing on their control displays were caused by a cyber attack on their SCADA systems. The final result was a blackout across the northeastern United States that left 50 million customers and parts of eight states and Canada without power. The outage cost an estimated $7 billion to $10 billion in financial losses and shut down parts of a two million barrel-per-day oil pipeline and airports in thirteen cities.

This grid failure was a complex event comprised of a cloud of events in the SCADA systems and diagnostic systems that control a number of collaborating grid systems over a four-hour period (12:00 ~PM to 4:15 ~PM). The ongoing Department of Energy (DOE) report (November 2003) lists thirty-five significant events in the failure, but not their causes or relationships.

According to the *New York Times*,[16] nobody had a global view of the developing complex event:

> In the end, then, it was not just a circuit breaker tripping or a transmission line sagging into a tree that caused the system to fail. Documents and interviews make clear that the blackout may well have resulted, just as

---

[15] Federally mandated Independent System Operators (ISOs), separate from the power generation companies.

[16] Eric Lipton, Richard Pérez-Peña and Matthew L. Wald, "Overseers Missed Big Picture As Failures Led To Blackout,"*New York Times*, September 13, 2003. www.nytimes .com/2003/09/13/us/overseers-missed-big-picture-as-failures-led-to-blackout.html

surely, from the fact that the people whose job it was to respond to those failures lacked much of the information about what was happening. They were, that afternoon, like air traffic controllers trying to keep order in the sky without knowing where all the planes were.

Both low-level grid events (e.g., "low voltage online," "power line open," "generating element tripped," "grid pathway closed" events) and higher-level policy events were involved.[17] For example, to take the strain off Cinergy's lines, the Midwest ISO turned to another power company, Allegheny Energy, asking it to help by reducing the electricity it was pumping out. But at 2:24 ~PM, an Allegheny controller told the ISO that the company's marketing staff wanted to do the opposite of what the ISO was asking so they could make money selling more power!

The overarching problem, of course, is that these electricity grids were one big connected system. Of the thirty-five events over four hours listed in the DOE report's timeline of events, the last twenty-five or so happened in the last ten minutes leading up the blackout. So a grid event monitoring system has to detect failure event patterns early in their process of happening in order to take remedial action. It has to have a global view of the whole system.

There have been similar grid failure blackouts in Europe as well. For example, most of Italy was blacked out in September 2003 as a result of a grid failure that started in southern France or Switzerland, depending upon which report you believe. However, not everyone in Italy was unhappy with the blackout. One newspaper report of the time quotes a twenty-one-year-old male student caught in a Rome night club when the lights went out: "there was panic, especially among the women." Similar blackouts in France and Germany have happened more recently.

A common element in all of these failures is lack of a grid event monitoring system that can monitor complex patterns of events to detect and correct possible failures before they happen.

Smart Electricity Grids

Some estimates put the number of current projects to develop smart electricity grids at well over one hundred worldwide. Investments in the United States in 2010 include Department of Energy (DOE) awards of $3.4 billion in stimulus grants toward upgrading the nation's energy grid, and an additional $4.7 billion in private funds invested through the DOE program.

---

[17]U.S.-Canada Power System Outage Task Force, "Final Report on the August 14, 2003 Blackout in the United States and Canada: Causes and Recommendations," April 2004. https://reports.energy.gov/BlackoutFinal-Web.pdf

A smart grid[18] is really two grids: a power transmission grid coupled with a two-way event driven monitoring and control grid. It is an essentially event controlled system. The overall goal is efficiency in the generation and use of power combined with reduction of costs.

The two grids are *coupled* in the sense that the SCADA measuring and control instruments on the power transmission grid are part of the control system, and conversely, the control system can send control events to the power transmission grid.

The control grid is where the complex event processing for the grid takes place.

There are twenty-year plans for developing smart grids that will use superconductive transmission lines to minimize power loss and will include intermittent electricity sources, such as solar and wind. These plans will use business event processing to support "business smarts" to control the grid and encourage the consumers to use power intelligently.

For example, the types of electricity usage and the pricing will vary with levels of consumption. Consumers can allow the grid to schedule power use within the home (e.g., turn on selected home appliances, such as washing machines, at off-peak hours). Factories can allow the grid to schedule selected processes to run at arbitrary hours and turn off those processes at peak times.

Event processing in the control grid will be bidirectional. Smart meters at consumer residences will monitor types of consumption and send report events back to local area control systems. The control system will respond by sending events containing instructions back to the individual meters. This will enable various types of consumption to be turned off or on automatically depending upon factors such as demand, power generation output, weather, and so on. Smart meters are being installed now by municipal utility companies in the United States.

The control grid must be capable of meeting the following requirements:[19]

- Defend against security threats from either inside or outside the system
- Allow use of alternative power generation sources that are intermittent
- Keep a stable power supply
- Control peak demand surges in order to ensure adequate reserves
- Use EP and CEP technology to control both global (grid control and power generation) and local (e.g., at the household level or even the appliance level in the household) uses of power (see Example 5.12)

---

[18]S. Massoud Amin and Bruce F. Wollenberg, "Toward a Smart Grid," *IEEE P&E Magazine* September 2005, Vol. 3, No. 5, pp. 34–41.

[19]U.S. Department of Energy's Office of Electricity Delivery & Energy Reliability, *The Smart Grid: An Introduction*, 2008, p. 37. www.oe.energy.gov/DocumentsandMedia/ DOE_SG_Book_Single_Pages(1).pdf

Example 5.12: Christmas Lights

A very simple example is the problem of timed Christmas lights, which can create large surges in power demand because they turn on at nearly the same time (e.g., sunset). A smart grid must schedule power supply so that these lighting systems do not create electric service reliability problems, such as power fluctuations, blackouts, or brownouts.

Plug-in hybrid vehicles might present a similar problem in the future, since they might tend to be plugged in to electricity sources at roughly the same times within a geographic time zone.

The event processing involved in smart grids and smart metering systems will raise capacity issues that need to be solved. A utility-planning department of a city with a population of about half a million expects that by 2012 the number of events flowing on their smart metering system between the control center and the household meters in their area will be on the order of 6 billion annually[20] (which is approaching 750,000 events an hour). Of course, we're not sure exactly what types of events are included. But the planners know that currently, the event transmission capacity in their networks won't allow this volume of event traffic.

Types of events flowing in the control grid will include many types of events from:

- Power generators
- Monitoring systems on power grid transmission lines and pathways
- Power transformers
- Local and regional control centers
- Utility company control centers
- Individual consumers (e.g., household and factory smart meters)

and doubtless many others. We can only guess at the types of proactive power consumption control events that may also eventually be carried on the control grid.

Security concerns will also lead to more types of event on the grid. A new generation of computer worms aimed specifically at industrial control software has recently appeared. A recent report on these security concerns is described in Example 5.13.

---

[20]Peter Alpern, "Smart Grid Inches Its Way Toward Reality," *Industry Week*, August 18, 2010. www.industryweek.com/articles/smart_grid_inches_its_way_toward_reality_22550 .aspx?Page=2

Example 5.13: Malicious Worms Aimed Specifically at SCADA Control Systems

The Stuxnet computer worm has triggered global anxiety by infiltrating an unknown number of industrial controls. The malware can secretly give false instructions to industrial machines and false readings to operators, and it is uncertain whether it can be effectively removed. Stuxnet is a validation of warnings by private experts and some former government officials that the electrical grid and other critical industries are susceptible to malevolent hacking, and that a new epoch of computerized attacks has commenced.

Previous cyber attacks have focused on inhibiting communications in countries such as Georgia or Estonia, but Stuxnet is the first piece of malicious software with a physically destructive purpose. Experts suggest that Stuxnet is most likely affiliated with a national government and may be a tool for terrorism, ideological motivation, or even extortion.

Fighting the worm is difficult due to poor communication between industry officials and computer experts. The malware would be especially threatening if its target is the electrical grid or nuclear power, as countries have invested in smart-grid infrastructure designed to interweave more industrial operations with the Internet.[21]

[21]Joseph Menn and Mary Watkins, "Stuxnet Worm Causes Worldwide Alarm," *Financial Times*, September 23, 2010. www.ft.com/cms/s/0/cbf707d2-c737-11df-aeb1-00144feab49a.html#axzz1TjqZYRGK

Summary

We have given a selection of examples of applications of CEP. There are many others and new ones are cropping up all the time. CEP is now being applied in diverse areas such as:

- Monitoring energy trading markets to detect patterns of activities similar to those that led to the Enron disaster[22]

[22]"The smartest guys in the room," http://www.pbs.org/independentlens/enron/.

- Monitoring gambling casinos to detect customer behaviors the house doesn't like
- Ensuring steady oil flow in oil pipelines

Event processing is a young field, and its potentials are just beginning to be explored.

CHAPTER 6

Patterns of Events

This chapter discusses classifying the problems we all face in dealing with the expected and the unexpected in the event cloud—and trying to avoiding false alarms. We will cover:

- Variables, templates, and patterns
- Single event patterns
- Patterns of multiple events
- Pattern matching
- Event patterns and state contexts
- Events and time: creation time, arrival time, time intervals
- Event patterns, state, and timing
- Causality, independence, and beyond today's event processing tools
- Expressing event patterns—requirements for event pattern languages

This chapter gets into some technical aspects of event patterns. Although it may look technical at first sight, in fact it's pretty simple stuff. If it gets to be hard going, skip it and move on—you can come back to it later. However, knowing some technical details about event processing helps to understand how a company can use events to solve some of the problems it may have to deal with. It also gives you some help in deciding what products have capabilities that would help with your problems.

Events contain information—here we're talking about event objects. Very often, events add up to actionable information, not simply one event at a time, but many events over a time interval. Each event may carry just a little information, which by itself gives us nothing actionable, but a set of events happening in a specific pattern over time may add up to something of importance. Most applications of event processing are based upon searching for and detecting patterns of events within the event input.

Everybody has to deal with patterns of events in everyday living. There are traffic patterns on the way to work, patterns of credit card use, or patterns of behavior in children, and so on. Everyone has an intuitive understanding of the concept of a pattern of events. Indeed, it is possible to give an hour's lecture on patterns of events without ever defining what a pattern is, and nobody complains! But that lecturer will find that there are many different ideas in the audience about exactly what he's been talking about for the past hour.

So we need to define precisely what we mean by *pattern of events*. It is important to separate the concepts from all the details of input languages and event processing implementations involved in using various event processing engines. We must not confuse *what the event pattern is* with *how we specify it* using XYZ pattern language, etc. That will make life much simpler—as far as talking about patterns of events.

In this chapter we tie down the basic concepts involved in defining and using patterns of events. They are very simple. In contrast, the systems that process patterns can be quite sophisticated, depending upon the kind of input information they're dealing with, how long it might take for a match of the pattern to show up, and whether the context in which a match happens is important. Some kinds of event pattern processing can happen in milliseconds; other kinds might take weeks or months. So entirely different kinds of systems may be employed in processing patterns of events. But the same basic concepts apply in all cases.

We go beyond the popular definitions of event patterns by introducing the use of *causality* between events in defining event patterns and its dual, *independent* events. Causality is a step into the future of event processing, since no commercial tools today provide explicitly for its use in event processing.

Events and Event Objects

As we saw in Chapter 3, event processing deals with event objects. Event objects represent events that happen or are thought of as happening. They contain information such as what the event is, where it happened, and the time that it happened. Also, we agreed to overload the two descriptions and refer to both events and event objects as simply *events*.

Overloading Two Meanings

Overloading is not new. It is used in programming languages to shorten the names of objects used in programs. That is, the same name is used for two different functions in the same program. Of course, there has to be some way to distinguish which function is being referenced (e.g., one function is used to compute temperatures and one to look up the times of day around the world). If there are no differences in their parameters or results, then they have to have different names!

Interestingly, the relativity physicists in the early twentieth century faced the same problem. The word *event* could mean either something that happens in the real world or a point in their four-dimensional relativistic model of the universe. They chose the same overloading solution for normal usage.[1]

Patterns and Pattern Matching

After *event*, the next concept in CEP is a *pattern of events*. One can find many different definitions of a pattern of events. And indeed, the concept of event patterns got very clouded during the early 2000s as commercial applications of CEP developed and the vendor community entered the picture. Each vendor had its own ideas, very much determined by its internal technical department's capability to grapple with both the definitional issues involved in specifying patterns precisely and the implementation issues involved in detection. In some cases, a particular application area was also an influence on pattern language features. Popular computer languages were frequently extended to specify patterns of events, common examples being extensions of Java and SQL. This profusion of definitions only served to confuse the marketplace and the event processing community.

Here, in our examples, we will take a declarative approach to specifying event patterns using simple logical operations. We want to focus on what kinds of patterns are needed in CEP, so we will ignore the diversions of grafting event patterns onto various existing computer languages.

Single Event Patterns

The very first kind of event pattern is a single event pattern.

Example: A single event pattern:

A car runs a red light.

---

[1]A. S. Eddington, *Space, Time and Gravitation: An Outline of the General Relativity Theory*, p. 45. (Cambridge, MA: University Press), 1920. www.archive.org/stream/ spacetimegravita00eddirich#page/44/mode/2up

What makes this a pattern? Well, it "matches" or denotes any event where some car, any make or model, runs any red light, anywhere. The pattern has variables, *car* and *red light*. An event, say E, such as

Car with California license 8XYZ-123 ran the red light at California and Van Ness in San Francisco.

is an *instance* of the pattern. That is, E is one example of the pattern. How so?

Well, if we take the actual objects (i.e., values) in E, namely "Cal license 8XYZ-123" and "the red light at California and Van Ness in San Francisco" and substitute them for *car* and *red light* in the pattern, then the result is E.

But the same pattern can also match:

My BMW ran the red light at El Camino and Embarcadero in Palo Alto.

Indeed, our example, "a car runs a red light," has a huge number of instances.

Definition: An *event pattern* is a *template* that specifies *event objects* called *instances* of the pattern.

A pattern contains variables. When the variables are replaced by objects (sometimes called values), the result is one of the events that the pattern denotes. And that event is called an *instance*.

Matching: The process of turning a pattern into an instance by replacing its variables by objects is called *matching*.

Another example of matching applied to a single event pattern is:

Tom buys a stock S for X dollars at time T

The variables are the stock S, the dollar price X, and the time of the transaction, T. But the name of the trader, Tom, is fixed—it is a constant in this pattern. So this pattern will only match buy transactions that Tom executes, like:

Tom buys IBM for 250 dollars at time 12:00 GMT.

This match is made by replacing the variables in the pattern by values as follows: S = IBM, X = $250, T = 12:00 GMT.

The first lesson here is that an event pattern definition must be able to express variable parts of events so that the definition can encompass many event instances. Natural language is not precise enough for today's machine-processing technology, so what we have at the moment by way of machine-processable pattern definitions is cumbersome. For example, one style of definition is:

BuyStock (Tom, S, X, T)

That's not very pretty, and it gets unreadable when used to express combinations of lots of events, but you get the idea! It would be called a *first order logic* specification of an event pattern.

Processing Patterns by Machine

The current generation of event pattern languages allows us to specify very clearly which parts of a pattern are variable, and also what types of values are denoted by the variable parts. There are a number of different ways this is done in commercial event processing languages.

Typically, the variables in event patterns are declared the same way as variables are declared in computer programs. Each variable is first defined as standing for values of a specific type such as integer, string, automobile, or traffic light. So machine-processable versions of our examples in the style of Java might look like:

Automobile car, Traffic light red_light; runs(car, red_light);
Stock Symbol S, Dollar X, Time T; BuyStock (Tom, S, X, T);

The pattern matcher, which is a computer program that detects instances, can tell using the declarations that *car* is a variable that must be replaced by an automobile and *red light* is a variable that must be replaced by a traffic light, and so on.

However, in our discussion we'll omit types and variable declarations in most examples since they are intended for us humans. Remember that when we give event patterns to machines to process, the declarations will have to be included!

Remarks: One or another kind of event pattern matching is the basis for most applications of modern event processing. As we shall see, sometimes the patterns are so simple that matching is little more than testing the values of constants or membership of events in a list. More complex kinds of pattern matching can lead to difficult implementation issues where processing time may be critical.

There are two main focuses of computational effort in pattern matching:

1. *Efficient detection of pattern instances*. The time taken to match a pattern increases with the number of variables in the pattern. Pattern

matching in its most efficient form should take an amount of time that is a linear multiple of the number of variables in the pattern. For example, if the pattern contains two variables, then the time the pattern matcher takes to match the pattern should be $2 \times N$, where N is some number that depends upon the pattern and the internal workings of the matcher. But it should not be, say, the square of N (i.e., N^{*2}). To achieve this can be a formidable problem for the designers of the pattern matching program.

2. *Early detection of impossibility of matching.* Equally important is recognizing when a pattern or a partial instance of a pattern has no hope of completing a match and therefore need no longer be tested as more events enter the input stream.

Patterns of Multiple Events Using Operators

Event patterns generally involve more than one single event template. We often want to define patterns of several events. The events may be related to one another—for example, they might have common values or variables. So one issue in defining patterns containing multiple event templates is the ability to express commonality between the event templates in a pattern. Another issue is the set of operators that are available in whatever pattern definition facility you're using.

For example, to express a coordinated stock trade, we might have a pattern such as:

when Tom buys a stock S for X dollars at time T **then**
Pete sells stock S for X + Δ dollars at time T' < T + 1 min

Notice there are two event templates in this pattern, and they have variables in common: S, X, and T. These common variables express that the same stock is being bought by Tom and then sold by Pete at a higher price within one minute. Commonality is expressed by the variables common to both templates.

This pattern could be used to detect collaboration between traders to sell on the uptick created by a buy event. Of course, most of its instances would be coincidental trades close together in time. But some instances could be illegal collaborations between traders. If instances of this pattern are frequently detected in stock market feeds, more complex patterns would be used to decide whether collaboration is taking place.

In our example, **when** . . . **then** . . . is an operator that combines two events into a pattern of trading. Common examples are Boolean operators like A **and** B and A **or** B.

Common Boolean operators and their meanings are:

A **and** B	both patterns A and B must match.
A **or** B	at least one of the patterns A or B must match.
not A	the pattern A must not match.
when A **then** B	whenever pattern A matches then pattern B must match.
if A **then** B	if a match of pattern A occurs, then search for a match of B.

These are Boolean operators commonly used in event patterns. Their meanings overlap; that is, patterns with some operators can be rewritten using other operators.

To match A **and** B, a pattern matching program must simply match both A and B in any order.

To match **when** A **then** B, the pattern matcher must first match A and then match B (**if** A **then** B has a similar meaning).

Note that **then** is used as a part of two different operators, "**when** . . . **then** . . ." and "**if** . . . **then** . . ." (**then** is not an operator itself, but a part of these two operators).

Example 6.1 gives a straightforward **and** combination of two event templates with common variables.

Example 6.1: Monitoring for Unusual Credit Card Activity

```
CreditCard Card;
DollarAmount S1, S2;
Location L1, L2;
Date D;
Charge(Card, S1, L1, D) and Charge(Card, S2, L2, D)
where Area(L1) ≠ Area(L2);
```

Two charges to the same credit card on the same day at locations in different processing areas will probably be logged as unusual activity. Various actions may be triggered when matches occur, such as putting the card on an alert list or contacting the card holder for an explanation.

Example 6.2: Monitoring for Violations of a Service-Level Agreement

if Complaint(C) **at** T **and not** ResponseTo(C) **within** (T + Δ)
and not ApologizeTo (C) **within** (T + 3*Δ)
then Alert

Most event patterns involve timing, which we'll deal with in the next section. In Example 6.2, the pattern would be used to monitor a call center that deals with enquiries and complaints from customers. The event input contains a stream of enquiries, complaints, responses, apologies, resolution reports, and so on. The pattern in this example will match if there is a complaint from a customer C and no response to that complaint is detected within a short time, Δ, and then there is no apology issued to that customer within 3*Δ. Event patterns such as this are used to monitor for violations of service level agreements, for example, at a call center. It is a common practice for a call center to have a contract requiring that customers must either receive a response or an apology in a timely manner.

Boolean operators can be used recursively in specifying event patterns. So it is quite common to see them nested in patterns. Sometimes nesting can get difficult to read, so most pattern languages will include facilities like pattern definitions for use to improve readability. Example 6.3 gives a clumsy example of nesting.

Example 6.3: Timely Handling of Loan Applications

Applicant A;
Property H;
Loan_Id L;
Date D;
If LoanApplication(A, H, L) **at** D
then (((IncomeReview(A, okay) **and**
HouseAppraisal(H, okay) **and**
CreditCheck(A, okay))
or Denial(L) **within** D + 3)
or RaisePriorityLevel(L) **at** D + 3;

As we can see, this pattern is a mess to understand! Here's an explanation; skip it if you want. Assume we are dealing with a cloud of loan applications in progress, each application going through various steps such as income review, house appraisal, credit check, and so on. In the days of easy credit, a large mortgage lender might be dealing with hundreds of applications per day, and the process steps might be farmed out to different specialty organizations around the world.

This pattern monitors the progress of each loan as it is processed. It requires a loan to pass the first three steps or to be denied within three days, or else to have its processing priority level raised at the third day.

We can use pattern definitions to improve readability and hence help us to see if the pattern correctly says what we want it to say.

Approval(A, H, L) = IncomeReview(A, okay) **and** HouseAppraisal(H, okay) **and** CreditCheck(A, okay)

So the pattern can be rewritten as,

If LoanApplication(A, H, L) **at** D **then**
Approval(A, H, L) **or** Denial(L) **within** D + 3 **or** RaisePriorityLevel(L) **at** D + 3;

This version of the pattern is easier to understand; more importantly, it is easier to see that it correctly expresses that a loan must either be approved or denied within three days or its processing priority must be raised.

Event Patterns and State

Often a pattern of events becomes important in specific circumstances. One example is traffic control. The rate at which cars are going through a set of freeway entrances will become a lot more important to a traffic-control system when the traffic density is high or there is an accident on the freeway. Another example is credit-card usage. A pattern of credit-card purchases might raise alarms in a monitoring system if the holder's credit rating suddenly changes. In these examples, the pattern processor is not only matching the pattern against incoming events but also concurrently querying databases or alert lists. We call this *pattern matching relative to state*.

However, one does not want to burden an event processor with lots of state checks when its primary purpose is to process incoming events and match patterns related to an application. So in its normal state, the processor will do no state checking. A change in a database, such as traffic density becoming high, or a customer's credit limit being reached, triggers changes in the state of the event processor. This could be as simple as adding an alert to a special alert list. Then the processor will check to determine whether certain circumstances apply when a specific person is the subject of a pattern check.

A common example of the use of state values is simply to count the number of times instances of a pattern have been detected in the recent past. If this number is high enough, then new instances of the pattern become more important than before—for example, an abnormal situation is happening.

Example 6.4: Monitoring for Epidemic Outbreaks

Int Count = 0;
Symptom S;
List_of_Symptoms Symptoms;
when (**exist** S **in** Symptoms **and** S **in** report) **then**
execute Count = Count + 1;
If Count > Threshold **and no** Alert **then**
execute Epidemic Alert;

Example 6.4 might apply to a cloud of input events that are SMS reports from field agents using mobile devices. Reports are processed in any order. The first rule increments values of Count and the second rule references those values. The **when** pattern matches whenever a report arrives that includes any symptom S on a list of symptoms. It references the list of symptoms in testing for a match. It then triggers an increment in a Count variable—which is another event. The **if** pattern matches when the value of Count goes above a Threshold and an Alert has not yet been issued. It then results in executing an alert. Count keeps track of how many reports with symptoms have been received. Symptoms is a database of disease symptoms. Symptoms and Count are called *state values*—that is, sets of values that are referenced in matching.

Another application of state in pattern matching is to market to customers with good records. Purchases made by good customers are treated as more important in Example 6.5.

Example 6.5: Marketing to Gold Card Members

If Purchase (SaleList, Customer, Amount) **where** (Amount > 1,000
and Customer **member** GoldCardList) **then**
Send SpecialOffer **to** Customer;

The trigger is a purchase event of items from a Sale List for an amount exceeding $1,000 by a Gold Card member. The state reference is to a database called the GoldCardList. When the pattern matches, it triggers an offer to the gold card member.

Event Patterns and Time

Time is of the essence in many situations today, and nowhere more so that in processing events. Events carry information that goes stale very quickly. The more "up-to-the-minute" a system or activity is, the more it requires immediate attention and response.

Patterns used to detect important situations in event feeds nearly always refer to time and contain timing constraints. Pattern languages must contain powerful features for referring to time in all of its different uses in event patterns. But there is no standard approach to expressing time in event patterns. Indeed, the syntax of timing in every commercial event processing language is different. Here we survey some of common uses of time together with the kinds of syntax that is in use.

Activity at a Point in Time

Example 6.6 is an illustration of this simple concept.

Example 6.6: A Pattern That Must Match at a Particular Point in Time

RingTheBell **at** 4.00 PM

Nothing could be simpler—the bell must be rung at 4:00 ~PM. The **at** syntax is used to specify a time value.

Timely Reporting and Response

Another very common use of time is to specify that if something happens at one time, then something else must happen at another time. Typically, if some event happens, then search for some other pattern, but only within a short time beyond when the first event happened. For example, if the boiler gets too hot then the alarm must go off, quickly!

As Example 6.7 shows, timing is often used to ensure that something happens within a specified time after something else.

Example 6.7: Timely Reporting of Sales

If Sale (Stock, Quantity, Price, Buyer, Seller) **at** Time1 **then** Report (Sale, Stock, Quantity, Price) **at** Time2 **where** Time2 < Time1 + Δ

This pattern would be used to monitor stock market feeds for timely reporting of sales. Note that the use of timing here serves not only to specify a boundary in which a report must be made, but also to limit the search for a match. A sale event at Time1 will lead to a partial match, and a search for the corresponding report event to complete the match. But that search is limited by the boundary Time1 + Δ. A failure to match will likely trigger an action such as reporting a failure to report a sale, as shown in Example 6.8.

Example 6.8: Timely Reporting of Sales

If Sale (Stock, Quantity, Price, Buyer, Seller) **at** Time1 **then** Report (Sale, Stock, Quantity, Price) **at** Time2 **where** Time2 < Time1 + Δ
else Alert "failure to report sale";

Time Windows and Focusing Search for Matches

Another use of time is to restrict the time in which an attempt to match a pattern needs to be made. Usually, the search is restricted to an interval of time, called a *time window*. A common notation for a time window is [T1, T2], where T1 and T2 are times and T1 ≤ T2. Example 6.9 shows one use of this strategy.

Example 6.9: Trading Strategies on Pairs of Stocks

StockSymbol X, Y;
if Price(X) **at** T > 1.02*VWAP(X, [T-1hr, T]) **then**

if Price(Y) < 0.98*VWAP(Y, [T-1hr, T]) **within** [T, T + Δ]
execute sell 1000 shares X **and** buy 5000 shares Y;

Those pairs of stocks X and Y that are deemed to increase and decrease together in normal market trading are monitored. If the price of X goes above its volume weighted average price (VWAP) over the past hour, then search within a time window Δ to see if the price of Y has dipped below its VWAP during the past hour. If that happens, then sell X and buy Y. The values, 1.02, 0.98, and Δ are of course usually secrets of the trading house, as are the stocks X and Y! The search for a decrease in the price of Y is triggered by the rise in the price of X, and is limited to a small time window, [T, T + Δ]. Usually there will be a similar pattern based upon Y going above its VWAP.

Realistic and Unrealistic Uses of Time as a Constraint

Time is often used to specify constraints on the performance of a system. Typically, if something happens, then a timing constraint will require something else to happen, within a specified time limit or a time window, as illustrated in Example 6.10.

Example 6.10: A Time Limit Requirement

if separation (aircraft1, aircraft2, sector) < limit(sector) **at** T **then**
(alert(aircraft1) **and** alert(aircraft2)) **within** T + Δ

Aircraft in the same control sector must be alerted within Δ time of a separation violation being detected. Detecting violations of this time limit requirement, say in a feed of real-time events from the air traffic control radars, is limited to a time window of length Δ from the time at which an instance of the separation trigger is detected. It is therefore an easy requirement to monitor.

But sometimes the use of time to specify system constraints can become unrealistic, difficult to understand, and more to the point, very difficult to monitor and to implement correctly. Example 6.11 expands the types of requirements.

Example 6.11: Timing as a Performance Requirement

for 95% **of all** Trades P **and** First Status Updates S(P) **in** Last 60 mins
Time_of S(P) − Time_of P ≤ 3 mins

While it is easy for humans to understand this requirement, detecting violations is far from easy. It requires that for 95 percent of trade reports, there is a report of the status of the trade within 3 minutes. But the requirement is checked over a time window that moves with time, the "Last 60 mins," called a sliding time window. So as time moves forward, the window slides and earlier trades become obsolete (i.e., they happened more than 60 minutes ago) and later trades enter the window and come under the requirement.

This causes a *race condition* in evaluating whether the requirement is being violated because as it is being evaluated, the set of trades to which it should be applied is changing. It is called a *race condition* between the edge of the window as it "slides" and the evaluation of the requirement for a potential violation. We regard this as an impractical use of timing.

Example 6.12 is another example of impractical use of timing.

Example 6.12: A Stock Trading Account Requirement.

for account X, **always** (weight of the top 5 securities in sector industrial) < 10% **of** total value account X

This requirement applies to those five securities in an account that belong to the Dow Jones Industrial sector and have the largest value in the account. Obviously, the actual five securities are changing all the time during the trading day. As a security is bought, it may enter the top five and displace another. While time is not mentioned explicitly, the **always** operator implies an invariant over all time. If the account is actively traded, monitoring this requirement could again involve race conditions between trade completions.

Proliferation of Timing Operators

There are many other operators that are in use in CEP tools put out by various vendors. Some of them are esoteric and peculiar to one vendor's event pattern language. Most of them can be defined using the basic set of operators given above, together with event timing constructs such as **at** and time intervals. Often, various notations are intended as convenient shorthand. Some notations assume that event input is either a stream of events, or that events are processed in their order of arrival,[2] as shown in Example 6.13.

Example 6.13: Monitoring Electric Power Grid Activity[3]

If 15 min Wattage moving avg **decreases by** 5%
followed by (remote equip alarm **and**
(substation stability warning **or**
Wattage spike > threshold) **within** 30 min)
execute send email; display on dashboard; call workflow resolution;

This is a pattern-triggered rule used in monitoring various power grid parameters that are being continuously computed. It can be assumed that there are streams of values of the parameters being measured. Also assume that the **decreases by** operator compares successive values of the Wattage average over a sliding window of 15 minutes. The **execute** action is triggered when a match of an event pattern, **if . . . followed by . . .** , is detected. If we ignore the specific meanings of the various measurements, the operator structure of the rule is:

If **F decreases by** 5%
followed by (A **and** (B **or** C > D) **within** 30 min)
execute Action1; Action2; Action3;

In this outline of the rule we've called the grid performance functions F, A, B, C, D. The meaning of the rule is that if a match of the pattern is detected in the event input then three actions are executed.

The pattern, **if . . . followed by . . .** could be expressed equivalently as

if . . . then . . .

(continued)

---

[2]See Chapter 3.

providing that we assume that the input is a stream of events such as values of wattage measurements, alarms, warnings etc., and that **followed by** means "followed by in order of arrival." However, all the events on a large electrical power grid are seldom nicely ordered, nor are they viewed by the control room of a single federally mandated independent systems operator (ISO).

---

[3]Due to Dr. John Bates, Apama, Inc.

Causality between Events

In CEP, an event pattern can include combinations of event templates together with timing conditions and state conditions. An important operator in CEP that is not yet available commercially is the *causal relationship* between sets of events.

It is very common to talk about events *causing* other events. For example, "did the car running the red light cause the accident?" Or "did that large sale of IBM stock cause the price to dip at 2:00 ~PM?" In fact, "cause" often goes by other names, a common one being "risk factor": Is smoking a *risk factor* in premature death?

However, it is interesting to note the current situation regarding the use of cause in event processing. No commercial CEP tools or products so far have an ability to define event patterns in which some events *cause* other events. There are several reasons for this.

First of all, the definition of causality is clouded in philosophy, mystery, and confusion. The English philosopher Bertrand Russell once remarked: "The average married couple has sexual intercourse four thousand times during their married life, and they produce 2.4 children. If one were to slam a door four thousand times and hear a bang 2.4 times, would one conclude that slamming the door caused the bang?"

Second, few if any technical engineering teams in industry know how to implement the tracking of causal relationships between events, even if they could settle on a clear definition.

Third, commercial applications of CEP have been successful so far without employing causality between events. They have been able to get away with operators such as **when** . . . **then** . . . or **if** . . . **then** . . . or

followed by applied to event streams. There has been little demand for causality from customers.

Fourth, causality would be a difficult concept to teach to marketing departments or to the current generation of customers for CEP.

And finally, in many event spaces it is often not known which events cause which other events. Or to say the least, such knowledge is far from complete!

Despite all these issues, there are many event spaces where causality is well known and easily determined—for example, in discrete event simulations and many event driven systems such as air traffic control systems, highway traffic systems, and natural disaster warning systems. The use of causality in specifying event patterns can lead to more precise and efficient detection of matches and avoidance of false alarms, because causality reduces the space of input events that need to be searched for possible matches.

No matter the trepidations of Bertrand Russell, there is a very simple definition of causality between events that is appropriate for event processing purposes. Notwithstanding the issues raised above, we predict that causality between events will become an important event operator in patterns in the future, both to improve the efficiency of the search for matches and to define important patterns precisely.

Causality: If event A had to happen in order for event B to happen, then A is a cause of B and we say, A *caused* B.

Note that this definition is given in terms of events (activities) rather than event objects. If there is a causal relation between two events, then it applies to the event objects representing those events. Also, an event may have several causes.

There is no universal test that can be applied to determine whether A is a cause of B. But in many event spaces, causality is well known. Each situation must be judged on the semantics of the event space individually. Consider Examples 6.14 and 6.15.

Example 6.14: Email

Event E1 is "I send you an email." Event E2 is "You reply to my email." Then E1 *caused* E2. That is, E1 had to happen in order for E2 to happen.

This causal relation is so universally accepted that it is customary for E1 to be appended to E2. Note that if E1 happens, it does not guarantee that E2 will happen; it is simply that E2 cannot happen unless E1 happens.

Example 6.15: Network Performance

Event E1 is a denial-of-service attack on networks in the United States at time T. Event E2 is my email server being unable to deliver email to recipients in the United States.

In this case it is quite likely that the DNS attack was the cause, or at least a cause, of my mailer failing. But unless other possible causes can be eliminated, such as Stanford's IT department doing network maintenance at that time, it is uncertain whether the DNS attack was a cause.

Remarks: This definition of causality was implemented in CEP tools in the Stanford CEP project going back to 1995 and used extensively in experiments in event processing applications—for example, in the analysis of discrete event simulations of processor designs and of network protocols. The tracking of causality between events in simulator output made analysis of the simulation results more efficient.

Causality between events is not to be confused with **followed by** in the order of arrival, or indeed in any stream order or time order. Events can arrive at a processing point in any order. That is, it is possible for A to cause B and for B to arrive before A at an event processor.

Operators for Causality and Independence

Causality between event patterns was expressed syntactically by the "→" operator in the Rapide event processing language.[4] It would be appropriate to add this operator to our list of basic operators in the previous section, "Patterns of Multiple Events Using Operators."

A → B means A *had to happen* in order for B to happen.

Note that "→" means the A is a cause of B, but it does not mean that A is the only cause of B.

The opposite relation to causality is independence. Two events happened independently of one another if neither is a cause of the other. The operator for independence in Rapide is "||."

A || B means A is not a cause of B, and B is not a cause of A.

These operators are demonstrated in Examples 6.16 and 6.17.

---

[4]http://complexevents.com/stanford/rapide

Example 6.16

The conformance-monitoring team of a global trading organization must track conformance to company policies in trading. The triggers for each trade must be recorded by the traders. Triggers are immediate causes or reasons for actions. Policy requires that the actions of traders at different offices are not causally dependent and also that all trades are immediately recorded in a central database. Here's one of the trading patterns the team might monitor for conformance:

> Trade A, B;
> Database update C, D;
> A(origin is NYC) **and** B(origin is Tokyo) **and** A ∥ B **and**
> A → C(origin is SF) **and** B → D(origin is SF);

The origin of an event is the place where it happens, and is one of its recorded attributes. The pattern uses ∥ (meaning "happens independently") and → (meaning "is a cause of"). The requirement says that trades A and B that are executed in New York City and Tokyo respectively, and independently (i.e., they had no knowledge of one another), must both be recorded by updating the database in San Francisco.

Example 6.17

A call center deals with a large number of customer calls. Many calls are being processed concurrently at any one time. Each call initiates a response thread that must lead to a resolution within a specified time. A single thread is a pattern of events such as,

> complaint → log → respond → (refund ∥ letter ∥ investigate) →
> resolve

Multiple events in a response to a complaint are processed concurrently and independently to save time. This use of independence between events is expressed by the "∥" operator.

It should be emphasized that independence between events does not imply that they happened at the same time; it only indicates that concurrency is possible.

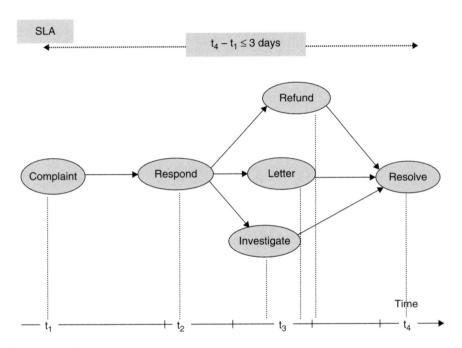

FIGURE 6.1 Causality and Independence between Events in a Complaint Resolution

Causality and Time

As one would expect, there is a relationship between causality between events and the time at which events happen. But it is weaker than one might expect.

Intuitively, an event that causes another event should be expected to happen earlier. That is usually the case, but not always!

If A causes B, it is possible for A and B to happen at the same time. But A cannot happen later than B.

This means that there's a weak relationship between cause and time.

On the other hand, independence has no relationship with time at all. If A and B happen independently, they can happen at the same time or different times, as Figure 6.1 shows. Independence between events simply means that the events are not causally related. They can happen at the same time, but that is not necessary for them to be independent.

Repetitive and Unbounded Behavior

Some patterns of events must allow for events to be repeated, and sometimes the number of repetitions is not known when the pattern is written. So the pattern language must be able to express repetitions both when the number of "repeats" is known and when it is not known in advance. An additional problem is the need to be precise about which matches of a repeated activity should be detected. For example, if there are ten *buy* events in an input stream, do we want to detect the first *buy*, the first two *buys*, etc., or just the maximal sequence of all ten *buys*? The last case is sometimes called *maximal match* semantics[5] and is usually what one wants. This is further discussed in Example 6.18.

Example 6.18: Communication Gone Awry

A communication protocol might send a message and wait for an acknowledgement. If an acknowledgement is not received within a preset time boundary, then the same message will be resent. A set of communication events might contain sequences such as:

Send(M, Id) **at** T1, Send(M, id) **at** T2, Send(M, Id) **at** T3, Send (M, Id) **at** T4, . . . Ack(Id) **at** T', . . . Send(M1, Id1) **at** T", . . .

The sender has timed out and resent the same message with the same identifier many times before receiving an acknowledgement. Then the identifier changes in all subsequent communication. One way to detect this kind of repetition, which may indicate a fault in transmission medium, is to use carefully set time windows in the monitoring pattern:

Message M; identifier Id; Time T, T';
not Send(M, Id) **at** T **and** Send(M, Id) **at** T' **where** T' − T > bound.

where the "bound" is greater than twice the expected transmission time between sender and receiver. This pattern would give the receiver time to reply to the sender's message—if he got it. If the pattern matches several times, then the sender is repeatedly sending the same message. This might indicate that the transmissions or else their acknowledgments are not being received, which could be due to a fault in the transmission medium.

(continued)

[5]Luckham, *The Power of Events* (Boston: Addison-Wesley, 2002) Section 8.9, p. 170, Example 1.

Another way to specify a communication monitoring pattern is to use a operator like the good old regular expression "*" operator.

not Send(M, Id)* **within** [T, T + bound]

The "E*" operator means "any number more than one of E events." If the input sequence contains many E events within the time window, say, E, E, E, E, . . . , a maximal match semantics will match once.

However, we may want to be more precise. We may want to see at least five Send events with the same message before we get worried about the transmission. This requires a more precise operator. Let's call it **repeat**:

[**repeat** 5] Send(M, Id).

This would be like a **for** loop in programming, meaning five repetitions of the Send event.

An ability to express the number of repetitions to be detected is important both for efficiency of the matching process and in order not to get inundated with large numbers of unwanted matches. That is also why maximal-match semantics is important in cases where the number of repetitions is unknown in advance.

The current generation of event processing languages contains some operators that express repetition. Each language is different. So again, there is no uniformity or standard way of expressing repetitive patterns. The best advice is always to try and decide on a time window in which the behavior you're looking for is most likely to occur, and use it in your pattern.

Examples 6.19 and 6.20 demonstrate some applications of event pattern matching with repeated events that have seen recent commercial application.

Example 6.19: Looking for What You Expect to Find in the Event Cloud

Sales at an online website involve sequences of events where a customer logs onto the site, chooses items, puts them in a shopping cart, and goes through a checkout process. Essentially, this is a sequence of several events, repeated over and over by different customers buying different items. In fact, we don't know in advance how many events will be in the sequence, because we don't know what each customer is going to buy. A shopping sequence might look like this:

Logon → Search → Choose → Add-to-cart → Discard → Checkout

But there are other possibilities, since a customer might, for example, repeat the choose and add-to-cart events. In fact, there are potentially an unbounded number of possible shopping sequences. Can we construct one pattern that can match all of them?

To do this the pattern language has to be powerful enough to express the repetitive behavior. If the event pattern language has the * operator, this is quite easy to express:

Logon → (Search **or** Choose **or** Add-to-cart **or** Discard)* → Checkout

This pattern says that after logging on, a customer can search, choose, add to the cart or discard any number of times, and then check out.

If, on the other hand, there is nothing like the * operator in a pattern language, it seems one will probably have to use approximations in which a specific number of repetitions is specified in the pattern.

Example 6.20: Detecting the Unexpected in the Event Cloud

A harder problem is to construct patterns to detect surprises, since it is difficult to define event patterns you don't expect! But it is just as important as the first problem; sometimes it is much more important. Let's take a couple of simple examples.

First of all, consider the online website shopping cart activity again. Customers often drop or "abandon" the cart right in the middle of shopping and walk away. Enterprises in online retail are often as interested in detecting the abandoned cart behavior as they are in completed sales. They want to know immediately the drop rates' increase above average. And then they want to know why. How can we write event patterns that will match a customer behavior that is not known in advance?

One approach is to use time windows in defining the expected shopping pattern. If the pattern fails to complete a match within the time window, a warning is triggered that perhaps there is a dropped cart. The pattern can also refer to customer history in defining the time window. In fact, the real issue here is event pattern languages design. To write these kinds of patterns so you don't get too many false warnings, the language has to be able to express time windows, history, and so on.

A very simple approach would be:

Logon(C) **at** T **and not** Checkout (C) **within** T + Bound.

A match of this pattern tells us that a customer logged on and then stopped somewhere in the expected shopping process, but it doesn't tell us just how far that customer went. Did they stop at the search or after choosing an item?

To find that out, we try

Logon **or** Logon → (Search **or** Choose **or** Add-to-cart **or** Discard)*

If the pattern matcher is using maximal-match semantics, this will match exactly the sequence of activities that the customer performed up to when they dropped the shopping cart. The first logon is needed in case they do nothing else.

Requirements for an Event Pattern Language

Perhaps this is where you hand this book, or this chapter, over to your IT group! It should help in discussing a choice between CEP products that you might consider purchasing.

Here is a summary of the features of event patterns that have been discussed in this chapter. This is a minimal set of features that should be provided in languages intended for event pattern searching in a general event input (i.e., an event cloud).

1. First, the language should be typed. Events are objects belonging to specified types. There can be many different types of events.
2. Single-event templates are typed patterns that contain variable parts and denote events.

3. Patterns are expressions that are composed recursively from single-event templates by applying a set of pattern operators to subexpressions. Common operators are:[6]

A **and** B	both patterns A and B must match
A **or** B	at least one of the patterns A or B must match
not A	the pattern A must not match
when A **then** B	whenever pattern A matches then pattern B must match
if A **then** B	if A is matched then search for a match of B
A $\rightarrow$ B	A causes B
A*	an unspecified number of A's

4. Patterns may contain constraints that are functional expressions requiring evaluation as part of pattern matching. These are called references to *state*. Common operators for state references are:

where state_expression, **if** state_expression

5. Patterns may contain timing constraints. A common set of timing operators include:

at T, **after** T, **within** [T1, T2], **during** [T1, T2]

where [T1, T2] is an interval of time between times T1 and T2

If the input is restricted in some way—for example, the events have special properties or the input is an ordered stream of events—then some of these features may be unnecessary.

Commercial pattern languages today contain most of these features. The notations, of course, differ about as widely as programming languages can differ. Graphical input for specifying patterns is a feature of most products, but graphics can only go so far. The fine details needed to specify a pattern precisely sometimes have to be given in programming language text.

Correctness and Other Questions

There has been little discussion in event processing literature of the correctness of implementations of pattern matching, nor indeed of the correctness of event processing engines in general. Also lacking is discussion of the adequacy of current event pattern languages, or whether users are able to express the patterns they want or understand the semantics of the pattern languages (e.g., does the pattern matching mean first-match semantics or maximal-match semantics).

---

[6]Note that *then* is a part of two different operators with slightly different meanings and is not an operator on its own.

Customers of CEP products should ask whether they are getting the correct matches, all the matches, only some matches, or perhaps only the first match or no matches where some do exist. But then, upon reflection, perhaps this situation is simply a symptom of software industry in general—and a reason for its users to evaluate products carefully and ask questions!

Clearly, these are research areas for event processing. But CEP tools are being applied in a wide variety of fields today, as we discussed in Chapter 5, and the fact that there are open questions is no reason not to go ahead with a CEP application. Simply recognize what you don't know!

CHAPTER 7

Making Sense of Chaos in Real Time: Part 1

This chapter discusses making sense of a large variety of types of events, as well as lots of events; reducing the numbers of events and concentrating the information; gross filters, filtering, prioritization, categorization and selective streaming, including:

- Organizing event flows and event processing strategies
- Categories of event processing strategies
- Gross filtering and prioritization

Most organizations have to deal with events from many different sources. This can become a major issue when, for example, a company tries to expand its business into new markets or is faced with marketing new products. And of course commercial entities and governments are already overrun with the expanding space of types of events that are "out there."

One of the first problems is how to deal with large numbers of different types of events. This requires different kinds of strategies from those used to dealing with large numbers of events of the same type or maybe just a few different types (as is usually the case in, e.g., stock trading).

Typically, events are flowing into a large enterprise on a worldwide basis from a myriad of sources and at greatly different event rates varying from thousands of events per minute to just a few events per month. Additionally, the quality of information contained in the events can vary greatly depending upon the sources. In some cases, much irrelevant stuff is mixed in with highly relevant data. CEP principles and techniques must be applied in *right now* time to deal with both ends of the spectrum of event input rates.

Obviously, there will be a mix of different kinds of strategies at work. What will be needed is a way to organize those strategies for maximal effectiveness, that is, a process architecture for event processing strategies.

Event processing strategy: A goal-oriented algorithm or heuristic program that takes events as input and produces events as output to achieve a specified goal.

An event processing strategy is designed to achieve a goal. For example, a *filtering strategy* is used to remove input events that are unrelated to a specific goal by applying very simple tests. It must be computationally fast, so the tests will be simple. But usually it will only remove some of the unrelated events. For example, in choosing a *filtering strategy* for algorithmic trading in technology stocks, any stock trade report whose subject is not on the technology stocks list will be removed. And to detect short-term upswings, only reports of price changes would be allowed through the filter. Other strategies would be used after the filter to determine whether the price changes indicate an upswing.

An event processing system can be viewed as an event flow through a tree of event processing strategies. The system may have several goals or purposes—typically to supply different levels of real-time information to different people or indeed to different programs.

Today's event processing systems are set up with a bunch of strategies, but little has been written about how to organize the order in which events flow through the strategies; we will address that in this chapter.

We start in Figure 7.1 with a very naïve view of an event processing system. Figure 7.1, in fact, shows only part of the event processing. Often a system will take a variety of output actions, such as sending alerts or triggering a business process, in addition to sending the output events to end users.

But in fact, strategies are seldom completely independent of one another, and the order in which strategies are applied can sometimes make a difference, both in terms of the quality of the information gathered and in terms of the computational efficiency of the system. Sometimes, when a number of strategies are put together, there can be surprising results (e.g., less important events get processed ahead of important ones, or some important events get omitted from further processing altogether).

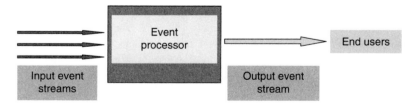

FIGURE 7.1 A Naive View of an Event Processing System

Best practices for composing event processing strategies need to be defined. Events flow through processing steps: each step consists of applying a strategy to the event flow, and the resulting events flow to the next step. The flow is not necessarily linear, as we shall see. The system should be architected with a view to how various strategies interact, the complexity of the strategies, and the computational effects of the order in which strategies are applied. One needs an event-flow architecture that has the flexibility to evolve as the set of strategies change and new ones are introduced over time.

The next two chapters discuss categories of event processing strategies and event flow architectures to deal with large numbers of events and with large event type spaces at the same time. This is the typical situation facing an information-driven enterprise that provides many different kinds of services, such as a government department, a communications organization, or a large international airline. But in some cases, it can apply to small businesses as well.

Event Type Spaces

Most event processing systems today are limited to processing small event type spaces.

What is an event type space? It is just a set of *types of events.* An event type space is usually associated with a specific application area, such as consumer relations or asset tracking. The number of events being input or output is one measure of the complexity of an event processing problem. But another measure is the number of different types of events being dealt with (i.e., a measure of the variety of events entering the system).

A large event type space system is one in which a large number of different types of events are being input to the system or output from the system, or both. The event inputs will be coming from lots of different sources. And the system has to satisfy many different demands. So one expects to see event processing operations like filtering and prioritization being applied early in the processing of incoming events, before the more precise goal-oriented strategies. Their objective is to channel the relevant types of events to specialized processing algorithms.

The first objective of event processing has two parts:

1. To extract information relevant to the goals of the enterprise from all types of event inputs
2. To make that information available to the various role players (i.e., people, applications, or devices) within the enterprise immediately

In large event type space problems, it often happens that both the spaces of input event types and output event types are large, and they can be very different. Also, there is usually another degree of complexity to the problem. Not only are the two event type spaces large and different, but they are fluid, changing all the time. New types of inputs are arising and new services are always being demanded. An event processing system must be easily reconfigured to deal with new types of inputs and outputs.

Restricting the Types of Event Inputs May Not Be an Option

Many types of events may seem irrelevant to the goals of the enterprise. They can be put on the back burner, so to speak. But should they be eliminated altogether from consideration? Experience shows that doing that can be dangerous. Obviously, some event sources can be ignored, but such choices must be careful and always subject to review. While some input events will be irrelevant to the goals of the processing, some will contain both useful and useless information all jumbled together.

Consequently, the enterprise is continuously faced with a choice between ignoring event sources or throwing more processing power at an ever-increasing filtering problem. Rather than ignore event sources, incoming events should be subjected to different kinds of operations varying in complexity from very simple and gross filtering operations at the beginning to sophisticated problem-specific strategies at the end. An array of different techniques is needed to process event inputs to concentrate relevant information.

Examples 7.1 and 7.2 are some well-known examples of the dilemma involved in choosing to restrict the types of input events.

Example 7.1: Trying to Restrict Event Inputs in Stock Trading

A stock trading operation might decide to take only stock market feeds as inputs. But as we all know, stock markets are influenced by many different kinds of information, not just the current prices of stocks.

For example,

- Industry production statistics
- Raw materials prices
- Labor union negotiations
- Weather reports
- Shipping news

and many other sources of events all have an influence on stock prices. In fact, nobody knows exactly what the total set of influences is; we only know that that set of influences is not constant; it varies from day to day.

Interestingly, recent discussion on this topic can be found in articles on stock-trading data feeds:

> Algorithms going forward will have to take into account news feeds and any data source that can affect the trading decision. Trading applications will have to be more adaptable and ready to absorb new and different information types.[1]

The lesson from this is that one cannot plan to restrict event input; instead, one must plan for exactly the opposite! A forward-thinking stock trader will factor the feeds from news aggregators and many other sources into the algorithms used in trading strategies. But doing this requires subjecting the input events to a variety of preprocessing strategies such as adapting to standard formats and putting a lot of effort into designing event filtering strategies. Indeed, how does one input news items to a trading algorithm? This has been a subject of secret, behind-the-scenes IT development on Wall Street for twenty years.

---

[1]Dow Jones Solutions for Algorithmic and Quantitative Trading, 2008.

Example 7.2: Restricting Event Inputs in Airline Passenger Scheduling Operations

An airline might be tempted to restrict the event inputs used in processing passenger schedule changes. For example, initially it might consider:

- Flight schedules
- FAA air traffic event feeds
- Current passenger schedules
- Flight connections and flight schedule delays of all connecting airlines
- Up-to-the-minute weather feeds from all operations areas

to be a sufficient list of real time event input feeds to a system that reschedules passengers making connecting flights at a large airport hub.

(continued)

But not for long!
The airline will soon find that

- Aircraft maintenance tracking
- Aircraft availability
- Flight crew availability
- Maintenance schedules and tracking
- Security line and other airport operations
- Homeland security and immigration advisories

and a host of other event sources and event types need to be added to the input to improve the results of its event processing systems.

Recent experience with CEP applications to airline management systems has shown the need to use types of event inputs that had not been in the original system planning. When the input event type space was expanded beyond original plans, the CEP application was found to be useful in other airline management and planning problems in several different areas of operations. This led to other demands on the system and to its further development to produce more types of output events.

As CEP is integrated into airline operations management, it turns out that the airlines find their operations management systems can be federated into cooperating systems across the various airlines to mutual benefit.

The Expanding Input Principle: Always Plan for New Types of Event Inputs and Event Outputs

Any strategy to simplify event processing by restricting the space of event inputs or outputs will eventually be defeated by the demand for more accurate and comprehensive information.

In essence, the stock traders have been stating this principle!

The reason for this principle is very simple. There is always an implicit feedback loop from the event inputs, the event processing, and the output information to the resulting performance of the enterprise and back again. Demand for better performance implicitly requires better information and improved processing algorithms. This loop will eventually lead to an expansion of the type spaces of event inputs and outputs. Consequently, simply trying to restrict the space of input event types will not work.

Event processing systems must be designed from the beginning to be *evolutionary*. They must be rapidly reconfigurable to accept more types of event inputs and produce more types of outputs. As we all know, businesses are always being challenged to respond to a changing environment, and to produce new alerts and execute new processes in response to new inputs. More about reconfigurability later!

Architecting Event Processing Strategies

An important consideration in setting up an event processing system is how to flow the events through a set of processing strategies. Some categories of strategies should be applied before others. This strategy architecture should be a primary design consideration in planning the system.

When a system is first set up, a choice of event input streams is made. The inputs are limited to those that are deemed most relevant or useful to the enterprise. Usually, this is done as the application is installed and is generally a decision involving consultants and business analysts. However, according to our expanding input principle, the initial set of inputs should always be adjustable to allow for adding different types of inputs later.

Figure 7.2 shows a paradigm for event flow architecture. The first-stage processing strategies are best described as *filters*. If we allow a large variety of inputs, we must first filter out the relevant from the irrelevant.

There are two families of event filters:

1. *Gross filters*: These are operations that eliminate events from further processing.
2. *Categorization and prioritization filters*: Operations that place events into various categories and determine the processing order of the various categories of events. The results of filtering are fed to the next level of event processors.

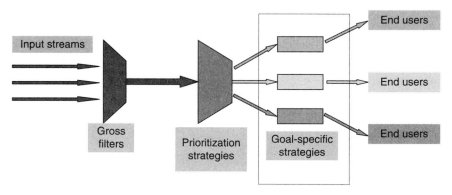

FIGURE 7.2 Event Flows through a Tree of Strategies

In the typical business system, these strategies are all executed on the same event-processing engine. But some systems will use several different event processors for the different strategies; usually those will be systems that deal with high volumes of event inputs.

Notice that although Figure 7.2 shows acyclic event flows, in practice it may well be that event flows through the various strategies do have cycles. Cycles are most likely to occur within the set of goal-specific strategies (i.e., in the box around the set of goal-specific strategies).

A third category, called *goal-specific strategies*, consists of strategies that are specialized to achieve the goals of the enterprise. They will be specific to the enterprise in question. Typically, they process the flow of events using various numerical algorithms, statistical measures, and strategies proprietary to the company to focus information in the events for different end users. They are placed last in the event flow processors, after filtering and prioritization, because they may be complex and take considerable compute power and time—so one doesn't want to apply them to events that are going to be filtered out.

In fact, the various processing paths through the event flow tree (Figure 7.2) will take different amounts of time to deliver their results. There will be fast-flow paths that deliver events after they have been through the filters and prioritization—that is, without applying any goal-specific strategies. Other paths will be slower, because they use heavyweight goal-specific strategies that take a lot of computation time.

There is a new principle of event processing embedded in Figure 7.2: that different people within the enterprise will want to see different views of the same event input. They have different uses and goals for the information they receive, so they need to see different types of events. A network manager, for example, will be interested in everything, but specifically in network activity, server loads, event throughput, network sources, and output loads from various event generators within his network. A business planner, on the other hand, couldn't care less about network statistics. He will be interested in new sales reports, supply chain events, perhaps sales reports of competitors, and so on—totally different types of events from the network manager. Event processing must get the right information to the right people; in fact, the event processing system might look to some end users as though they have their own separate dedicated system!

Gross Filters

Gross filters are strategies that simply exclude events in the input feeds according to criteria that are very simple and use little processing power. Usually events are eliminated based upon their attributes or data contents.

Examples of common attributes used in gross filters:

- Event type (e.g., delete all events of type T)
- Origin (e.g., delete all events generated by sensor S)
- Topic (e.g., delete all events on yesterday's weather)
- Creation time (e.g., delete all events created before time T–1 hour)
- Data content (e.g., delete any trade of a non-Fortune 500 company)

Gross filters must be fast so that there is little degradation in the speed of the input streams. These kinds of filters depend only upon attributes of the events and the data in them and do not refer to context, history, and state. In some systems, the input events may be flowed through several layers of gross filters.

Patterns of events can be used as filters to eliminate events that do not match the pattern. Usually, these are very simple patterns that err on the side of allowing an event if there is any doubt about whether it might be useful.

Examples: deletion of events from input stream using event patterns:

- Delete all "truck stop" and "truck start" events.
- Delete all "customer is idle" events.
- Delete all "Bought A" events dated earlier than yesterday if there have been no "Sold A" events since then.
- Delete the activities of customer C unless customer D is online at the same time.

Prioritization: Split Streaming, Topics, Sentiments, and Other Attributes

Strategies for separating events are then applied to input streams that have gone through the gross filters, as shown in Figure 7.2. They are various forms of prioritization and categorization. It is assumed that all remaining events might have some relevancy to the processing goals. So rather than being eliminated from consideration, event inputs are run through a set of ordering and categorization strategies before they are subjected to the next layer of goal-specific strategies. The essential idea is that the "more relevant" inputs should be processed before the "less relevant" inputs.

But relevancy is difficult to determine. Prioritization and categorization strategies are usually very problem specific. There are no general guidelines. In this area of processing, techniques are specialized to a given application area and in some cases depend upon categorizations and ontologies that have taken years of work and trial-and-error feedback experiments to develop.

Again, these strategies are required to be fast. But they are more complicated than the gross filters. For example, in automated stock trading, some systems split the stream of input events into many streams based upon predetermined relevancy criteria using keywords contained in the events. The streams are then prioritized.

A typical example of prioritization can be found in the use of news reports in automated stock trading. News feeds are available nowadays in which the reports are in an XML format with keywords called *tags* added to describe the content of each report (see Examples 7.3 and 7.4). The XML tags indicate not only the usual key economic indicators, but also trading attributes, such as sentiment and surprise values. Adding tags to news items is based upon sophisticated natural language processing of news articles.[2]

Example 7.3: Elementized News Feeds

Elementized news feeds deliver news items in a specified format that includes an added set of data tags. Examples include economic and corporate news items with added XML-tagged "topic" fields.

Elementizing news items involves automated language analysis to determine the presence of news on topic categories such as (an incomplete list):

- Earnings & Earnings Guidance
- Merger Announcements
- Analyst Upgrades & Downgrades
- Executive Changes
- Bankruptcy
- Stock Splits
- Significance & Unexpectedness

The topic categories on significance and unexpectedness are examples of "sentiment tags" added to all corporate news for analysis of potential impact of that news item.

(continued)

---

[2] "Dow Jones Launches XML Data Feed for Algorithmic Trading," *Finextra*, March 6, 2007. www.finextra.com/fullstory.asp?id=16606

These feeds are advertised in the Finextra.com article cited above as "an ultra-low-latency service delivering economic and corporate news." Their purpose is to eliminate the need to parse unstructured text. The elementized news feeds are input directly to quantitative-analysis models and automated trading programs used in financial services operations, such as algorithmic trading, quantitative analysis, and order execution management. According the article, this approach enables "trading models to process, interpret and take action on breaking news in milliseconds."

Example 7.4: Market Commentary on the Introduction of Elementized News Feeds in 2007[3]

Assuming that the information is reliably encoded, these feeds should enable the creation of additional sophisticated trading and risk management algorithms.

Consider for a moment what currently occurs with the monthly release of U.S. employment data. The financial markets pause that first Friday morning of each month to digest the various statistics that are released at 8:30 ~AM ET and then trading activity often picks up a frantic pace based upon whether the economy is perceived to be stronger or weaker than expected.

By having such employment data fed directly into a quantitative algorithm, the computers can more rapidly than humans make decisions about what, if anything, should be bought or sold at which trading venue. Alternatively, the quantitative algorithms might raise a flag (or technically 'create an alert event') indicating that the employment data is out of some pre-determined norm and all electronic trading instructions should be stopped until there is human intervention.

[3]"Dow Jones Elementized News Feed was named 'Best Data Solution' in the 2008 Financial News Awards for Excellence in IT." www.stevieawards.com/pubs/awards/403_2591_19349.cfm

Complex Filtering and Prioritization Using Event Patterns

There are cases in which it makes computational sense to run the input events through filters that are more sophisticated than gross filters. The prioritization schemes may also use complex event patterns. The complexity in the initial processing step results in fewer and more relevant events being passed on for further processing, thereby saving time downstream. Usually, in these cases much of the event processing, including filtering and prioritization, is goal-specific from the beginning.

A second approach to prioritization is to prioritize not only single events based upon their data tags, but also sets of events that match one or more event patterns on a specified list. Events that are given priority are treated as most important and passed first through the processor. Consider Example 7.5.

Example 7.5: Monitoring and Controlling a Fleet of Delivery Trucks

Let us return to the example given in the "Transportation" section in Chapter 5, in which a single human fleet supervisor is monitoring the progress of a company's fleet of 400 delivery vans in a large metropolitan area.

The event processing system that supports the supervisor is receiving input events from each van's radio and GPS system, and

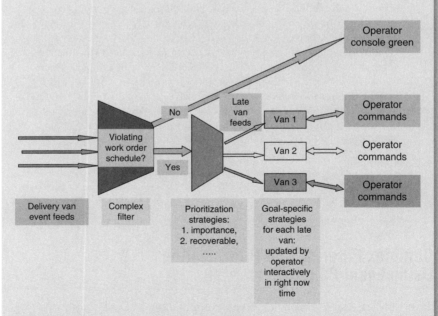

FIGURE 7.3 Delivery Van Fleet's Event Processing and Control System Showing Complex Filtering of Incoming Events

additional input events from customers, suppliers, traffic reports, weather, and other sources.

The event processing system displays output events resulting from its processing on the supervisor's graphical screen. As Figure 7.3 shows, the input events are put through an initial complex filter that checks the event flow for each van against the van's work order schedule. This is not a gross filter, in contrast to the processing scheme shown in Figure 7.2. It is a complex test involving matching the incoming events with event patterns that represents the van's schedule, timing constraints, and expected progress. If the van is on schedule, no further action is taken—the van is simply displayed on the operator console as green.

Event feeds from vans that are violating their work order schedules are then passed through the filter for further processing. At the next step the event flows are prioritized according to the importance of a van's cargo, whether the van can recover from its lateness (which may involve many factors, including traffic reports), and other criteria. The prioritized late-van event feeds are then passed on to a goal-oriented processing stage where the goal-strategies are directly under the control of the operator. The operator interacts in *right now* time with these late van feeds to try to get them back on schedule. For example, the operator may elect to alter a van's work schedule because some of its delivery or pickup orders are highly important.

This is an example of *management by exception.* Normal situations are simply ignored. No action is taken unless a truck gets into an exceptional situation. This is an approach to dealing with today's information glut. CEP gives us a way to implement management by exception. There is a growing number of demanding business scenarios where the volume, latency, and complexity of the event data are exploding.

Summary

Event processing systems apply strategies to flows of incoming events. Strategies can be classified into three main categories, which are applied in the following order:

1. *Filtering strategies* are applied first to reduce the numbers of events that must be further processed.
2. *Ordering and prioritization strategies* are applied after filtering.
3. *Goal-specific strategies* are applied last, after filtering and ordering.

In many systems, the strategies can be altered in *right now* time as the event flows are being processed.

The overall objective of applying the categories of strategies in this order is to improve efficiency and speed by reducing the number of events that must be processed at each stage without eliminating events that contain information important to the goals of the enterprise.

As we discussed in the beginning of this chapter, the goal of reducing the numbers of events being processed tends to be defeated by increasing pressures for more accurate information for wider numbers of users. Event-processing systems are being required to deal with ever-wider varieties of event inputs. We take up this topic in Chapter 9.

Typically, events are processed in these systems by flowing through a tree of strategies whose paths branch toward delivering events of interest to its various users, as illustrated in Figures 7.2 and 7.3. Different users want different kinds of information. So each path through the tree gets more and more specialized toward delivering a particular kind of information.

This chapter has described strategies that tend to be applied early in the processing tree. Chapter 8 describes some of the strategies that can be used later in the event flow to abstract information in events for different users in the enterprise.

CHAPTER 8

Making Sense of Chaos in Real Time: Part 2

This chapter describes more advanced event processing strategies that may be employed on event inputs after they have been put through gross filtering:

- Abstracting patterns of events
- Levels and views
- Hierarchies of events and why they are important
- Methods of defining event hierarchies
- Using computable event hierarchies
- Drilling down, reversing abstraction, and retrieving information when you need it

The event processing techniques described in this chapter go beyond the capabilities available in the CEP tools in the current marketplace.[1] But as event processing matures, we believe that these techniques and the tools to apply them will appear in the marketplace. Within a few years, the event processing techniques described in this chapter will become part of common practice. In fact, in special cases it can be argued that they are already in use!

One of the main problems today is information overload. As we have seen, restricting event inputs is a dangerous practice, because it puts the enterprise in danger of missing vital information. The standard approach to tackling this problem is the use of gross filtering strategies described in the previous chapter.

Another approach to solving the information-overload problem, one that complements the gross filtering strategies and can be used in conjunction

---

[1]The year 2011.

with them, is to organize events into levels of abstraction. Organizing events into levels of abstraction is one of the goal-specific strategies that can be used in processing flows of events (see Chapter 7, Figures 7.2 and 7.3).

Different levels provide different views of the information contained in the flows of events as they arrive, in real time. The objective is to deliver *the right information to the right people*. This requires matching event patterns to the input events that have passed through gross filtering and then using the matches that are detected to create higher level abstract events.

Interestingly, if you look at commercial CEP applications today, you will see abstract events being created all over the place. But nobody pays any attention to the *concept* of abstraction. The immediate problems can be solved without thinking explicitly about the underlying principles or how one abstract event relates to another. At present, the power of event abstraction is used in unconscious, ad hoc, and informal ways. We should stop muddling along and apply abstraction more precisely! This is a next step in establishing longer term commercial applications of event processing.

Abstract Events and Views

An abstract event can be used to summarize the data contained in a set of events. This is a technique in CEP called *abstraction*. One advantage of abstract events is to reduce the number of events being processed while retaining the information that is relevant to our goals. Consider Example 8.1.

Example 8.1: Abstractions of Stock Market Feeds

For example, look back at the market trading application discussed in Chapter 3, in the section on "Event Streams" and in Figure 3.7. An event processor is computing on the data in trading events from two stock market feeds. There are probably thousands of events per minute arriving in this input. The processor computes the volume weighted average price (VWAP) of each of the stock symbols over a time window and outputs a stream of events that contain the VWAP values of the trades in each stock over each time window.

For example, suppose the time window is five minutes, and IBM trades reported during one of the five-minute windows are (1) 100 shares at $166.25, (2) 500 shares at 165.8, and (3) 200 shares at 165.5. Then the processor will output a VWAP event for IBM of 165.78 over that five-minute time window. Three trade events were input and one VWAP event abstracted their data over the time window. The processor computes one VWAP event for each stock symbol that arrives in the input streams no matter how many trades of that stock were reported in the five-minute window.

The VWAP processor is creating a particular kind of abstract view of trading activity that traders find useful without having to look at all the individual trades.

Abstraction is often used as a tool to *concentrate information* that is spread out in little pieces over a large set of events and maybe also over a large time window.

Abstraction: An event is an *abstraction* of a set of events if it summarizes the information contained in the events in the set.

An event created for this purpose is called an *abstract event*. Notice that an abstract event need not contain *all* the information in the set of events, but just a summary of that information. How a summary is computed from the information in the set of events is left open.

We don't often think of some popular kinds of event processing as computing abstractions. But in fact, they usually are (see Example 8.2).

Example 8.2: Online Retail Website Monitoring[2]

During the online operation of a retail website, hundreds or thousands of customers may be logged on to the website at any time. Customer visits are tracked in real time. Each completed customer visit is represented by a sequence of events in which a customer logs onto the site, searches a catalogue, reviews items, chooses items and puts them in a shopping cart, and then "pushes" the cart through a checkout process. Of course, there are cycles where an item is chosen and later discarded, but let's filter out those cycles from the shopping sequence. For different customer visits, the sequences are different and contain different numbers of events. But each completed visit could be abstracted by a single event, *completed visit*, containing only the data the website owner wants to keep: for example, customer name, date, amount of sale, length of time of the visit, and traffic density (i.e., the number of other customers visiting the website at the same time).

---

[2]In Chapter 6, we discussed how to define patterns of customer visits to a website. Here, we discuss how to abstract those patterns of behavior.

In Figure 8.1, the input events are flowing at a high rate—say, several hundred per minute. The figure shows real-time functions that compute abstractions of the input activity, as it is happening, by recognizing event patterns in the input. For example, the financial summary event will be an abstraction of patterns of those events in which a customer purchases items. A behavior profile event will be an abstraction of the events tracking a customer's activity on the website (e.g., type of items viewed, enquiries made, type of items purchased, and so on). Obviously, there are many ways to compute abstractions of a customer's behavior. These are higher-level events. The numbers of higher-level events are far fewer than the numbers of input events, as they are intended to abstract or summarize sets of events in the input activity.

For example, eighty raw events of customer activity might match a pattern consisting of a Login, followed by several iterations of (Search **or** Choose **or** Add-to-cart **or** Discard), followed by Checkout and Logout events. This pattern would be abstracted to a few executive summary events.

The executive summaries would depend upon the interests of various departments within the website organization. For example, the shipping department might want a summary event containing the number of items checked out and purchased, their weight, and the customer's

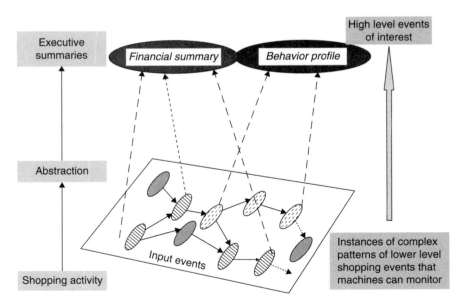

FIGURE 8.1 Abstractions Applied to Patterns of Events from Consumer Activity on a Retail Website Can Lead to Different Views of the Same Events

delivery address. The marketing department might want an update of the customer's profile, with the categories of items purchased.

Our interest is in how to define those higher-level events that give us the abstractions.

There are many methods of defining an abstraction of a set of events. In Example 8.2, on monitoring customer's behavior on a retail website, one abstraction might be the total price of the customer's purchase at the end of shopping. Other abstractions could be the categories of articles purchased or a behavior profile of how the customer spent the time shopping—did they spend a lot of time discarding items and then choosing others, and so on?

Different abstractions provide different views of the same set of events as illustrated in Figure 8.1.

Views: A *view* is a set of abstract events that are frequently used together in the same context. A view is specified by the set of types of the events in it.

One use of abstraction is to provide real-time views of the event activity being monitored. The goal is to condense information that is spread out over a large number of events into a smaller set of abstract events. A view has a specific purpose—for example, to profile or categorize a customer according to different measures, to compare sales in different areas of the country, or to monitor for violations of service-level agreements and other policy constraints.

Figure 8.2 illustrates different uses of higher-level events to analyze the input flow of events in real time. There is a continuous flow of input events from the different sources that are being monitored. These are shown at the bottom. This input is searched continuously for patterns of events that are specified in advance in the event pattern rules engine but may be changed at any time. Whenever an instance of a pattern is detected, a rule is triggered, resulting in creation of a higher-level event containing data from the events in that instance of the pattern. These data provide a view of the pattern instance.

The higher-level event could be called a "view" of the lower-level activity. Different pattern-triggered rules can give totally different views for specific purposes. For example, the state of a business process, the possibility of an SLA being violated, or changes in a sales environment.

One implication of using abstractions is that we will want to create new abstractions, or improve previous ones, all the time. Once we start using views, we will be continuously improving them to suit the demands of the business. This implies that the methods of defining views should be easy and accessible online.

Note: The creation of an abstract event does *not* imply the deletion of the set or pattern of events (i.e., *event objects* that represent the

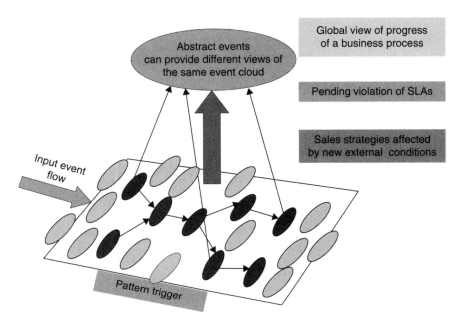

FIGURE 8.2 Pattern-Triggered Rules Abstract Information in Higher-Level Events Used for Making Management Decisions

events) that it abstracts. Those event objects should always be retained for recording and analysis of the performance of the method of abstraction although they may take no further part in the processing. And remember, an event (i.e., the thing that happens) can never be deleted from history! The equivalent of deleting an event object is to filter it out of the event processing (i.e., forget it).

Levels of Abstraction and Views

Not only are there different views of the events in an activity, but some views are more abstract than others. This leads to the concept that there are different *levels* of abstraction and viewing, as shown in Figure 8.3.

Figures 8.1 and 8.3 are related. Figure 8.1 shows how higher-level events can provide different views of the activity of customers in a retail website. Each view consists of a set of higher-level events. Figure 8.3 shows how views can be organized into different levels according to their abstraction.

The lowest-level view contains the actual operations performed behind the scenes by the implementation of the website. They are invoked when a

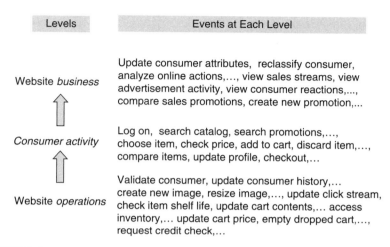

Levels	Events at Each Level
Website *business*	Update consumer attributes, reclassify consumer, analyze online actions,…, view sales streams, view advertisement activity, view consumer reactions,…, compare sales promotions, create new promotion,…
Consumer *activity*	Log on, search catalog, search promotions,…, choose item, check price, add to cart, discard item,…, compare items, update profile, checkout,…
Website *operations*	Validate consumer, update consumer history,… create new image, resize image,…, update click stream, check item shelf life, update cart contents,… access inventory,… update cart price, empty dropped cart,…, request credit check,…

FIGURE 8.3 Levels of Views of Activity

customer uses the features and operations available to users at the interface of the website. Second-level views consist of visible activities specified in the website interface that the customer actually performs. And third-level views give a business summary of what customers buy and how they behave. The third-level views are clearly abstractions of second-level events.

Example 8.3: Mappings between Levels That Create Abstract Events

At the consumer activity level (Figure 8.3) we might have the following set of events: "customer C logs on," "C views website catalogue," "C selects a category of items," "C searches for the cheapest item," "C selects an item," "C purchases the item," "C logs off." The website activity viewer may contain an event pattern that would be matched by a subset of these events—say, "customer views catalog," "customer selects an item," "customer purchases the item." And the activity viewer might then create a business-level event that gives a business view of that instance of the pattern. For example, it might create a business-level event, "customer assigned score A at time T," in which A is a cumulative sum of the prices of items purchased in that shopping activity during time T. In this way, the activity viewer would be mapping sets of events at the consumer-activity level to events at the website business level.

Example 8.3 is an example of a rule triggered by an event pattern that maps sets of events at one level to events at the next level. A computable event hierarchy is implemented by sets of these mappings between the various levels in the hierarchy.

Figure 8.4 illustrates possible applications of the views at the three levels in Figure 8.3. The first level of website operations provides a view that is useful for managing the network operations.

At a higher level, a view of consumer activity events is used in consumer relations, sales promotions and product planning. An even higher-level view, abstracted from consumer activity, provides a business intelligence view of website operation, its profitability, trends in sales, consumer interest, and so on.

It must be emphasized that the different levels of viewing are taking place in real time, as the website is in operation and customers are using it. So there is a continuous flow of events at all three levels. The events at level 2 are being created from patterns of events at level 1 by pattern-triggered rules. Similarly, the events at level 3 are created from patterns of events at level 2.

So we come to a concept of levels of abstraction or levels of views. How can it be said that one view is a *higher level* than another? There is no accepted standard for organizing views—of events in a website or any type of events anywhere else—into levels. For example, some people might argue that the activities (and corresponding events) shown in the view at level 2 in Figure 8.3 are not any higher or "more abstract" than those at level 1. A counter argument would be that the level 2 events are composed of sets of level 1 events.

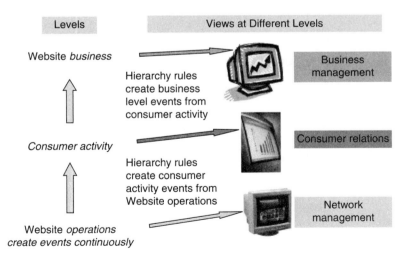

FIGURE 8.4 Different Views for Different Purposes

A level 2 event is created whenever a particular pattern of level 1 events happens and triggers a rule that creates the level 2 event. But there can be little argument that events at level 3 are higher than those at level 2.

Again, there might be disagreement as to whether the events listed at level 3 all belong at one level! The definition of computable event hierarchies will probably be the result of a lot of consensus formation within a particular IT technology sector. As we said at the beginning of this chapter, this is new ground in applying event processing.

Organizing Views

The decision to classify or name a set of types of events as a view is quite arbitrary. At the moment, there are very few standards to which one can refer.[3] And having defined some views, it is another issue as to how they can be compared and organized into a hierarchy. Indeed, some views might be considered to be as abstract as one another (i.e., at the same level of abstraction). Other views might be very clearly at different levels of abstraction, one being more abstract than the other. On the other hand, there will be many cases of pairs of views for which there is no general agreement as to whether one is more abstract than the other. Unless views are defined from the beginning to be comparable to one another by mappings, most views will be incomparable as far as abstraction is concerned.

However, to develop methods of viewing the activity within an enterprise and dealing with information overload, the set of views to be used should be organized from the bottom up. The base view must use the event sources that are available, the raw events. Starting from the base, views can be developed on demand, in response to what is needed.

One way to establish levels of views is to define how the events in one view can be composed from sets of events in the other view. Thus, in organizing sets of events into views and views into levels, as shown in the previous figures, there are two decisions that must be taken:

1. Decide which types of events belong in the same view
2. Define how events in one view are composed of sets of events in lower views

---

[3]Two well-known examples are the TCP/IP messaging hierarchy: R. Braden, Editor, "RFC 1122: Requirements for Internet Hosts—Communication Layers" *Internet Engineering Task Force*, available online at http://tools.ietf.org/html/rfc1122, and the Open System Interconnection Reference Model: Rachelle Miller, "The OSI Model: An Overview." SANS Institute Reading Room, available online at www.sans.org/reading_room/whitepapers/standards/osi-model-overview_543

This is new territory, and its commercial value is as yet unexplored. One obvious use is to provide a real-time flow of different views of the events created in a system to observers (either people or programs) that have different interests in the events in that system. Typically, enterprises are hierarchical in their organization, and different role players within the enterprise—from network managers to the CEO—will require different views of the raw events and information in them, as Figure 8.4 illustrates. Thus a hierarchy of views of the raw events will correspond to the organizational levels within the business or enterprise and the requirements of its role players.

But as we mentioned at the beginning of the chapter, the overall problem is to deal with information overload—and that is where levels of abstraction and views have application. The numbers of events at higher levels of abstraction decrease rapidly with increasing levels, because sets of events are being mapped into single higher-level events.

Computing Abstractions by Event Pattern Maps

In CEP, an abstraction is required to be computable. This means that to create abstract events that summarize the information in a given set of events, there must be a computable method of creating those abstractions.

Having decided upon the abstractions to be used in viewing the enterprise's activities, the next question is to develop real-time methods of computing those abstractions and the corresponding views. In fact, the computable method should be part of the definition of the abstractions and views.

Computable abstraction: An event is a *computable abstraction* of a set of events if it summarizes the information contained in the events in the set and there is a method of computing that event. Example 8.4 gives a practical use of this concept.

Example 8.4: VWAP Events Are Computable Abstractions of Streams of Stock Market Trades

The VWAP is an abstraction of a set of stock market feeds. Chapter 3, in the section on "Event Streams," describes a method for computing the VWAP over a time windows of events in stock market feeds.

One method of computing abstract events is by means of event pattern mappings.

Event pattern map: *An Event pattern mapping* is a function that takes as argument a pattern of events and creates an event as the result of its computation.

Two event pattern maps are illustrated in Figure 8.1. Map f computes financial summaries from the raw events in an input cloud, while map g computes customer behavior profiles from the same sets of input events. These maps are computed continuously in real time as the input events flow into the enterprise. So Figure 8.1 illustrates a continuous flow of abstract events being computed from the input flows.

An event pattern map can be defined by a set of reactive rules, each of which is triggered by a pattern of events. When a rule is triggered, it creates an event that summarizes the information in the set of events that triggered it. A map may consist of several pattern-triggered rules. If we want to see what the code for a map might look like, Example 8.5 gives the code for a map that summarizes the patterns of shopping activities of customers over periods of time as abstract shopping report events, and Examples 8.6 and 8.7 show practical applications of the event pattern map.

Example 8.5: Summarizing Retail Website Activity

map Shopping Reports
Customer C, Item I;
whenever C Logs on to Website **at** T1 **and** C checks Items **and**
C adds I to cart **followed by** C checks out **at** T2 **and**
C Purchases I **at** T3 **followed by** C Is Approved
then create Shopping Report (C, I, T1, T3)

Examples 8.6 and 8.7 are some more examples of mappings that compute abstractions of patterns of activity.

Example 8.6: Profiling Internet Activity from Outside Sources

Monitoring the activity in a large organization's network that is originating from outside Internet sources can be automated by event pattern mappings. Such a map is a function that computes summaries of network scans from outside IP addresses and creates an abstract event containing the summaries for a specific time window.

(continued)

The function takes as input a sliding time window of the events from outside sources. The input events are level 1, let's say. It creates an abstract event that summarizes the activity during the time window from each outside IP address. There are many different possible output formats for the summaries. For example, a summary event might contain an array indexed by the outside IP addresses that are sources of scanning activity. The elements of the array would contain the internal network IP addresses that were scanned within a given time window, and the time spent scanning that internal IP address. These abstract events form level 2, let's say.

It would be possible to go further and create a set of level 3 events that characterize the nature of the network activities that are summarized by the level 2 events. This could be done (1) by using knowledge of the outside source IP addresses as, say, "friendly," "known local," "unknown," "suspected botnet," etc., and (2) by analyzing the nature of the attempted accesses, as say, "remote callback," "synchronizing grid heartbeat," "port scan," "DNS attack," and so on. Level 3 events would contain suspected classifications of the nature of the network activity from the outside sources.

Example 8.7: Viewing Activity of a Feet of Delivery Trucks

The online human operator monitoring a fleet of 400 trucks in a previous example needs a little help. Instead of viewing the progress of each truck on its delivery schedule, the monitoring system should compute views that summarize the fleet activity. There are many ways to do this. For example, the area map displayed on the monitor (Figure 5.1) can be divided into sectors.

A *sector view* could summarize the on-time progress of each truck in the sector. If a sector is green, then every truck in that sector is on schedule; if its view goes yellow, then there are one or more trucks in that sector that have deviated from their schedule in some way (e.g., they are at least ten minutes behind schedule). A red sector would indicate serious problems such as a breakdown or accident. The operator should be able to drill down by clicking on a sector to see the actual truck activity and their statuses.

A different view might be a *trip plan view* of the truck fleet. The progress of each truck is monitored for consistency with its preassigned delivery plan. As long as a truck's progress is within specified consistency bounds with its plan, the view shows a green light. If a truck deviates from its plan beyond the specified bounds, the view changes to show the truck's position on the map and the parameters of its deviation from its schedule. The trip plan view might then trigger a process to plan getting the truck back on schedule.

Computable Event Hierarchies

Too much information contained in large numbers of events is just as self-defeating as too little. That's where event pattern maps and computable abstractions can be useful! They give us a method of organizing the viewing of the raw input events into higher-level views of the information. We can slice and dice information for different people according to their roles and needs within the enterprise and, at the same time, reduce the number of events that must be viewed. Essentially, event pattern maps are a tool for the efficient use of information—providing of course that we can define maps for computing our abstractions.

The basic plan is very simple. Various role players in an enterprise need specific information related to their jobs. So we use event pattern mappings to compute the views of the incoming information that various role players need.[4] This is illustrated in the previous figures.

Next, we must deal with the problem of relating the views. How are different abstractions and views related? And is there a way we can organize them to keep the growth of different abstractions of the enterprise's information under control? One approach is to use event hierarchies.

Hierarchical structure is ubiquitous in everyday life. There have been standard hierarchies in some areas of science for many years, for example in hardware design and in networks. The Open Systems Interconnection (OSI) Seven-Layer Model[5] of messaging operations was developed in the 1970s. Its purpose was to develop a standard for layers of messaging operations, with the assumption that operations at each layer were "conceptually similar functions that provide services to the layer above it and receives service from the layer below it."

---

[4]The role players will be consulted throughout the setup of an event viewing system for a company.

[5]Rachelle Miller, "The OSI Model: An Overview." SANS Institute Reading Room. Available online at www.sans.org/reading_room/whitepapers/standards/osi-model-overview_543

Notice that open-ended phrase, "conceptually similar functions"! And notice also the idea that functions at one level "provide services" to functions at the level above. In our terminology this means that there are event pattern mappings whereby a function invocation at one level is composed of a set of function invocations at the level below.

The OSI standard does not specify how an event at one level is composed of sets of events at the level below it. The relationships between layers were left open. There have been arguments both for and against the layering idea.[6]

In CEP, we view an event hierarchy as consisting of *levels of types of events*. The types of events at a level are conceptually similar to one another. But, more than that, we require two conditions.

Computable event hierarchy: **a hierarchical organization of sets of types of events into levels so that:**

1. The types of events at one level are abstractions of sets of types of events at the level below, level 1 being the raw input events.
2. There are event pattern maps between levels that compute the events at one level in terms of sets of events of the types in the levels below.

The abstraction relationships between events at different levels are computable both up and down the hierarchy. Figure 8.5 illustrates this idea. Each map computes events at the next level from sets of events at the level below.[7]

Flexibility of Hierarchy Definitions

Notice one other property of an event hierarchy—*flexibility*. Event hierarchies are flexible in the sense that they can be easily changed. A new level of events can always be inserted between existing layers or added at the top or bottom, and an existing level can be deleted. To do this, the mappings between levels must be added or changed.

For example, to add a new level between, say levels N and N + 1, one must add the event types of the new level and two sets of mappings, one from level N to the new level, and another from the new level to the

---

[6]*Some Internet Architectural Guidelines and Philosophy*, OSI Internet Working Group, 2002. http://tools.ietf.org/html/rfc3439, section 3.

[7]More generally, a map may use events from several lower levels below level N to compute an event at level N.

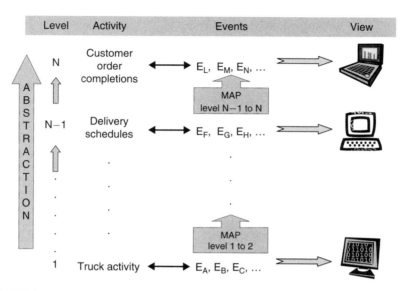

FIGURE 8.5 A Computable Event Hierarchy Using Mapping between Levels

old level N + 1 (which is now level N + 2). A computable event hierarchy is never set in stone!

Computable event hierarchies let us focus events within the enterprise for specific purposes at each level of activity and management. Experience also shows that the numbers of events decrease at higher levels, sometimes exponentially, as the information contained in sets of lower-level events is concentrated into single higher-level events. Intuitively speaking, higher-level events are *bigger* in the sense they contain more information than lower-level events, but there are *fewer* of them!

Classifying event types into a CEP hierarchy, as shown in Figures 8.3, 8.4, and 8.5, gives us a computable method of organizing the use of event abstraction. This is a fundamental concept of CEP. But it has to be done with care and precision to be useful.

Drill Down and Event Analysis

The complementary concept of *drill down* in a computable event hierarchy is equally important. It is the means of explanation. And it is to be considered a part of event abstraction.

Retrievability in a computable event hierarchy: Given an abstract event in a computable event hierarchy it is possible to retrieve the set of events that it abstracts.

For example, to analyze a successful sale event in the retail website we must be able to recall the sequence of events of that particular website visit. Note that two identical successful sale events (i.e., same customer, items, sale amount, but at different times) might well abstract different sequences of website activity. Perhaps on the first visit the customer chose and then returned some items, whereas on the second visit the customer knew exactly what was wanted.

The reason that retrievability is possible in event hierarchies is that computable event pattern maps can be reversed.

Every computable event pattern map has an inverse, called the *reverse map*. A reverse map, if given an event E at level N + 1 will retrieve the set of events at level N that comprise E.

Reverse maps allow *drill down* to provide explanations as to how higher-level events were constructed from sets of lower-level events, as illustrated in Figure 8.6.

For example, we can view a financial summary as being made up of financial accounting events. If a company-wide financial summary arrives on the CEO's desk, he might well ask to see the next level of detailed accountings that were used to compose that summary. This might result in a drill down through more levels of details. The next level down might consist of financial summaries by geographic or logistical region; at an even lower level, one might see the costing and profits from each type of company activity in a region.

Drill down in a real-time event hierarchy must be an automated operation; consider Example 8.8.

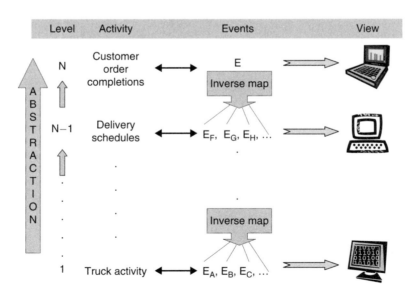

FIGURE 8.6 Inverse Mappings in a Computable Event Hierarchy

Example 8.8: Truck Feet Monitoring Revisited

The previous example of monitoring the activity a fleet of delivery trucks can be abstracted to allow two or three levels of monitoring for different purposes. Three possible levels, going top down from level 3 to level 1, with examples of the possible event types at each level, could be as follows:

3. *Top level: Sales and service profiles.* This level would monitor events such as the status of service agreements with customers, customer orders, sales and promotions, publicity on new products, demand forecasts and product manufacturing forecasts, . . .
2. *Middle layer: Supply chain forecast and management.* New product orders, product manufacture orders, warehouse management, restocking, delivery planning, delivery schedules, . . .
1. *Bottom layer: Fleet management.* Personnel schedules, truck maintenance schedules, truck status, warehouse stocks, immediate delivery planning, truck trip plans, . . .

Reverse maps between these layers would enable a manager of the delivery fleet to see explanations of events at the highest layer. For example, if there was a complaint from a customer about the timeliness of a delivery completion, the customer's order completion event could be expanded using a reverse map to immediately see in real time the events that were executed in the associated delivery schedule. If a number of separate deliveries were involved in the order, each of those deliveries would be second-level events. These second-level events could also be expanded using reverse maps in real time to see the timing of the delivery truck movements, loading, route execution, and deliveries. If the customer's complaint was correct, the actual components of the order that were behind schedule could be traced, together with the causes for the contract violation. Diagnosis might suggest corrective actions.

Every detail of these abstraction examples can be argued with: which events should be at each level, are there events that should have been included at a particular level, pairs of events that should or should not be at the same level of abstraction, and missing levels of abstraction. All of which illustrates a crucial point in applying the notion of hierarchy to organizing events: the need for *flexibility* to modify an event hierarchy, add new levels of events, delete levels and change, or delete or add mappings to the hierarchy.

Summary: Dealing with Information Overload

The need for analyzing large numbers of raw events and concentrating the information they possess for different purposes and different users will increase the importance of the CEP abstraction and hierarchy techniques we have described. When this technology is introduced, we predict that the separate demands of the different users will surface and be made more explicit.

Bearing in mind that the input sources of events will be ever expanding and that the variety of types of input events will continue to grow,[8] here is a short summary of the advantages and capabilities of computable event hierarchies:

1. *Focused information.* A primary advantage is to provide different role players in an enterprise with the kind of information they need abstracted from the available event sources. Each job requires a different kind of information. Network administrators need lower-level network events and statistics, while managerial levels need more abstract information (see Figure 8.4). The views in a hierarchy should reflect those requirements.

2. *Efficiency of event processing.* The numbers of events at each level in a hierarchy will decrease exponentially. Processing higher-level views will be less demanding in terms of scale of input event throughput, although making the best use of higher-level views may require sophisticated analytical techniques.

3. *Understandability.* The principle that each event contains a fragment of the information needed means that a human must look at lots of lower level events to gain an understanding of that information. If the views in the hierarchy levels correspond to the "right" abstractions that the stake holders require,[9] then fewer higher-level events are needed to provide a humanly understandable view of the information.

4. *Flexibility.* A computable event hierarchy can easily be modified to meet the changing requirements to add new views of incoming events, to integrate new types of event sources into the views, or to eliminate existing views. Adding a new level of events is achieved by defining that level and the mappings between it and the levels above and below. Deleting a level involves composing the two layers of

---

[8]See Chapter 6, the section entitled, "Patterns and Pattern Matching," and the expanding input principle.

[9]Defining the hierarchy requires the end users be kept in the loop at all times.

maps into a single layer of maps spanning the gap between the levels below and above. Usually this is a straightforward functional composition of the maps.

5. *Ease of process construction.* Fewer higher-level events will be needed to construct event-driven business processes. It is easier to define or modify event-driven business processes when the events are humanly understandable and the event patterns that trigger the processes involve small numbers of events.

6. *Correctness.* Questions of correctness of event-driven business processes are easier to analyze when humanly understandable events are involved, which usually means higher-level events.

CHAPTER 9

The Future of Event Processing

Complex event processing (CEP) will become part of the supporting technology service within the enterprise information infrastructure of the future. Some of the systems that use CEP as a supporting technology will evolve into global holistic event processing systems:

- Event processing becomes a supporting technology within the IT infrastructure
- Large-scale holistic event processing systems appear
- CEP disappears under the hood of these event-driven systems
- Businesses take a global view of information and events
- Five example areas where holistic event processing systems will emerge:
  1. Unifying air traffic control
  2. Pandemic watch
  3. Monitoring "the consequences" (Al Gore)
  4. Solving gridlock in the metropolis
  5. Tracking your information footprint

This chapter is about the kinds of *holistic event processing* systems that can be expected to emerge in the future and the role CEP will play in them. It is not about what will happen with absolute certainty. Rather, it is a vision of what may probably happen in the longer term and the reasons why that vision might turn out to be correct.

Taking Stock

At the present time, CEP is an event processing technology that is being marketed either as a standalone tool or as a visible component of a suite of business intelligence tools. Eventually, it will become a foundational technology within large application systems.

We believe CEP will become largely invisible to the average user of business event processing systems. This does not imply that CEP is somehow a failure; on the contrary. it will become an all pervasive essential technology—just as the TCP/IP network protocols are critical to our Internet systems today. The features of CEP described in Chapters 6 through 8, such as event patterns, abstract events, hierarchy definitions, and abstraction mappings, will be part of a technology arsenal used by technical support engineers and knowledgeable business specialists in building and using enterprise management systems. CEP technology will be available to users online through graphical interfaces and other user-friendly tools.

This is the final stage in the development of CEP technology, which we described in Chapter 4 in the section entitled "Ubiquitous CEP." It is what we mean by *disappearing under the hood* of large application systems.

At present, the range of market areas for event-processing applications is expanding, as we described in Chapter 5. Sales of CEP in these markets are increasing. And new markets and new kinds of CEP products are appearing all the time. We are well into the stage of *creeping CEP*,[1] and beginning to enter the next stage when CEP becomes an established information technology. From this position, we can look forward a few years and predict the longer-term future of CEP and of event processing in general.

First of all, present-day event processing applications are *small event type space*[2] applications (e.g., the examples in Chapter 5). They deal with a small number of different types of event inputs and produce a small number of different types of results. Of course, they may be processing large numbers of events and high volumes of event throughput. But the point is that each of these applications is dealing with a *limited variety of types of events*, and they are specialized to produce a *small number of types of results*.

For most of the current generation of commercial event processing applications, small event type space processing is all that is needed. And it is worth noting that many of the present applications have become

---

[1]See Chapter 4.

[2]See Chapter 7 for a definition of event type spaces.

important components of various commercial information infrastructures. They will endure for many years. We shall refer to these kinds of event processing systems as *specialized systems.* There will always be a need for these systems, and they are not going to disappear!

But over time, a new category called *holistic event processing systems* will emerge from the melting pot of IT systems. Holistic systems will have a global span, processing event inputs from different types of sources from all over the world in order to produce a wide variety of different types of results. The event types will be a mix of structured and unstructured kinds of data, and they will be continually expanded to include more events from *outside* of the company (e.g., news feeds; market data feeds; Web click streams; feeds from trade associations and government agencies; communications from mobile phones such as text messages, social computing sources such as Twitter, Facebook, etc.; GPS data; perhaps new types of sensors; and of course data from application systems that do not currently emit events). The actual set of types of event inputs may be configurable dynamically during operation.

Essentially, holistic systems will be *large event type space* systems in contrast to today's systems. They will employ many different, specialized technologies in their components (e.g., statistical analytic systems and predictive analytics, Monte Carlo simulation systems, constraint-based optimization systems, and rule engines) in order to satisfy the demands of different goals and objectives. CEP will be but one of these specialized technologies. Holistic systems will be open-ended, extensible event-processing systems.

This development in event processing is a natural consequence of increasing demands and expectations. Limiting the number of input event types not only helps to keep the event processing simple, but it also limits the results that the system can produce.[3] Most systems will start life as small event type space systems. This is just a matter of limited planning and goals, and of course, economics. But in the future, as the number of different kinds of applications of event processing increases, large global businesses and governments will demand more results from these systems. Therefore, we can expect some event processing systems to evolve to a point where they will see simultaneous use for many different purposes. They will become not only global systems, but also *holistic event processing* systems.

You can already see this trend in some of the examples in Chapter 5. In the case of businesses, it is a trend toward developing management

---

[3]The expanding input principle; in Chapter 7, see the section entitled "Restricting the Types of Event Inputs May Not Be an Option."

systems that encompass the total operation of the business. The idea is to achieve greater efficiency all round by using a single management system that has all aspects of the business within its reach.

There is a compelling example of broadening the space of input event types in the area of stock-trading systems. Some trading systems are now using event feeds from news aggregators, weather reports, and political news, together with sentiment attributes tagged onto each individual item of news, as additional input to trading algorithms. The idea is to factor in the old adage that "sentiment moves markets" into trading. One effect is to increase the number of types of event inputs beyond normal trading data.

Other kinds of businesses are now also exploring the use of public sentiment tagging and social media websites in the logistics that run their sales and marketing operations. The number of different types of events used in business operations is increasing, and some of these inputs would not have been predicted a short time ago!

The Evolution of Holistic Event Processing Systems

The term *holistic event processing*[4] applies to a class of event processing systems that process many different types of event inputs and combine many event processing applications on a global scale. These systems will evolve gradually over time by combining lots of smaller, specialized event processing applications.

Holistic Event Processing System: An automated event processing system, usually global in scope, based upon the integration of a large number of diverse event processing applications, processing many different types of event inputs, and producing many different types of results.

How many EP applications and different types of events and event sources? There are no specific numbers at which point an event processing system passes some invisible boundary and "goes holistic"! Holistic systems are *large event type space* systems. They will often be implemented as a loosely coupled network of event processing applications running on separate engines, each application being specialized to a particular problem area. But other configurations are possible, such as a network of satellite processors doing event gathering at local areas and some preprocessing before passing events onto a large central system.

Holistic event processing is a term used to describe a *scale* of event processing greater than today's systems. A holistic system will involve new

---

[4]The term *holism* was introduced by the South African statesman Jan Smuts in his 1926 book, *Holism and Evolution*. Smuts defined holism as "The tendency in nature to form wholes that are greater than the sum of the parts through creative evolution."

technology for combining sets of event processing applications and for making predictions from combinations of outputs of sets of applications. Its outputs will go well beyond the functionality of current systems, due to the use of large sets of types of event inputs and the combination of widely diverse event processing applications. The predictive capabilities will definitely involve new technology. You will recognize a holistic event processing system when you see one. We will give examples.

Example 9.1

One could imagine a holistic event processing system based upon satellite communications and composed of a dynamic global network of mobile smartphones—field agents, in effect. The phones would act as EPAs in the network, gathering and forwarding input events. They would feed input events, after filtering and a first level of event processing, to central processors that would correlate and abstract the event inputs, and produce output events. Output events would be fed back to the field agents for action. Field agents would possess different kinds of event gathering and processing capabilities. They may differ in the types of events they gather and process. Overall the system would be processing a large event type space. One of the dynamic aspects of this kind of network would be that field agents could come and go, entering and leaving the network at random.[5]

---

[5] The architectures of some tsunami warning systems follow this model nowadays, except that the input events are gathered by deep ocean buoys, not cell phones.

The reason that holistic event processing systems will evolve is to achieve demands beyond the reach of existing individual event processing applications. These demands will require combining the results of many different event searches and event computations. Existing systems will be incapable of meeting these demands without their capabilities being extended. So event processing systems will be cobbled together, gradually one by one over time, to form a wider reaching system. Truly, Aristotle's dictum will apply whenever such evolutionary compositions of applications are successful: *"The whole is greater than the sum of the parts."*

Holistic event processing systems will not be planned or designed or built as such. They will result from evolutionary development, usually by haphazard extensions of existing systems and many trial-and-error experiments and failures.

The following points are to be emphasized:

- Holistic event processing systems will result from a series of evolutionary steps, incorporating sets of specialized EP applications over many years.
- An enabling force for holistic event processing will be the development of new methods of combining the results of different kinds of event processing using sets of event processors operating in different event type spaces to yield new types of results for which demand has arisen.
- Holistic systems will result from the changing requirements for *right now* information and predictions from different departments within a company or different communities within a nation. This is coupled with the need to meet economic constraints on the costs of developing new event processing systems. Instead of building new separate systems, old systems will be added to and extended beyond their original designs.
- A holistic system will produce predictions that result from abstracting the output events from sets of its component EP applications. Many of its outputs will share the results of common components. And predictions may take the form of abstract events.
- CEP concepts and tools will be employed in various roles during the evolution of a holistic EP system.
- CEP will disappear into the event processing infrastructure of holistic EP systems and will no longer be visible to the user. It will become simply an enabling technology.

What kinds of new results might be demanded? There are many examples. A retail company may want to track demographic and social trends so that it will be continuously aware of opportunities to expand its business or make acquisitions to introduce new directions in response to trends in styles and fashion. Pharmaceutical manufacturers may find advantages in tracking and predicting epidemiology events, perhaps on a worldwide scale. And of course large oil companies should be monitoring pretty much everything from the weather to politics!

Event patterns and event abstraction, supported by distributed networks of event processing engines, will be an important technology in combining widely different types of event inputs to yield understandable views from which decisions can be made and actions taken *right now* (consider Example 9.2).

Example 9.2: A Large National Bank Seeking to Expand into New Areas of Business

A large national bank has maxed out its opportunities in traditional areas of banking. In its current retail banking business it processes about 50 types of input events for servicing bank accounts, credit cards, funds transfers, mortgages, and so on. Its inputs include customer life events (e.g., change of address, home purchases, births, and so on) in addition to the normal bank account management events. However, the bank is planning to expand its lines of business to include commercial banking, commodities trading, and eventually travel planning, cruise ships, hotels, and even wider business sectors. It is planning to eventually process more than 1,000 different types of event inputs across its new businesses and to develop the event processing network necessary to support this. It plans a two-tier CEP architecture. The first tier of CEP engines will do filtering and routing of raw input events, and then send the events to the second tier network. This tier will contain specialized CEP applications for fraud detection, sales and cross-sell/up-sell applications, etc. There will probably be multiple CEP applications for security and fraud and multiple applications for focused areas of sales. Eventually, the bank will be doing holistic event processing across a very large space of types of event inputs.

There will be demand for holistic systems in areas well beyond business. One area is earth sciences where there is a pressing need for more accurate predictions of earthquakes, tsunamis, and other natural disasters, as well as for long-term global climate-monitoring systems. Another area is predictive systems in epidemiology, where the evidence of emerging disease epidemics is often misjudged because contributing events arise from diverse sources at different times and are not correlated to build an accurate picture of what is happening. Management of world resources, such as food and energy, is an area in which holistic event processing may evolve in support of monitoring and planning systems. And there are many areas of automation in government where holistic event processing will play a supporting role. We shall return to these example areas.

Note: Holistic event processing systems go beyond the concept of a *federation*[6] of subsystems. A holistic system must incorporate technology

---

[6]L. M. Haas, E. T. Lin, and M. A. Roth, "Data Integration through Database Federation," *IBM Systems Journal*, Vol. 41, No. 4, 2002, pp. 578–596.

for combining the events that are output by the separate CEP systems, for making predictions based upon the results, and for applying hierarchical abstraction to the resulting sets of events. It is not simply a single-access system to multiple sources. However, a federation of CEP systems may well be a step in the evolution of a holistic system.

Crossing Boundaries

The evolution of holistic event processing will have to cross boundaries. The first are the boundaries of individual CEP products and vendors, since holistic EP systems will involve combining and integrating many different CEP applications from many suppliers. Indeed, boundaries may exist within the same company between different business units with their own CEP applications and boundaries. The second are sociopolitical boundaries. In some cases, these kinds of EP systems may be seen as a threat to various social and political issues, such as privacy, the rights of the individual, and other matters beyond the scope of our discussion.

Crossing boundaries will depend upon progress on a number of technical and nontechnical enablers:

1. *Comprehensive standards* in event processing.
2. *Technical innovations* in applying CEP to special problem domains in implementations of distributed networks of specialized CEP engines and in predictive analytics based upon large sets of events that are output from the specialized engines.
3. *Event processing infrastructures* that solve the scalability issues and permit the development of CEP capabilities for processing large event type spaces.
4. *Political will* involving agreement, collaboration, and funding between different business enterprises or government departments, or indeed the governments of many nations.

Progress on some of these enablers is already happening—for example, enabling infrastructures. The advent of cloud computing should be seen as a promising foundation for building the next-generation event processing infrastructures needed for holistic systems. And the proposed Internet of Things[7] may turn out to be a very large-scale holistic system indeed, even if only parts of it such as global sensor networks come to exist.

Some efforts are also underway within official standards organizations that should eventually lay down basic standards for event processing, such

---

[7] http://en.wikipedia.org/wiki/Internet_of_Things

as standards for event representations. As for technical innovation, that is happening all the time, although it is hard to predict.

Note: These enablers do not have to happen first before any progress towards holistic systems can take place. Development of the enablers and the holistic systems that they enable can, and most often do, take place simultaneously.

Indeed, it is hard to predict to what extent standards for event processing will be necessary. We guess that most standards will come after the first holistic systems emerge and become recognized as such, when the advantages of these systems become clear from the lessons learned. The evolution of holistic systems will be open-ended, opportunistic, and haphazard.

The Beginnings of Holistic Event Processing Systems

Today there are many examples of systems that may evolve into holistic event processing systems. This is a result of various pressures to expand the existing systems. As we described previously, some of these pressures include:

1. Economies of scale: Doing more for less
2. Unification of separate EP systems: Reaching goals and satisfying demands that can only be achieved by using the results of sets of the individual components
3. Competition within the marketplace
4. Social, political, and economic pressures

The first three pressures apply to many kinds of information systems. Example 9.2, describing a large national bank that plans to expand its lines of business beyond the domain of banking, is the result of these kinds of pressures within a single business organization.

Point 4 is an observation that powerful forces are beginning to arise in favor of achieving economic and humanitarian goals that can only be attained with the help of global event processing. Some of these we have already mentioned, such as a need for organizing warning and response systems to natural disasters like earthquakes and floods, worldwide food shortages, and disease epidemics. There are also pressures to build systems that *predict* these kinds of emergencies.

Some possible future holistic systems are already in the early stages of evolution today, and their evolutions are haphazard, as we predicted. This is happening:

- With little or no knowledge of CEP techniques
- With an implicit assumption that networking will be an adequate support platform for the huge amount of event inputs of many event types that are already available

- With little planning to how to support all the different kinds of event processing technologies that will be needed (e.g., event causality, correlation and abstraction, event hierarchies, communication between event processing systems, and the aggregation of the results of separate event processing systems)

Nobody is thinking about these emerging systems as being "holistic," but that is what they will evolve to become!

Example 9.2, the large national bank that is planning to expand its businesses, is a possible example of an embryonic holistic event-processing system.

A compelling example is the United States Geological Survey (USGS) Natural Hazards website, described in Chapter 4. See the section on the creeping CEP stage of development, and Figures 4.4 and 4.5. The USGS NHSS website displays near real-time information from a large number of different types of event sources, including satellites, deep ocean buoys, surface buoys, and land-based remote automated weather stations (RAWS) around the United States,[8] and in some cases around the globe, earthquake sensors, volcano monitors, water monitoring stations, forestry monitoring sensors, National Weather Service reports, and many other sources. All inputs are real time or near real time. Refresh and update rates for inputs vary from minutes to two hours. All in all, the actual number of input event sources to this facility must number in the tens of thousands.

The NHSS information is displayed on a dashboard with an interactive world map. There are graphical tools for manipulating the map, such as zoom and focus, and for displaying location specific information. For example, as a hurricane nears a shoreline, NHSS users can see its proximity to their current location and they can access real-time information on stream levels, wind speeds, and tide conditions for their location. The system also provides historical weather and natural hazard information for locations on the displayed map.

The goal of the USGS website is to construct a facility that provides national and local government authorities, fire and police departments, first aid planners, road work crews, and a host of other potential users (including private individuals) with an early warning system for potential natural disasters. As a system, it is clearly attempting to integrate a number of other systems. For example, the system of RAWS within the United States was developed to provide weather data to assist

---

[8]There are nearly 2,200 remote automated weather stations (RAWS) located throughout the United States (USGS, 2008).

land-management agencies with monitoring air quality, rating fire danger, and providing information for research applications. But the RAWS system alone is not sufficient to make predictions about future hazards, even in the near term.

The USGS Natural Hazards Support System (NHSS) could evolve into a truly holistic event processing system, processing many thousands of event sources and producing many different types of predictive events. At present, users must make their own interpretations and conclusions from the information it displays. If, for example, they miss some of the information, their conclusions may be drastically wrong, as say in the case of trying to predict hazards that might result from earthquakes.[9]

The NHSS system needs to evolve to another level of service. One possible next step would be to add different types of event abstraction. Predictive models need to be incorporated into the system. These might enable inferences to be made from events appearing on the website. As new events appear, the predictions would be continuously updated. Data from previous events can be stored to test these models.

As Figure 4.5 in Chapter 4 illustrates, an event aggregation facility is needed that could correlate events at close locations from the present and recent past, together with terrain knowledge and historical data, to develop potential hazard warnings for possible imminent threats such as avalanches, mudslides, wildfires, high tidal waves, floods, and so on. Abstracting from different sources of events together with historical data to create alert events, and doing it for different kinds of hazard situations, would certainly put the system into the sphere of holistic applications.

But the types and numbers of event inputs for the continental United States are far more numerous and detailed than for the rest of the world, so at the moment the USGS NHSS is far from being the worldwide system it could be.

That said, the NHSS system is an event processing system that is evolving into a holistic system. It has all the ingredients: a large space of input event types, a large community of possible users requiring different types of information as outputs, and the need to process incoming events in real time. What is needed are predictive capabilities, political will, and economic backing. And its evolution may well be helped by the advent of new predictive methods in earth sciences.

---

[9]The effects of the Richter 9.1 Sumatra-Andaman earthquake in December 2004 (http://en.wikipedia.org/wiki/2004_Indian_Ocean_earthquake) were underestimated, and those of the Richter 8.8 earthquake in the Pacific off the coast of Chile in February 2010 (http://en.wikipedia.org/wiki/February_2010_Chile_earthquake) were overestimated by current methods.

Of course, there are many components to effective natural disaster warning systems beyond event processing predictive systems. Long-term planning includes building codes, shelters for the community, education, response systems involving police and the military, and many other facets, as in the case of the Japanese earthquake and tsunami of 2011.[10,11] Such long-term planning takes the political will to do it. Even so, warning systems take time to react. And while the Japanese situation would have been much worse without the long-term planning, there was almost no time to react. Hawaii, in contrast, was much better prepared for the same event. Because of the National Oceanic and Atmospheric Administration (NOAA)'s Pacific warning system, Hawaii had time to react to its warnings and prepare for the tsunami.

Where would the necessary political will to develop the NHSS system in the United States come from? It is quite possible that if a natural disaster with large economic consequences happens in the United States, there could be political pressure upon various government agencies such as NOAA to develop a comprehensive disaster prediction and warning system. In response, those agencies might see the NHSS system as a promising starting point. The rest would depend upon funding.

In the following sections, we shall make a case for believing that several other examples of event processing systems are now in an early stage of evolution toward becoming holistic systems.

Future Air Travel Management Systems

Air travel systems today are a good example of business systems in chaotic bits and pieces all over the place—systems on the "garage floor," so to speak. Here are the titles of some articles on the airline industry that have appeared over the past few years:

- "Increasing air travel, air freight, private aviation, light weight air limousine industry and proposed 'flying cars'"
- "Climate effects of aviation"
- "Crowded air space"
- "Current air traffic control systems are outdated 50 year-old technology"
- "Safety, efficiency, scalability—an autonomous, globally integrated ATC system is needed"

---

[10] Max Fisher, "Why Japan Was Ready," *The Atlantic*, March 14, 2011. www.theatlantic.com/international/archive/2011/03/why-japan-was-ready/72429

[11] Japan Meteorological Agency, "What Is an Earthquake Early Warning?" www.jma.go.jp/jma/en/Activities/eew1.html

The simple statistics describe the situation. In 2009, the world's air transportation system flew 2.3 billion people safely on 35 million flights—the equivalent of between a quarter and a third of the entire world's population. The air traffic across the north Atlantic itself was some 185,000 flights going in each direction. According to the U.S. Federal Aviation Administration, there were around 7,000 aircraft in the air over the United States at any given time in 2010.[12]

The current air traffic management systems (ATMs) have evolved from systems that were developed in the 1960s. Some of the components have been improved, and some new components have been added. But there are many separate systems in the air and on the ground that should interoperate but do not. The whole structure is creaking at the seams. As a consequence, there are plans by various government agencies in the United States, Canada, China, and Europe to put new air traffic management systems in place.

A future air traffic management system will be a holistic event processing system par excellence. It will no longer be ground-centric. The primary basis for air traffic control will be air-to-air communication between aircraft based upon satellite location. It will manage not only the movement of aircraft in the air across the nation, but also on the ground through airports. It will incorporate advanced planning to smooth the total flow of air traffic in the face of weather and other outside events. The system will manage all air traffic across the nation; eventually it will evolve into a worldwide ATM system.

A good example of the evolution toward future air traffic management systems is found in the United States' plans for the NextGen[13] system, which is a transformation of the entire National Airspace System (NAS). NextGen is planned to be developed in stages between 2010 and 2025. Various components will be developed and tested within the existing air traffic control system.

To understand the scope of the event processing involved in this system, we go into a bit more detail. NextGen has five core event driven components:

1. ADS-B, an on-board aircraft control system
2. SWIM (System Wide Information Management), which supplies the same second-by-second data to controllers and pilots

---

[12] U.S. Federal Aviation Administration website. http://www.faa.gov/air_traffic/briefing

[13] Automatic dependent surveillance-broadcast (ADS-B). http://en.wikipedia.org/wiki/ADS-B

3. NextGen Data Communication systems that supply air traffic control data to the cockpit computers and display screens (enabling controllers on the ground and pilots in the air to see the same screens)
4. NNEW (NextGen Network-Enabled Weather), a real-time picture and summary of weather data across the nation in four dimensions, delivered to all concerned
5. NVS, a single voice communication system or voice switch, for air/ground and ground/ground voice communications for the entire National Airspace System

At the core of the NextGen system is an on-board aircraft control system, ADS-B (automatic dependent surveillance-broadcast technology), which is a satellite-based technology. Using ADS-B, each aircraft broadcasts its identification, position, and speed with once-per-second updates. ADS-B on-board transponders receive GPS signals and use them to determine the aircraft's precise position in the sky. This and other data are then broadcast to other aircraft and to air traffic ground control. At the same time, each aircraft is receiving similar data from every other aircraft and ground station in its vicinity (see 9.1).

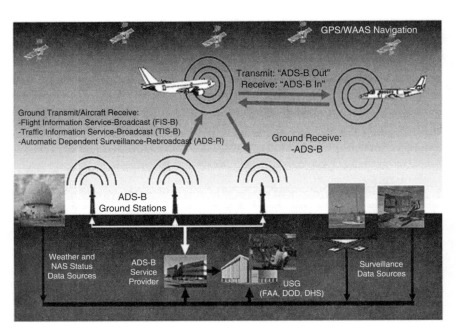

FIGURE 9.1 ADS-B System for On Board Flight Control and Routing

So a lot of different types of *right now* events are being received and generated by each aircraft. The goal of every aircraft using ADS-B is to give both pilots and air traffic controllers the same real-time display of the air traffic situation. If everyone is on the same page, so to speak, the result should be improved safety.

NextGen designers envisioned a future in which a series of event stream communications is used to define a flight. It will be a case of flight-deck computers exchanging streams of events with computers on the ground. Pilots and ground controllers, both using ADS-B, will simply confirm the flight paths that are planned by the system.

Obviously, NextGen itself will be a very large event processing system. Pilots and dispatchers will have the freedom to select their own flight paths, rather than follow a path on today's railroad-like grid of predefined flight paths in the sky. Each airplane will transmit and receive precise information about the time at which it and others will cross key points along their paths.

The hope is that NextGen, with ADS-B in place, will shorten virtually every commercial airline route, save fuel and time, enable the amount of air traffic in the skies at any one time to be increased, and finally also reduce aircraft engine emissions.

There is a parallel development effort for a new European Union air traffic management system called SESAR[14] or Single European Sky ATM Research, planned since 2004 and expected to be deployed by 2020. It will interoperate with NextGen. SESAR plans full integration of airport operations as part of ATM.

One of the issues with NextGen is how it will impact airlines, both from a financial and an event processing perspective. Nobody really knows yet!

On the financial side, figures anywhere up to $40 billion over the next 10 years have been mentioned. The costs to airlines for new equipment are estimated at half of this, which has been a stumbling block. Nobody wants to pay, not the government and not the airlines.[15] But there are also estimates that the costs of doing nothing will be higher. In resolving the complicated politics of NextGen, *political will* must play a very large role!

---

[14]European Commission Mobility & Transport, "What is the SESAR Project?" April 15, 2011. http://ec.europa.eu/transport/air/sesar/sesar_en.htm

[15]Between 2007 and 2011 bills to finance the FAA for NextGen were stalled 18 times in the U.S. Congress: Jad Mouawad, "Untangling the Skies," *New York Times*, April 2, 2011. http://query.nytimes.com/gst/fullpage.html?res=9F05EFDB1130 F931A35757C0A9679D8B63&scp=1&sq=jad%20mouawad%202011%20 untangling&st=Search

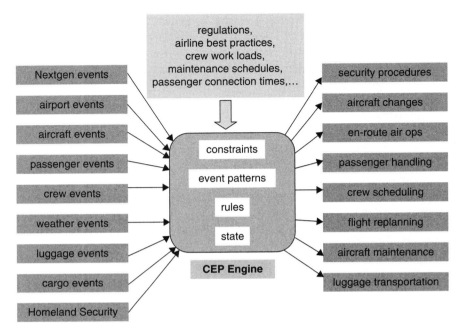

FIGURE 9.2 Numerous Event Spaces Contribute to a Large Airline's Future Unified Operations System

Consider the future operations management system for a single airline by the time NextGen is operating. From an event processing perspective, extrapolating from the situation today, a single airline's unified operational system will handle a very large number of different types of events coming from all the different systems that the airline will deal with. NextGen is only one of the event sources. Figure 9.2 schematically depicts a small part of the event processing for the operations of a large airline. By 2025 or thereabouts, the events could span everything from passengers and crew and airports to the core domain of flight operations.

This will be a *holistic event processing system*:

- *Input-event types.* Input-event types, like "NextGen events" (see Figure 9.1), include all the types of events flowing between each of the airline's aircraft and other aircraft and all the NextGen subsystems during the course of a flight. And then there are all the other types of events involved in crew scheduling; passenger-booking system events; security; airport operations such as runway control; gate management; airline connection updates; and support systems such as aircraft maintenance, and the like . . . Plus there are more events from partner airlines. You can imagine the rest! There are hundreds of different types of input events.

- *Output-event types.* These are the types of events that drive an airline's operations in *right-now* time. They span all operations and directives dealing with passengers, crew, aircraft, airports, flight schedules and delays, weather reports, catering supplies, and on and on. Again, there is a large number of varied output types.

- *State.* Finally, the state of the airline's operations system itself—which will be a system distributed over many server clouds worldwide. This will contain regulations, the airline's policy guidelines and other constraints on operations, event patterns that are being monitored *right now*, and reactive rules that codify the airline's best practices. This state is being continuously updated.

- *CEP.* CEP technology will be used in a number of subsystems. Some obvious examples are:

  - *Security.* As we have seen in Chapter 5, event patterns play many roles in security and in command-and-control operations. CEP should be used in much the same roles in the security for all the operations of an airline.[16]

  - *Airborne operations.* These are event patterns for on-board prediction and early recognition of emerging air traffic situations during the operation of any flight. This part of the system is critical to the *right-now* operation of aircraft in an ever more demanding environment.

  - *Flight planning.* A library of common real-time air traffic patterns for all areas of operations will be a basic resource in planning the operation of each flight. These event patterns will become quite complex, including not only air-traffic event patterns but also the operations of airports, the patterns for handling passengers, weather patterns for areas en route, and many other factors.

  - *Support-systems prediction.* All airline operations are affected by supply chains and support systems, such as aircraft parts for maintenance, the operations and performance of subcontractors, airport operations, and so on. Conversely, many of the events that occur in airline operations affect the supply chain management systems that are running in other companies (suppliers, customers, freight forwarders, agents, etc.), so the airlines will need to send supply chain prediction events to their subcontractors and partners, too.

---

[16]One of the criticisms of the NextGen plans has been the lack of planning for the security of its operations.

■ *Sales and services.* Passenger and cargo systems involved in sales and services.

Holistic airline operations-management systems will *evolve* from the current systems piece by piece. They will not be designed and built anew, but will evolve while in use. At every turn in their development, they will cross different boundaries. Various international and government regulations, technical IT boundaries as the component pieces are gradually unified, employee union issues, and the problems of collaborating with the existing operational systems of partners, or perhaps merging with other airlines. It will be a chaotic evolution.

Will such systems ever happen? If one reviews the development scenario we have just outlined, one would have to be skeptical. There is a very good chance that such an evolution will progress partway and stop at some point in the future. The airline would then be running on several separate unconnected EP systems, an intolerable situation! On the other hand, there will be increasing pressures for efficiency and interconnecting airline operations, as well as economies of scale that argue in favor of unified holistic operations-management systems for airlines. So we argue that whatever the outcome, the new systems that do emerge, even if they go only partway to what we have described, are quite likely to be holistic event processing systems.

Monitoring Human Activities

It is difficult to select just one example of a system for monitoring worldwide human activities to illustrate the role of event processing and CEP as an enabling technology. There are so many existing systems—and none of them are coping adequately with the problems they are intended to address. For example there are:

■ Pandemic watch systems
■ Drug-trafficking and money-laundering detection systems
■ Basic resources monitoring systems (food, energy, water)

that are currently operated by separate organizations such as the United Nations (UN), the World Health Organization (WHO), and various national agencies. They all lack a basic event-driven IT infrastructure. These systems are now used to monitor events in different activity areas on a worldwide basis. Some of them drive enforcement systems as well—rather badly, in fact. All of them are event-driven IT systems, although the EP technology is hidden from view and is never mentioned at a level of operating the system. It is well recognized by the organizations concerned that these systems need to be improved. But the question is how to do it.

As a first step, there needs to be a lot more use made of event pattern detection and other CEP technology in these systems, because they are essentially tasked with doing event correlation, event-pattern detection, and abstraction to achieve their goals.

Longer term, as they develop, it is a good bet that these human activity monitoring systems are destined to become holistic event processing systems. Their scope of application will expand due to the pressures we have outlined previously.

For example, a worldwide drug-trafficking system has to monitor resources such as the movement of money, ships, planes, and people, while also factoring in all manner of demographic and economic events. So its input-event space certainly overlaps with the event spaces of the other systems.

Perhaps one day, far in the future, these systems may all finally evolve into a single global system, although many obstacles, both technical and political, will have to be overcome. Certainly, federation may be an evolutionary step. But abstracting combinations of the monitoring results and predicting longer-term outcomes cannot be achieved by simply federating the separate systems.

Here we choose to focus on future monitoring systems for outbreaks of infectious diseases as our example of holistic event processing in the area of monitoring human activities.

Pandemic Watch Systems

Early detection systems that watch for outbreaks of infectious diseases with the potential to grow into epidemics are in their infancy at the moment. Progress needs to be made toward developing epidemic warning systems that span the world. For example, here are some recent quotes from various WHO officials and reports:

- "Infectious diseases are now spreading geographically much faster than at any time in history." (WHO report, August 22, 2007)
- "Over the last five years alone, WHO experts have verified more than 1,100 epidemics of different diseases."
- "With more than 2 billion people traveling by air every year, an outbreak or epidemic in one part of the world is only a few hours away from becoming an imminent threat elsewhere."
- "The question of a pandemic of a human form of avian influenza virus (H5N1) is still a matter of when, not if."

As Dr. Larry Brilliant, an expert on disease pandemics, puts it:

> . . . simulations of a Bird Flu pandemic today show that it will happen very quickly, from first observed case to global involvement, 3 weeks.[17]

There are many examples of infectious disease outbreaks where early detection systems would have helped curtail outbreaks and save lives, had they existed. Perhaps the latest is the 2009 outbreak of the H1N1 virus, which started on a pig farm in central Mexico sometime in 2008. It mutated into an infection that jumped from pigs to humans. Despite attempts to contain it in Mexico, it broke out in the United States early in 2009 and spread into a world epidemic during that year.[18]

But luckily H1N1 flu was a relatively mild form of this disease. There are far worse highly infectious diseases out there. The real problem is the speed with which they can travel between continents and populations these days.

This is clearly an area where holistic event processing can and will be used.

We can get a good idea of the kinds of event processing required in a pandemic watch system by studying existing systems. Notable among these are the Canadian Global Public Health Information Network (GPHIN), PROMED-mail,[19] and the National Health Service (NHS) QFLU system for detecting flu outbreaks in the United Kingdom.

GPHIN

GPHIN was created in 1998 by Health Canada's Laboratory Centre for Disease Control, in collaboration with WHO. It has since undergone continuous development. It is a fee-based electronic reporting service that continuously searches electronic media sources from around the globe. It gathers news reports related to public health and other topics from news wire services, including foreign language services such as Factiva and Al Bawaba (Farsi news reports), as well as thousands of website. The reports are processed and provided to subscribers. In some cases, email alerts to subscribers are triggered.

---

[17]Larry Brilliant, "Larry Brilliant Wants to Stop Pandemics," TEDtalks, July 2006. www.ted.com/talks/larry_brilliant_wants_to_stop_pandemics.html

[18]2009 Flu Pandemic. http://en.wikipedia.org/wiki/2009_flu_pandemic#Epidemiology

[19]Since October 1999, ProMED-mail has operated as an official program of the International Society for Infectious Diseases, a nonprofit professional organization with 20,000 members worldwide.

Input reports from the sources are subject to an automated translation step: The non-English articles are "gisted" into English using a machine translation engine. The purpose of the gist is to provide a report in English with the essence of the original article.

Inputs are then passed through an automated processing step that filters them for relevancy to public health issues, sorts them into eight categories, and then ranks them for importance. Those of high-enough rank are published to the GPHIN database. Articles with relevancy below the "publish" threshold are presented to a GPHIN analyst, who reviews the article and decides whether to publish it, issue an alert, or dismiss it. Those judged to be of "immediate concern" result in email alerts to subscribers.

Additionally, the GPHIN analyst team conducts more in-depth tasks, including linking events in different regions, identifying trends, and assessing the health risks to populations around the world.

Subscribers can access a stream of reports on the GPHIN website 24 × 7. Normally, about 4,000 reports are published per day, but in times of crisis this number has risen as high as 20,000. Subscribers receive alerts and can review the reports in one of several different languages (currently, Arabic, English, French, Russian, Simplified and Traditional Chinese, and Spanish).

GPHIN tracks a broad range of topics, such as disease outbreaks, infectious diseases, contaminated food and water, bioterrorism and exposure to chemical and radio nuclear agents,[20] and natural disasters. GPHIN also monitors issues related to the safety of products, drugs, and medical devices. Events that may have serious public health consequences are given the highest rank.

GPHIN alerted the Western world to the Severe Acute Respiratory Syndrome (SARS) outbreak in 2002. This occurred in Guangdong Province in mainland China; it was detected and reported by GPHIN as early as November 27, 2002, three months ahead of the official WHO alert on February 25, 2003. Interestingly, GPHIN was alerted to monitor for SARS by an input that was a financial report about a pharmaceutical company's increased sales of antivirals in the Guangdong Province. The report attributed the increased sales to the unusual outbreak occurring in that region.[21]

This example illustrates the need for epidemic warning systems to process a wide variety of different types of events. So, although its main function is clearly in the medical event area, the GPHIN system is tending to "go holistic" in the number of different types of input events.

---

[20] Radio nuclear agents are radioactive chemicals capable of causing injury.

[21] Michael Blench, "Global Public Health Intelligence Network (GPHIN)," Proceedings of the 8th AMTA Conference, October 2008, pp. 299–303.

In summary,

> *Input events* are pulled from several hundred different sources and
> enter the system at a rate of a few thousand per day. These inputs
> are processed by a system that is partially automatic, but has
> human analysts in the loop.
> *Output events*, both to the GPHIN website and in the form of alerts and
> notifications to subscribers, are at the rate of a few hundred per
> day. A report may take several days or even weeks to reach the
> website or result in an alert. This was barely adequate in the year
> 2002, and in today's world it will prove to be too slow.

The human-in-the-loop aspect of GPHIN certainly slows it down.

The need to improve the speed of reporting and to extend the reach
of the system beyond Internet sources is well understood. As one of
GPHIN's core implementers put it:

> We need to increase the "grass roots" sources because that is where the
> "early warning" aspect lies. "Cream skimmers" like AP [the Associated
> Press news service] rarely venture to the local newspaper in some small
> village in rural China where some strange malady has struck.

Other alerting systems, such as the Program for Monitoring Emerging
Diseases (PROMED-mail)[22] and the United Kingdom's QFLU have a similar
underlying dependence upon event processing technology. PROMED-mail
is completely based upon the Internet for information gathering and
reporting. Interestingly, PROMED states that it maintains independence
from governments on the grounds that independence helps it avoid issues
of governmental delay or suppression of disease reporting for bureaucratic
or strategic reasons. There are ongoing projects to make information flowing into PROMED-mail available on Google maps.[23]

GOARN

The Global Outbreak Alert & Response Network[24] (GOARN) is a complementary system to GPHIN to respond to alerts. It was set up by member nations of the WHO in 2000 and now has a network of more than

---

[22] International Society for Infectious Diseases, ProMED-mail website. www
.promed-mail.org

[23] www.cdc.gov/eid/content/15/5/689.htm

[24] WHO, Global Outbreak Alert & Response Network. www.who.int/csr/outbreak
, network/en/

120 partner nations throughout the world. The partners pool resources, including personnel, equipment, and laboratories.

GOARN's outbreak response teams are assembled and mobilized to countries where a disease outbreak is occurring. The teams offer medical and logistics support to the national health authorities to coordinate and direct activities in response to an outbreak. The SARS outbreak was the first time that GOARN responded to an outbreak that was rapidly spreading internationally.

During the first six months of 2006, WHO/GOARN mobilized more than seventy operational interventions in response to avian influenza (AI) outbreaks and human transmission. Currently, GOARN responds to more than fifty outbreaks in developing countries each year. For example, a recent GOARN mobilization was in response to an outbreak of cholera in Haiti.[25]

Today the mission includes operating a "comprehensive event management system to manage critical information about outbreaks and ensure accurate and timely communications between key international public health professionals, including WHO Regional Offices, Country Offices, collaborating centres and partners in the Global Outbreak Alert and Response Network." Exactly how this event-management system is implemented is not clear, nor is its response delay time, but it is almost certainly "human-in-the-loop."

Future Epidemic Warning Systems

In the best of all worlds, there would be a single unified system for detecting and responding to epidemic outbreaks and other emergencies anywhere in the world. It could take many forms—for example, a federation of separate systems covering specific areas.

It would have to be a holistic event processing system correlating a wide range of inputs. Figure 9.3 shows some of the event processing in such a system. It is at best a sketch, but it illustrates that a holistic event processing system would be needed.

The range of input-event types spans everything from field messages, both text and voice, from mobile phones, PDAs, and other handheld devices to official alerts and reports from health agencies:

- *Mobile phone and text messages.* This class of inputs are events closest to the "grassroots" (i.e., possible locations of outbreaks). They will come from area inhabitants, field workers, and local health personnel

---

[25] Pan American Health Organization, "GOARN Team Deployment to Haiti," blog entry, November 24, 2010. http://new.paho.org/blogs/haiti/?p=1377

and may be in multiple languages. In rural areas, mobile phones may be the only communication devices available. In fact, a recent study shows that the number of mobile phones in use worldwide has topped 5.0 billion, boosted by soaring demand in emerging markets India and China.[26] So these events will probably be the most important in terms of early detection. But they are also the most in need of event filtering and correlation—in other words, quite advanced event processing at step one!

■ *Social networks.* The adoption of this activity by the inhabitants of rural areas in, say, southeast Asia, is quite surprising and on the increase. The use of social networks such as Twitter by field workers and observers is a prominent feature in the planning of some of the future epidemic monitoring systems. It provides a scalable and rapid method of making field observations available to a very wide audience. And it is easily accessed using cell phones. But there are dangers in using this medium that we'll discuss shortly!

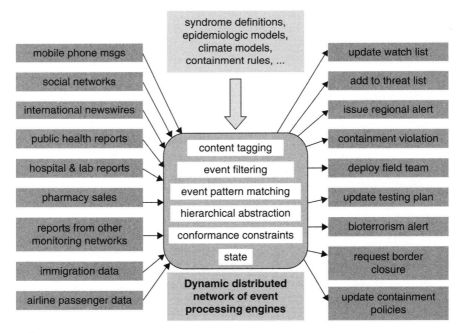

FIGURE 9.3 Event Processing in an Epidemic Warning and Containment System

---

[26] A study by Swedish telecom giant Ericsson, March 31, 2011, cited in "Mobile Phones in Use Worldwide Top 5.0 Billion: Study," Physorg.com, July 15, 2010. www.physorg.com/news198405924.html

- *Newswires.* These are often a second source of rumors and early news of emerging outbreaks. Again, their content is not reliable and needs careful review.
- *Clinics and hospitals.* Local-area medical facilities are also likely to produce early reports. Usually, these reports eventually find their way into reports from the area public health authorities, if such exist.
- *Pharmacy sales.* These can also be an indicator of an emerging epidemic, as in the case of SARS.
- *Travel and immigration data.* This information from airlines and border authorities will soon become important in tracking the spread of an epidemic and in predicting where medical resources may be needed.
- *Reports of other monitoring networks.* Networks such as GPHIN and PROMED-mail would probably act as confirmation to alerts issued by an effective warning system. The system would collaborate with other monitoring networks.

Output-event types vary from cautious early actions, such as adding a new event to a watch list or updating containment policies, to active actions, such as alerts for possible bioterrorism, to decisive emergency response actions, such as deploying field teams to the location of an outbreak or requesting border closures. This implies human-in-the-loop systems.

A broad range of input-event types is needed to correlate events from different sources and factor out unreliable reports. Moreover, an epidemic warning system has to pursue a careful line of decision making:

1. *It must minimize false positives.* Precautions against issuing alerts based on insufficient information (e.g., where an outbreak report is not confirmed or turns out not to be of international public health significance) must be taken to limit the economic impact on trade and travel.
2. *It should be able to uncover attempts to hide an outbreak.* For fear of economic impact regional authorities and governments have been known to be slow to issue health alerts that would have helped limit an outbreak.

For these reasons, all the inputs types we have described (and perhaps others) will be needed.

As for response times, we should expect the first types of cautious outputs (such as updating watch lists) within twenty-four to forty-eight hours of initial observations from the field. Reaction times for alerts and mobilizations will depend upon the rapidity and volume of inputs and how they correlate. This again argues in favor of processing the widest possible range of types of input events.

There are many possible uses of CEP in future epidemic warning systems. Much of the preliminary processing of incoming reports will be automated. It is here that CEP may be used in roles that would have been assigned to human agents in the earlier systems. We can expect CEP to play important roles wherever the detection of patterns of events is required—for example, in the recognition of potential outbreaks. And patterns of events will be used in the processes for (1) updating watch lists and containment policies, (2) formulating testing plans, and (3) identifying conditions for issuing alerts. CEP is likely to play a role in the formulation of these rules as well.

Monitoring the Consequences

The effects of human activities on the environment in which we all live have been studied by earth scientists for several decades. They have also been a topic of contentious political debate between those who understand the results of the scientific work and those who choose to disbelieve them for one reason or another—usually motivated by short-term self interests.

The results are not good, and one of the "effects" is more extreme weather events. This is generally referred to as *climate change*. Former Vice President Al Gore talks about a "period of consequences." Today, it is obvious that we are well into a period of suffering the consequences that Al Gore predicted.

The effects on the Earth and its environment are everywhere. They can clearly be seen in the new edition of *The Times Comprehensive Atlas of the World*:

> We can literally see environmental disasters unfolding before our eyes. We have a real fear that in the near future famous geographical features will disappear forever.[27]

Changes in the atmosphere and the oceans are already well-documented. The ocean, for example, is 30 percent more acidic than it was in 1800, and this trend is having critical results on the human food chain.[28]

We have wired our planet with measuring devices, and all of them generate countless numbers of events. There are more than enough earth

---

[27] Mick Ashworth, editor-in-chief of the *Times World Atlas*, 2007.

[28] Daniel Grossman, "UN: Oceans are 30 Percent More Acidic Than Before Fossil Fuels," *National Geographic Daily News* (website), December 15, 2009. http://newswatch.nationalgeographic.com/2009/12/15/acidification

observation and forecasting systems (EOFS) in existence to track every one of the human activity effects in the minutest detail: sensors on satellites, aircraft, balloons, deep ocean buoys and surface buoys, polar ice cap stations, land-based observation stations, stream gauges in rivers, and on and on.

There are many international organizations and partnerships aimed at processing the events from the earth observation devices and making the results available to everyone. They have put up open-ended websites that host event processing toolsets, grid computing, numerical analysis, predictive models for forecasting hazards (e.g., floods, coastal surges, tsunamis, landslides, etc.), data fusion tools and other stuff. Anyone can join in and contribute.

Among these environmental monitoring projects we mention:

■ *Global Monitoring for Environment and Security (GMES)* [29], a joint initiative of the European Commission and the European Space Agency. It is aimed at achieving an autonomous and operational Earth observation capacity to be fully operational by 2014. It will pull together "all the information obtained by environmental satellites, air and ground stations to provide a comprehensive picture of the health of Earth." The major unknown is how the information in all the collected events will be made available and what computing facilities will be available to study that information. That is not clear. The project seems to be following a path of chaotic evolution.

■ *Global Earth Observation System of Systems (GEOSS)* [30] is being built by the Group on Earth Observations (GEO), a partnership of 75 cooperating nations, including the United States, with a ten-year implementation plan from 2005 to 2015. It is a highly ambitious plan, shown in Figure 9.4, that may well fall short of some of its goals. The IT architecture to support this effort is not yet clearly specified. It will probably turn out to be an Internet portal with various tools that allow access to large quantities of data from all the measuring systems worldwide. If things turn out well, it may be based upon data representation standards that are yet to be determined.

■ *The Planetary Skin Institute (PSI)*,[31] an R&D project founded jointly in 2009 by Cisco and NASA to "cut across institutional, disciplinary, and national boundaries and create a space for flexible pooling of assets and ideas between stakeholder networks." It aims to develop

---

[29] European Commission Enterprise and Industry, "GMES: Observing Our Planet for a Safer World." http://ec.europa.eu/enterprise/policies/space/gmes

[30] Group on Earth Observations website: www.earthobservations.org

[31] Planetary Skin Institute website: www.planetaryskin.org

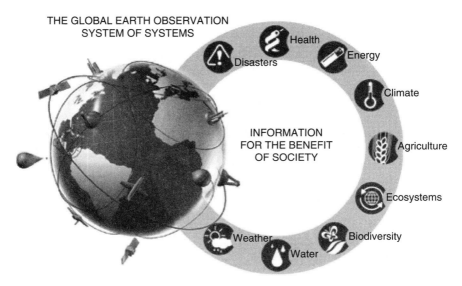

FIGURE 9.4 Graphic Used by GEOSS to Illustrate the Scope of Its Planned Missions

systems for monitoring the demand for water, energy, food, and land, and the resulting environmental degradation and climate change. As part of its mission to advance global multi-stakeholder collaboration, PSI is committed to building a decentralized peer-to-peer network for research and innovation, anchored by eight regional hubs in Brazil, India, China, South Africa, Japan, Middle East, the European Union, and the United States.

- *Various Advisory and Standards Panels* sponsored by international organizations, devoted to environmental monitoring, and possibly overseeing the implementation of systems that contribute to the *right-now* availability of monitoring data, (e.g., the Global Climate Observing System (GCOS)[32] and the Global Ocean Observing System (GOOS)[33]).

And there are many others. We cannot possibly list all the Earth monitoring projects that are ongoing at the moment.

Despite the official write-ups of GEMS, GEOSS, PSI, and the others, today's trend is toward making the vast amounts of observational

---

[32] GCOS website: www.wmo.int/pages/prog/gcos/index.php

[33] GOOS website: www.ioc-goos.org

events and the data they contain accessible using very simple and widely available Web-based "pull" technology. That is, most of these projects plan to put the observational events on Internet portals that can deliver access to the information in a way that is optimized for PDAs and smart-phones. The goal is instant access to everyone.

For example, a beta version of the PSI ALERTS platform is "an online cloud-based platform for near real-time global land change detection, and is available at no cost as a global public good to members of the public." It "provides visualization, layering, and customization tools for identify-ing and characterizing land use change. Users can view changes in space and time on the ALERTS geospatial platform, and subscribe to personal-ized alerts that will notify them via email whenever land use changes are detected in geographical areas of interest."[34]

All of these efforts are in the very good direction of dispelling disbe-lief and getting the true picture of our Earth's dilemma out there for all to see and understand. The political will to take positive action to correct the environmental situation must be energized.

But there are problems with all these well-meaning plans:

- The various subsystems have typically operated in isolation from one another as a conglomeration of separate projects.
- They are run by different organizations and governments.
- There is a need for integration technology: standards for formats, pro-tocols, and practices.
- These systems piggyback on existing networks—there is no scalable independent unifying event processing infrastructure. The plans rely on the Internet, and most projects are still being researched.
- The computing power needed may present a boundary. For example, Cisco estimates the global Internet traffic to be 63.9 exabytes per month in 2014.[35] Also, some estimates guess that in 2010 Google used more than 450,000 servers worldwide at a cost on the order of $2 million per month in electricity charges.[36]

---

[34] University of Minnesota, College of Science and Engineering, "Computer Scientists Launch Beta Version of New System to Track Global Land Change," http://cse.umn.edu/admin/comm/newsreleases/2010_12_07_planetary-skin.php

[35] Cisco Systems, "New Peering Standards for Ethernet Exchanges: Simplify Interconnections and Enable New Revenues," White Paper, 2010. p. 1. www.cisco.com/en/US/prod/collateral/routers/ps9853/c11-609224-00_ethernet_exchanges_wp.pdf

[36] Randall Stross, *Planet Google* (New York: Free Press, 2008) p. 61.

Perhaps NOAA's website describes the issues as well as any (emphasis has been added):[37]

> Today the many thousands of separate data systems in constant use usually don't work together. Decision-makers and users at many levels—farmers making planting choices, emergency managers making evacuation decisions, companies evaluating prospective building sites, nations battling drought and disease, parents checking daily weather reports—all take advantage of data from satellite remote sensing, aerial surveys, land or ocean-based monitoring systems and a vast array of socio-economic information. *But the Earth observation data being collected are just a fraction of what could be put to excellent, perhaps life-saving use in every region of the world.*
>
> Without comprehensive, integrated data sets, there are gaps in scientific understanding. Nature doesn't work just on land, in the sea, or in the atmosphere, and *taking the pulse of the planet requires an understanding of the intrinsic links of these Earth systems.*
>
> GEOSS is emerging to fill the gaps. With human ingenuity and the political will of 80 governments, GEOSS is a robust effort dedicated to building an integrated, comprehensive and sustained "system of systems" from many thousands of individual Earth observation technologies around the globe. This essential approach is as integrated as the planet that GEOSS is designed to observe, predict and protect.

NOAA pins our future hopes well and truly on the GEOSS consortium and planning. Indeed, the U.S. Environmental Protection Agency follows exactly the same plans.[38]

Any undertaking to monitor the consequences is going to be a truly holistic event processing project. A comprehensive supporting event processing infrastructure will be needed to make all of this worldwide event collection accessible in *right-now* time. It must process millions of events per second from a vast number of different types of sources, and then apply complex event pattern abstractions to produce higher-level events that allow humans to make decisions and take *right-now* actions.

Figure 9.5 does not do the project justice, but serves to illustrate parts of the input and output event type spaces and the holistic event processing

---

[37] NOAA, "Earth as a New Frontier: The World-Changing Capability of the Global Earth Observation System of Systems (GEOSS)." www.noaa.gov/eos.html

[38] U.S. Environmental Protection Agency, "Global Earth Observation System of Systems (GEOSS) and the Group on Earth Observations (GEO)." www.epa.gov/geoss

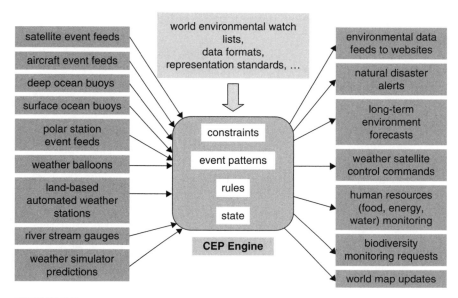

FIGURE 9.5 A Possible Snapshot of the Holistic Event Processing Involved in a Unified System for "Monitoring the Consequences"

that must be involved in supporting its implementation. The system would monitor event pattern constraints that detect trends toward situations that should not happen and should trigger alerts. It will execute rules that codify agreed policies and processes. The sets of constraints and rules would undergo continuous changes—a process that itself is challenging, since it will involve changes to processes that are currently executing.

The goal of a unified system: Continuous real-time estimates of long-term effects of human activity on the environment.

The most likely final implementation: A dynamic distributed network of millions of event processing engines, dynamic in the sense that some processors will enter or leave the network. It will evolve by a gradual federation of specialized event processing systems.

The magnitude of the holistic event processing that would be involved in a unified system for monitoring the consequences are enormous. This must raise doubts about whether such a system will ever evolve successfully from the bits and pieces that currently exist or are planned for the near future.

However, there are also arguments in favor of the evolution of such a system. First, there are commonalities between environmental monitoring and epidemic monitoring. For example, links between ocean temperatures and cycles such as El Niño and epidemics of infectious diseases such as malaria and dengue fever in many parts of the world have been established.[39,40]

Secondly, the quote from NOAA (above) states the case for such a system. GEOSS is only a first step. And *understanding the links* between separate earth monitoring systems is a step in earth science that will have to happen for there to be the political will to make a unified system a reality. Recall the enablers for holistic event processing systems:

1. *Comprehensive standards* in event processing
2. *Technical innovations* in applying CEP to special problem domains
3. *Event processing infrastructures* that solve the scalability issues and permit the development of CEP capabilities for processing large event type spaces
4. *Political will* involving agreement, collaboration, and funding between different business enterprises or government departments, or indeed the governments of many nations

Solving Gridlock in the Metropolis

Traffic congestion is a well-known hazard of large metropolitan areas the world over, and the economic costs have been the subject of both highway studies and political debate.

For example, in its study of 439 urban areas around the United States, the Texas Transportation Institute (Texas A&M University) found that American travelers are spending about 36 hours per year on average in traffic jams, and much more in the nation's largest cities. Collectively, Americans spent nearly 500,000 years stuck in traffic in 2007—nearly 4.2 billion hours. In 2009 the cost of traffic congestion was estimated at $115 billion in wasted fuel and lost productivity, or $808 per traveler per year.[41] Various government transportation secretaries, both in the United

---

[39] The Board of Global Health and the Institute of Medicine, "Climate, Ecology, and Infectious Disease," in *Global Climate Change and Extreme Weather Events: Understanding the Contributions to Infectious Disease Emergence: Workshop Summary*, www.ncbi.nlm.nih.gov/books/NBK45744/
National Academies Press (US); 2008. ISBN-13: 978-0-309-12402-7

[40] The World Health Organization, "El Niño and its health impact." www.allcountries.org/health/el_nino_and_its_health_impact.html

[41] Texas Transportation Institute, "2009 Urban Mobility Report and Appendices." http://mobility.tamu.edu/ums/report

States and the European Union, have made speeches on the costs of grid-lock in recent years.[42]

We can try building bigger highways and prioritizing "high occupancy vehicles," or taxing cars entering the metropolis. But these "solutions" have all been tried without really solving the problem. What comes next?

One direction in traffic research is to take the human driver out of the loop altogether and automate the management of the traffic. Highway systems that control traffic lights and the flow of cars on the roads are already in service. They are event driven systems. A next step is to make the car part of these systems—so-called drive-by-wire cars that drive them-selves and communicate with the traffic system and with one another to automate the management of traffic flow.

Building a drive-by-wire car depends upon solving four technical problems. The car must:

1. Understand its immediate environment (sensors technology)
2. Know where it is and where it wants to go (the navigation system)
3. Find its way in the traffic (the motion planning system)
4. Operate the mechanics of the vehicle (actuation)

Arguably, two and a half of these problems are already solved: navigation and actuation have been solved completely, and sensors have been solved partially, but are improving fast. The main unsolved part is the motion planning.[43]

The other half of the problem is to automate the highways. Highways must provide navigation and traffic information in a form that the new guidance systems in cars can use.

Work toward building driverless cars is in various experimental stages in the United States, Europe, and Australia. So far, experimental pilot proj-ects have combined magnetic sensors, forward-looking sensors, mobile wireless in cars, video cameras both in cars and on the highways, display technologies, and networks of computers spread out along the highway system. There have been several demonstrations of such systems around the world during the past fifteen years.

---

[42] For example, the E.U. telecoms commissioner at the time, Viviane Reding, said that 24 percent of driving time in Europe is spent in traffic jams, which could cost the E.U. economy €80 billion by 2010 (*Agence France Presse*, August 2008).

[43] Shawn Langlois, "The Car of Tomorrow Will Drive Itself—and Fly," *MarketWatch*, June 17, 2011. www.marketwatch.com/story/the-car-of-tomorrow-will-drive-itself-and-fly-2011-06-17

A totally automated traffic system, cars and highways, will certainly involve a lot of sophisticated event processing. It will entail using event patterns, real-time pattern matching, and event pattern abstraction to analyze traffic behavior and long-term trends. Hopefully, this use of event processing technology in automated traffic systems will contribute to reducing traffic congestion and increasing safety on the roads.[44]

The drive-by-wire car approach in the United States is an R & D project of the Department of Transportation based upon a dedicated wireless communication channel. Dedicated short-range communications[45] (DSRC) is the communications media of choice because:

- It operates in a licensed frequency band.
- It is primarily allocated for vehicle safety applications by FCC Report & Order—February 2004 (75 MHz of spectrum).
- It provides a secure wireless interface required by active safety applications.
- It supports high-speed, low-latency, short-range wireless communications.
- It works in high vehicle speed mobility conditions.
- Its performance is immune to extreme weather conditions (e.g., rain, fog, snow, etc.).
- It is designed to be tolerant to multipath transmissions typical with roadway environments.
- It supports both intervehicle and vehicle ↔ infrastructure communications between cars and the highway system.

That's a lot of events and event processing.

Note that DSRC[46] is preferred over wifi because the proliferation of wifi handheld and hands-free devices that occupy the 2.4 GHz and 5 GHz bands, along with the projected increase in wifi hot spots and wireless mesh extensions, could cause intolerable and uncontrollable levels of interference that could hamper reliability and effectiveness. Also, car safety applications require response times measured in milliseconds. DSRC enables vehicles to

---

[44] According to the National Highway Traffic Safety Administration (NHTSA), there are about 40,000 traffic deaths per year in the United States and a far higher number of serious injuries. www.nhtsa.gov

[45] www.intellidriveusa.org

[46] DSRC is similar to IEEE 802.11a except it operates in a 75 MHz licensed spectrum around 5.9 GHz, and it brings better wireless channel propagation with respect to multipath delay spread and Doppler effects caused by high mobility and roadway environments.

receive safety messages (e.g., road blocks ahead) and immediately determine if they should respond.

"Cars that drive themselves—even parking at their destination—could be ready for sale within a decade," is a quote from the director of research for General Motors Corp. in January 2008.

However, there is a question: Does the political will to "cross the boundaries" exist? The politics of traffic systems planning is complicated. Big money is involved!

For example, most experts agree that technology allowing cars to communicate with each other—and with the infrastructure—would make our highways safer and more efficient. But they disagree about who should have access to vehicles' computer systems and at what level. "Right now, automakers rigidly control access to their automotive operating systems in a way that even Apple Computer might find constricting."[47,48]

The European Union is actively researching drive-by-wire cars and infrastructure for an efficient and safe European road network. For example, the COM2REACT[49] project is to develop new technology that allows a group of vehicles to exchange data automatically with each other and with traffic control centers. The vehicle-to-vehicle communication has been tested in several urban traffic environments. And one of the stated goals of the project is to bring the cost per vehicle down to €100.

Building on this project, the European Safe Road Trains for the Environment (SARTRE) project[50] now aims at developing car-to-car communication so that cars can self-organize into platoons on highways at the usual rush hours times of the day. Each platoon has a professional driver in the lead and the other cars fall in behind and maintain distance by communicating with each other. Their drivers do nothing and can even take a nap during the trip.

An automated traffic system of the future will certainly involve holistic event processing. It will process event feeds from all surface traffic control systems (vehicles, video cameras, traffic lights, highway access controls, roadside sensors, etc.), police information systems, road works, media events, weather, airline and train schedules, and much else. It will factor

---

[47] Bryan Laviolette, "Experts Debate How Cars Will Talk to Each Other," *The Detroit Bureau*. www.thedetroitbureau.com/2010/08/experts-debate-how-connected-vehicles-will-talk-to-each-other, August 4, 2010.

[48] The U.S. DOT will decide by 2013 about requiring DSRC receivers in vehicles or possibly develop another communications system.

[49] The COM2REACT website: www.com2react-project.org

[50] The SARTRE Project website: www.sartre-project.eu/en/Sidor/default.aspx

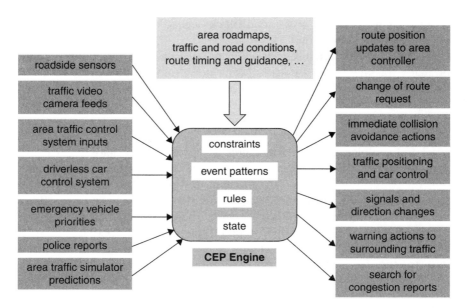

FIGURE 9.6 Holistic Event Processing Guiding Driverless Cars in Metropolitan Areas with Automated Wireless Traffic Control Systems

in traffic simulator predictions for the area, all in *right-now* time. It must produce directives for the automated traffic control systems, congestion and hazards alerts and rerouting guides, as well as highway situation forecasts for the emergency authorities.

We attempt to sketch the scope of the holistic event processing required for controlling a driverless car within an automated traffic system for a large metropolitan area in Figure 9.6. There are a wide range of different types of input events to the area traffic management system from the highway sensors, communications with cars, police traffic systems, weather forecasts, and many other sources. Similarly, the output events range from immediate motion planning of the car and traffic positioning to route planning and predictions.

Monitoring Your Personal Information Footprint

One of the most challenging uses of CEP might turn out to be to track the use of personal information on the Internet and protect it from misuse. The Internet has become a way of life. We all use it daily for such things as email, online banking, and credit card purchases. Bits and pieces of our personal information are out there, and few of us know what happens to all of it.

Today we face a continuous erosion of privacy. More and more data on individuals are collected electronically and made available to anyone for a small price—usually without the individuals' knowledge. Privacy laws do not keep pace with technology, and laws governing public records do not stop those records from being misused.

Personal Information Footprint: The totality of an individual's personal data, including, e.g., name, address, parents' names, social security number, passport number, bank accounts, medical records, Internet passwords, family history, and the like.

The problem: As individuals do more—shopping, talking, working—online, they leave private information behind in databases stored on servers that are not under the individual's control. Most companies store proprietary data on networked servers connected to the Internet; Internet vendors are a prime example. Computer security experts struggle to develop technology and best practices to protect this information from unauthorized intruders or inadvertent leaks. It's a losing battle!

The individual is powerless to control how his information footprint is used. The general situation is that once one's personal information is "out there," it may be subjected to many different uses.[51] Commonly, it can make its way from one mailing list to another, be sold to online marketers, used for targeted advertising, or misused in ways that cause direct loss to the individual. In the worst case, personal information is used to impersonate the individual to apply for credit cards or to steal directly from the individual's bank accounts. The costs of identity theft are high.[52]

In addition to the crooks, the individual must also worry about what happens to his information when it finds its way into a data fusion center.

As of July 2009 there are more than 72 state, local, and regional fusion centers in operation around the United States, and more in development. They are a relatively new tool for law enforcement, emergency management, and homeland security. Supposedly, fusion centers allow federal, state, and local public safety agencies to work side by side, collecting and sharing data from a wide variety of sources. Analysis of the

---

[51] See, e.g., Robert L. Mitchell, "12 Tips for Managing Your Information Footprint," *Computerworld*, January 27, 2009. www.computerworld.com/s/article/9125098/12_tips_for_managing_your_information_footprint

[52] The U.S. government estimates state that 8.1 million U.S. adults were victims of identity theft in 2010, at a total cost of $374 billion. (California Office of Privacy Protection, "Identity Theft First Aid," June 1, 2011). www.privacyprotection.ca.gov/identity_theft.htm

data is intended to result in actionable intelligence that leads to safer communities.[53]

However, some fusion centers do not host the data, but rather refresh them regularly. That means their analysts are not subject to the Freedom of Information Act (FOIA) or being dragged into court for misuse of information.[54,55] This is potentially disastrous for private citizens who are trying to pin down responsibility for mistaken information that is turning their lives upside down!

As with all technologies, event processing and CEP can be used for both legitimate and illegitimate purposes. On the negative side, for example, event processing can be used to implement spying programs that steal personal information. These days it is often used to spy on an individual's activities and their communications for commercial and maybe even political ends.

The current methods of defense available commercially are, to say the least, inadequate. One can buy protections such as:

- *Fraud prevention.* A service that places fraud alerts on your data with the three major credit bureaus. Credit issuers are forced to contact you before opening an account in your name.
- *ID theft detection.* Software systems that send email alerts when triggered by events in public records, such as a change of address, a credit report inquiry, or a public record name change.
- *Activity monitors.* Programs that record emails, chats, instant messaging, website visits, Internet searches, programs that are run on your computer, keystrokes typed, files transferred, and screen snapshots. Activity monitors might help to warn an individual to avoid risky behavior, but they are more likely to be used by employers spying on their employees during working hours!

---

[53] American Civil Liberties Union (ACLU), "Questions to Ask About Fusions [sic] Centers," November 21, 2007. www.aclu.org/national-security-technology-and-liberty/questions-ask-about-fusions-centers

[54] Fusion centers are often run by private companies under contract. For example, the largest collection of medical records in the United States is maintained by an insurance industry organization, the Medical Information Bureau (MIB).

[55] For a list of the types of data a fusion center collects on private citizens with no criminal record, see: Charity & Security Network, "Texas Law Enforcement Memo: Beware Nonprofits Promoting Tolerance," April 9, 2009. www.charityandsecurity .org/news/Texas_Memo_Beware_Nonprofits_Promoting_Tolerance

These are disparate commercial services, each covering only a very small piece of the individual's information footprint. They do not solve the privacy problem. They cost more money than they turn out to be worth in most cases. They only deliver after-the-fact reporting. And they certainly don't stop identity theft from happening!

Perhaps the best suggestion toward monitoring your information footprint may be to use alert services such as Google Alerts, which will continuously search the Web to track topics you're interested in. Alert services can be configured to find out what information about you is being published on the Web. These services continuously search the Web for instances of personally identifying information such as your name, address, phone number, social security number, and so on. For example, when Google finds matches, it will send you an email with links. The downside may well be that you will be inundated with alerts that you know about or gave permission for.

The *privacy of the individual* is a continual battleground, because new tracking and collection methods are appearing all the time. It has become the subject for the formulation of new laws—e.g., requiring "opt out" features on website that collect data on visitors. But these laws are not likely to solve the problem.

On the positive side, holistic event processing systems probably represent the best line of attack toward building programs that can track and inform individuals as to what is happening to their information and proactively alert them to suspicious circumstances as they are happening and before damage is done.

Protecting Your Information Footprint. Holistic event processing systems that:

1. Monitor all known Internet sources of data on an individual, including the collection points and distribution points for that data, fusion centers, local, state, and national government agencies, and the individual's own Internet activities.
2. Inform you as to what's in your public information footprint—where it is, who's looking at it, and who is using it!
3. Execute preemptive vetting of requests for your data from all sources, and uses of that data—e.g., in possible identity theft attempts—and enable you to terminate such requests and uses.

Figure 9.7 shows the scope of the kinds of event processing that could be needed to protect an individual's personal data and enable that individual to keep track of what's happening to the information. Possibly, event processing can be used to increase the individual's awareness of his Internet behaviors and potential dangers thereof. Finally, it might be able

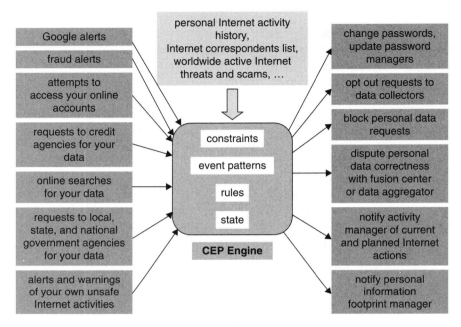

FIGURE 9.7 Sketch of Holistic Event Processing for Protecting Your Information Footprint

to enable an individual to block uses of personal information. However, the potential for false alarms and burdensome demands upon an individual's attention is obviously a possible drawback with such protection systems.

People have different reactions to the idea of a system that tracks and protects your information footprint. Some specialists in event processing think this may be the ultimate "police application," and it will take fifty years to develop.

Others see a need for this kind of protection of the individual. They think it can be achieved in incremental steps, and that some tools for preventing personal information misuse—*catch it as it is happening*—can be built now; also some of the components already exist.

Summary: The Future of Complex Event Processing

These five examples of possible applications of holistic event processing are but a few of the possibilities. Some of the examples we have given may not happen. But some other large-scale future applications of event processing will evolve, and they will be holistic in the sense that they process large numbers of different types of event inputs, combine different kinds of event processing, and provide predictive capabilities for interpreting their outputs.

Complex event processing technology will be an essential component of holistic systems for enterprise management. Event patterns, rules, rules engines, and event hierarchies will be part of the technology available in these systems to technical support engineers and knowledgeable business specialists. But CEP will be under the hood and hidden by sophisticated graphical interfaces from the average user. In many cases, users will probably not know that their requests for information *right now* are being implemented underneath the user interface by event pattern detection engines—but of course, some users will also be specialists in event processing!

Who will be responsible for the evolution of holistic event processing systems? That is harder to predict than anything else about event processing! But one thing is likely true:

Some of the people who read this book will be contributors to the evolution of holistic event processing systems.

I encourage you to go forward with whatever application of, or new technology for, *event processing* catches your interest.

Of one thing I am certain. We have barely scratched the surface of discovering the ways events can be gathered and processed, and the results applied, *right now*, for the good of all of us here on this Earth.

APPENDIX

Glossary of Terminology: The Event Processing Technical Society

(EPTS) Glossary of Terms—Version 2.0

Compiled by
David Luckham & W. Roy Schulte
and
EPTS Glossary Working Group Members:
Jeff Adkins
Pedro Bizarro
H.-Arno Jacobsen
Albert Mavashev
Brenda M. Michelson
Peter Niblett
David Tucker

February 2010

Permission to copy and display this glossary in any medium without fee or royalty is hereby granted, provided that you include the copyright notice as shown herein and link or URL to the Material on the EPTS website.

DISCLAIMERS:

This material is provided "as is," and the Event Processing Technical Society (EPTS) and its members make no representations or warranties, express or implied, including, but not limited to, warranties of merchantability, fitness for a particular purpose, non-infringement, or title; that the contents of this material are suitable for any purpose; nor that the implementation of such contents will not infringe any third-party patents, copyrights, trademarks, or other rights.

To the fullest extent permitted by applicable law, the EPTS and its members will not be liable for any direct, indirect, special, incidental, or consequential damages arising out of any use of this material or the performance or implementation of the contents thereof.

No other rights are granted by implication, estoppel, or otherwise.

Acknowledgments: We are indebted to many correspondents who have made contributions, suggestions, and comments over the past year. They are too numerous to mention individually, but we owe them our thanks.—David Luckham, Roy Schulte

PREFACE

Purpose

The purpose of the EPTS glossary of terms is to facilitate industry use of event processing technology by providing a common language for developing applications and software infrastructure that use event processing concepts.

The event processing glossary has three goals:

- Accelerate the learning of the event processing concept
- Further community communication by enabling practitioners to utilize common concepts and terms
- Provide a foundation for analysis and the development of best practices, publications, and industry standards

Organization

The glossary is presented according to the logical order of the terms. An alphabetical listing is available at the beginning of the document for convenience.

Content

This glossary covers a small set of basic terms related to event processing. It will be frequently periodically updated with additional terms in response to suggestions from the event processing community for improvements and additions.

Our approach is to define each term independently of any particular implementation, product, or domain of application. So, for example, the term *event object* has popular meanings as a tuple, a vector, a row, etc. These are all realizations of events in particular approaches and products.

Even the most basic term, *event,* is problematic. Essentially, there are two distinct meanings:

- An activity that happens
- Something that represents that activity in a computer system

It is tempting to introduce two separate terms such as *event* and *event object.* However, in any discussion longer than a paragraph or two, this becomes intolerably clumsy and one finds the distinction being misused, forgotten, or dropped altogether. For example, using the two separate terms would dictate that *event processing* (see below) should be *event object processing.* The best solution is to overload the word *event.* The context of each use becomes the indicator of which meaning is intended. This has been standard practice in the field of event driven simulation for the past thirty years. It was the approach taken by the physicists of the early twentieth century in discussions of relativity where *event* also has two meanings. We have chosen to follow their example in the knowledge that it did not lead them into ambiguity problems.

Alphabetical List
of Glossary Terms

Cause

Clock

Complex event

Complex event processing (CEP)

Composite event

Constraint (event pattern constraint)

Derived event (synthesized event, synthetic event)

Event

Event (event object, event message, event tuple)

Event abstraction

Event attribute (event property)

Event channel

Event cloud

Event consumer sink (event sink, event handler, event listener)

Event driven

Event driven architecture (EDA)

Event management

Event pattern

Event pattern detection

Event pattern discovery

Event pattern triggered reactive rule

Event processing

Event processing agent (EPA) (event processing component, event mediator)

Event processing language (EPL)

Event processing network (EPN)

Event producer (event source, event emitter)

Event stream

Event stream processing (ESP)

Event template

Event timing

Event type (event class, event definition, event schema)

Instantaneous event

Pattern instance (event pattern instance)

Publish-and-subscribe

Publisher

Raw event

Relationships between events

Rule (in event processing)

Simple event

Subscriber

Time interval

Timestamp

Virtual event

Window (in event processing)

Glossary of Terms

Event Anything that happens or is contemplated as happening.

Examples:

- A financial trade
- An airplane lands
- A sensor outputs a reading
- A change of state in a database or a finite state machine
- A keystroke
- A natural occurrence such as an earthquake
- A social or historical happening (e.g., the abolition of slavery, the battle of Waterloo, the Russian Revolution, and the Irish potato famine).

Event (event object, event message, event tuple) An object that represents, encodes, or records an event, generally for the purpose of computer processing.

Examples:

- A purchase order (records a purchase activity)
- An email confirmation of an airline reservation
- Stock tick message that reports a stock trade
- A message that reports an RFID sensor reading
- A medical insurance claim document

Notes:

1. Events are processed by computer systems by processing their representations as event objects. The same activity may be represented by more than one event object; each event object might record different attributes of the activity. In many event processing systems, for example simulation systems, events are immutable. In such systems, a modification or transformation of an event must be achieved by

creating a new event object and not by altering the original event. Deletion would entail removing an event from further processing.

2. Overloading: Event objects contain data. The word—*event* is overloaded so that it can be used as a synonym for *event object*. In discussing event processing, the word—*event* is used to denote both the everyday meaning (anything that happens) and the computer science meaning (an event object or message). The context of each use indicates which meaning is intended.

Virtual event   An event that does not happen in the physical world, but is imagined, modeled, or simulated.

Examples:

- Instruction executions modeled by a hardware design simulation
- Events predicted by a weather simulation
- Events modeled by a war game
- Events that take place in a dream ("these dreams of you, so real and so true"—Van Morrison)
- Events in virtual reality

Note: A virtual event can refer to either an event object or a thing that happens.

Event type (event class, event definition, or event schema)   A class of event objects.

Examples:

- The type of all price quotations
- The type of all sensor readings for any kind of sensor

Notes:

1. All events must be instances of an event type. An event has the structure defined by its type. The structure is represented as a collection of event attributes (below).
2. Event types should be defined within the type definition system of a modern strongly typed computer language such as XML Schema or Java. Any standard for representing events will usually specify certain predefined data (attributes), examples of which might be:

    - A unique event identifier used to reference the event
    - The type of the event

- The time stamps of the event's creation
- The source of creation for the event

Event attribute (event property)   A component of the structure of an event.

Note: An event attribute can have a simple or complex data type.

Event processing   Computing that performs operations on events, including reading, creating, transforming, or discarding events.

Note: The overloaded meaning *event object processing* is intended in this context.

Clock   A process that creates an ordered ascending sequence of values of type Time with a uniform interval between them.

Note: Each value is produced at a tick (or clock tick). The length of the interval between clock ticks is called a chronon (the clock's granularity).

Event timing (timing)   The time value attributes of an event.

Timestamp   A time value attribute of an event recording the reading of a clock in the system in which the event was created or observed.

Examples:

- *Creation time*: the time interval or time at which an event was created
- *Arrival time*: the time at which an event arrived at a point of observation

Notes:

1. An event can contain timestamps according to one or more clocks. For example, it can contain both its creation time according to a clock where it was created and its arrival time at a system location according to a clock at that location.
2. In systems with multiple clocks, the issue of clock synchronization is an ongoing topic of research. Not all timing attributes are timestamps. Timing in derived events, for example, may be derived from timing of the source events.

Time interval   A period of time bounded by two timing attributes called the interval's *start time* and *end time*.

Instantaneous event   An event that happens at a point in time.

Note: If they are recorded, the start and end times of an instantaneous event are the same.

Cause   An event A is a cause of another event B, if A had to happen in order for B to happen.

Examples:

- The birth of a father and the birth of a son of the father
- Sending an email and a reply to that email

Note: This is a definition of computational causality. It requires A to be necessary for B to happen. For example B's father is a cause of B, but so is B's mother. Other definitions of causality are possible (e.g., probable cause). The meaning and definitions of intentional or philosophical causality have been debated in countless books on philosophy.

Complex event   An event that summarizes, represents, or denotes a set of other events.

Examples:

- The 1929 stock market crash—an abstraction denoting many thousands of member events, including individual stock trades
- The 2004 Indonesian tsunami—an abstraction of many natural events
- A CPU instruction—an abstraction of register transfer level (RTL) events
- A completed stock purchase—an abstraction of the events in a transaction to purchase the stock
- A successful online shopping cart checkout—an abstraction of shopping cart events on an online website

Notes:

1. A complex event can be an event object or anything that happens, depending on the context.
2. All derived events are complex, but not all complex events are derived from event objects (they may arise from other sources).
3. An event that is regarded as complex in one application might be viewed as a simple event in another application.
4. A complex event can convey additional information that was not present in any of the events that gave rise to it.

Event abstraction   The relationship between a complex event and the other events that it denotes, summarizes, or otherwise represents.

Note: This definition applies to the use of abstraction in an event processing context. The term *abstraction* is used elsewhere in computer science in other ways.

Derived event (synthesized event, synthetic event)   An event that is generated as a result of applying a method or process to one or more other events.

Examples:

- An event reporting that company B has entered the bidding to take over A with probability 0.9, might be derived from an event reporting that the price of company A's stock has jumped 10 percent in 5 minutes.
- The absence of an event, say in a given time interval, can lead to a derived event reporting that the first event did not happen.

Notes:

1. A derived event is an event object.
2. A derived event is a kind of complex event, although not all complex events are derived.

Composite event   A derived event that is created by combining a set of other simple or complex events (known as its members) using a specific set of event constructors such as disjunction, conjunction, and sequence. A composite event always includes the member (base) events from which it is derived.

Notes:

1. A composite event is an event object—something that happens cannot be a composite event.
2. A composite event is a kind of complex event.
3. A derived event is not a composite if its method of derivation lies outside a specified set of allowed constructors.
4. The terminology *composite* and *constructor* originated in the field of Active Database research.

Relationships between events   Events are related by time, causality, abstraction, and other relationships. Time and causality impose partial orderings upon events.

Notes:

1. Regarding the relationships of composite, derived, and complex events: A composite event or a derived event is a complex event. The converses are not necessarily true.

2. The term *aggregate event* is sometimes used for some forms of composite or derived event.

Simple event   An event that is not viewed as summarizing, representing, or denoting a set of other events.

Notes:
1. All events are either simple or complex. Simple event is the complement to complex event.
2. Simple and complex are relative terms. A simple event to one observer may be complex to another.

Raw event   An event object that records a real-world event.

Note: A raw event may represent a simple real-world event (e.g., the phone rang) or a complex real-world event. For example, the stock market crash of 1929 was a complex real-world event that can be recorded by a complex raw event.

Event hierarchy   A model that represents the relationships between events that are at different levels of abstraction with respect to each other.

Note: A complex event is usually at a higher level in the hierarchy than the events that it denotes, summarizes, or otherwise represents.

Complex event processing (CEP)   Computing that performs operations on complex events, including reading, creating, transforming, abstracting, or discarding them.

Note: CEP ultimately creates complex events, even if some or all of the source events are simple events. See also the definitions for event stream processing (ESP), event streams, and event clouds, below.

Event producer (event source, event emitter)   An event processing agent that sends events.

Examples:
- Software module
- Sensor
- Clock

Event consumer (event sink, event handler, event listener)   An event processing agent that receives events.

Examples:

- Software module
- Database
- Dashboard

Event channel   Any means of conveying event objects.

Notes:

1. A channel can carry events of multiple types.
2. Events transported by a single channel may be consumed by multiple event consumers (the channel is said to *fan out*).
3. Events transported by a single channel may originate in multiple producers and be delivered to one consumer (the channel is said to *fan in*).

Event template   An event form or descriptor, some of whose parameters are variables. An event template matches single events by replacing the variables with values.

Examples:

- Send of any message
- String Msg; Send(John, Msg)

Event pattern   A template containing event templates, relational operators, and variables. An event pattern can match sets of related events by replacing variables with values.

Examples:

- A pattern of events defining those sets of events in a completed sales transaction
- A pattern of events in an email correspondence: String Msg, Time T1, T2; Send(John, Msg, T1) and Receive(John, Msg, T2)
- A pattern defining the events in any successfully resolved customer complaint: Customer C, Agent A, Problem P, Time T1, T2, T3; Complain(C, P, T1) → Engage(A, C, T2) → Resolved (P, T3)

Note: Event patterns can often be specified graphically.

Pattern instance (event pattern instance)   A set of related events resulting from an event pattern where the variables are replaced by values.

Example: Send(John, See the NYT today, 15.00 EST) and Receive (John, See the NYT today, 12.05 PST).

Constraint (event pattern constraint)   A Boolean condition that must be satisfied by the events observed in a system.

Example: A service level agreement limiting the time taken to complete a mortgage transaction from the time an application is received.

Event pattern discovery   Finding new event patterns.

Event pattern detection   Finding instances of an event pattern.

Notes:

1. The process of deciding whether a set of events is an instance of a pattern is called matching.
2. Discovery deals with finding new patterns, whereas detection deals with matching a given pattern.

Rule (in event processing)   A prescribed method for processing events.

Examples:

- Whenever three timeouts have happened, send an alert to the network manager.
- If more than ten shopping carts have been active for more than five minutes, then activate the website reaction time monitor and display an amber alert on the dashboard.
- Whenever IBM trades 2 percent above its one-hour VWAP and then within fifteen minutes trades 5 points below, then buy 1000 shares of IBM.

Note: Event processing rules may be prescribed in many different ways, including by finite state machines, UML diagrams, graphical methods, Java code, SQL code, ECA (event-condition-action) rules, or reactive rules that are triggered by event patterns (below).

Event pattern–triggered reactive rule   A rule that prescribes actions to be taken whenever an instance of a given event pattern is detected.

Event processing agent (EPA) (event processing component, event mediator)
An entity that processes event objects.

Notes:

1. An EPA may perform different kinds of computation on events such as filtering, aggregating, and detecting patterns of events.
2. An EPA can be recursive—it can be an EPN consisting of multiple EPAs and channels.
3. Event source and event sink are roles that an EPA may play. An EPA could act in both roles—it could be an event producer at one moment and an event consumer at another time.

Event processing language (EPL)   A high-level computer language for defining the behavior of event processing agents.

Event management   An IT discipline that encompasses event governance, event policy management, and the design, development, testing, deployment, maintenance, and administration of events, event models, event metadata, and related aspects of systems that process events.

Event stream   A linearly ordered sequence of events.

Notes:

1. Usually, streams are ordered by time (e.g., arrival time).
2. An event stream may be bounded by a certain time interval or other criteria (content, space, source), or be open-ended and unbounded.
3. A stream may contain events of many different types.

Window (in event processing)   A bounded segment of an event stream.

Example: The events in the last ten minutes (i.e., a ten-minute moving window).

Note: Windows define subsequences of an event stream typically to focus the event processing on specific data or to improve event processing performance; however, they may also have other uses.

Event stream processing (ESP)   Computing on inputs that are event streams.

Example: Applications that use stock market feeds as inputs and process events in their order of arrival to compute running average stock prices, volume weighted average prices over time windows, etc.

Notes:

1. ESP has its origins in active databases and data streams management.
2. The terms ESP and CEP are conceptual classifications. They can be useful in delineating philosophies of event processing and intended applications, but do not specify precisely the underlying capabilities of event processing engines.

Event cloud   A partially ordered set of events (*poset*), either bounded or unbounded, where the partial orderings are imposed by the causal, timing, and other relationships between the events.

Notes:

1. Typically, an event cloud is created by the events produced by one or more distributed systems.
2. An event cloud may contain many event types, event streams, and event channels.
3. The difference between a cloud and a stream is that there may not be an event relationship that totally orders the events in a cloud. A stream is a cloud, but the converse is not necessarily true.
4. CEP usually refers to event processing that assumes an event cloud as input, and therefore can make no assumptions about the arrival order of events.

Event Processing Network (EPN)   A set of event processing agents (EPAs) and the channels they use to communicate.

Notes:

1. The runtime deployment of an event processing network may be distributed across multiple physical networks, computers, and software artifacts.
2. An EPN can be an EPA (i.e., EPAs and EPNs can be recursive).

Publish-and-subscribe (pub-sub)   A method of communication in which messages are delivered according to subscriptions.

Notes:

1. Subscriptions define which messages should flow to which consumers.
2. Event processing applications may use publish-and-subscribe communication for delivering events. However, publish-and-subscribe is

not definitional to event processing—other communication styles may be used.

Publisher An agent that sends events that are disseminated by a publish-and-subscribe protocol.

Subscriber An agent that submits a subscription for publish-and-subscribe communication.

Note: In most publish-and-subscribe systems, the consumer must be the subscriber. However, in some systems, the subscriber can be a third party.

Event-driven The behavior of a device, software module, or other entity whose execution is in response to the arrival of events from external or internal sources.

Examples:

- A cell phone
- An event-triggered rule
- An operating system
- A bank's trust department where the personnel spend their time putting out fires (i.e., event-driven rather than goal-driven or directed)

Event-driven architecture (EDA) An architectural style in which components are event-driven and communicate by means of events.

Notes:

1. Architecture is the fundamental organization of a system embodied in its components, their relationships to each other and to the environment, and the principles guiding its design and evolution (from IEEE).
2. An architectural style is a coordinated set of architectural constraints that restricts the roles/features of architectural elements and the allowed relationships among those elements within any architecture that conforms to that style (from Roy T. Fielding).

Glossary According to Lexicographic Order (definitions only)

Cause: An event A is a cause of another event B if A had to happen in order for B to happen.

Clock: A process that creates an ordered ascending sequence of values of type Time with a uniform interval between them.

Complex event: An event that summarizes, represents, or denotes a set of other events.

Complex event processing (CEP): Computing that performs operations on complex events, including reading, creating, transforming, abstracting, or discarding them.

Composite event: A derived event that is created by combining a set of other simple or complex events (known as its members)—using a specific set of event constructors, such as disjunction, conjunction, and sequence. A composite event always includes the member (base) events from which it is derived.

Constraint (event pattern constraint): A Boolean condition that must be satisfied by the events observed in a system.

Derived event (synthesized event, synthetic event): An event that is generated as a result of applying a method or process to one or more other events.

Event: Anything that happens or is contemplated as happening.

Event (event object, event message, event tuple): An object that represents encodes or records an event, generally for the purpose of computer processing.

Event abstraction: The relationship between a complex event and the other events that it denotes, summarizes, or otherwise represents.

Event attribute (event property): A component of the structure of an event.

Event channel: Any means of conveying event objects.

Event cloud: A partially ordered set of events (*poset*), either bounded or unbounded.

Event consumer (event sink): An event processing agent that receives events.

Event driven: The behavior of a device, software module, or other entity whose execution is in response to the arrival of events from external or internal sources.

Event driven architecture (EDA): An architectural style in which components are event-driven and communicate by means of events.

Event hierarchy: A model that represents the relationships between events that are at different levels of abstraction with respect to each other.

Event management: An IT discipline that encompasses event governance, event policy management, and the design, development, testing, deployment, maintenance, and administration of events, event models, event metadata, and related aspects of systems that process events.

Event pattern: A template containing event templates, relational operators, and variables. An event pattern can match sets of related events by replacing variables with values.

Event pattern detection: Finding instances of an event pattern.

Event pattern discovery: Finding new event patterns.

Event pattern–triggered reactive rule: A rule that prescribes actions to be taken whenever an instance of a given event pattern is detected.

Event processing: Computing that performs operations on events, including reading, creating, transforming, or discarding events.

Event processing agent (EPA) (event processing component, event mediator): A software module that processes events.

Event processing language (EPL): A high-level computer language for defining the behavior of event processing agents.

Event processing network (EPN): A set of event processing agents (EPAs) and a set of event channels connecting them.

Event producer (event source, event emitter): An event processing agent that sends events.

Event stream: A linearly ordered sequence of events.

Event stream processing (ESP): Computing on inputs that are event streams.

Event template: An event form or descriptor, some of whose parameters are variables. An event template matches single events by replacing the variables with values.

Event timing: The time value attributes of an event.

Event type (event class, event definition, or event schema): A class of event objects.

Instantaneous event: An event that happens at a point in time.

Pattern instance (event pattern instance): A set of related events resulting from an event pattern by replacing the variables by values.

Publish-and-subscribe (pub-sub): A method of communication in which messages are delivered according to subscriptions.

Publisher: An agent that sends events that are disseminated by a publish-and-subscribe protocol.

Raw event: An event object that records a real-world event.

Relationships between events: Events are related by time, causality, abstraction, and other relationships. Time and causality impose partial orderings upon events.

Rule (in event processing): A prescribed method for processing events.

Simple event: An event that is not viewed as summarizing, representing, or denoting a set of other events.

Subscriber: An agent that submits a subscription for publish-and-subscribe communication.

Time interval: A period of time bounded by two timing attributes, called the interval's *start time* and *end time*.

Timestamp: A time value attribute of an event recording the reading of a clock in the system in which the event was created or observed.

Virtual event: An event that does not happen in the physical world but is imagined, modeled, or simulated.

Window (in event processing): A bounded segment of an event stream.

About the Author

David Luckham has held faculty and invited faculty positions in mathematics, computer science, and electrical engineering at eight major universities in Europe and the United States. He was one of the founders of Rational Software Inc. in 1981, supplying both the company's initial software product and the software team that founded the company. He has been an invited lecturer, keynote speaker, panelist, and U.S. delegate at many international conferences and congresses. Currently, he is Professor Emeritus of Electrical Engineering, Stanford University.

His research and consulting activities in business and software technology are aimed at building real-time event driven enterprises. Topics include event driven systems, complex event processing, business activity monitoring, enterprise middleware, multiprocessing and business process languages, event driven systems architecture modeling and simulation, and artificial intelligence (automated deduction and reasoning systems).

He has published five books and more than one hundred technical papers; he has received two ACM/IEEE Best Paper Awards, and several of his papers are now in historical anthologies and book collections. His 2002 book *The Power of Events* laid the foundations for high-level event processing in real-time business and intelligence-gathering systems: www .amazon.com/exec/obidos/ASIN/0201727897/ref%3Dnosim/katehartsh osp-20/002-4874956-4852829.

This book builds on *The Power of Events*. It describes for a general audience of readers the explosion that has taken place since 2002 in applications of high-level event processing to businesses, enterprise management, and more generally, to building the Information Society.

Index